ILLMAN'S
English / Zulu Dictionary
and
Phrase Book

ILLMAN'S

English / Zulu Dictionary
and
Phrase Book

Asikhulumeni - Let's Talk

Shirley Illman

authorHOUSE®

PREFACE

I grew up on a farm called Daviddale in the Lothair district in Southeast Mpumalanga. My parents, John and Rylda Greene, had a shop, butchery and bakery on their small holding. Dad and Mom supplied the surrounding area and Swaziland with bread and meat. Growing up in the sticks, as people would call it, was a terrific experience for all of us.

I, my brothers, Ray and Graham, and sisters Lyn and Yvonne, could have not asked for a better place to grow up. Besides the finer things in life, like the tennis courts, swimming pool, squash court, rolling lawns surrounded by beds of exquisite flowers and shrubs, we also learnt the basics of life. We were all fortunate to grow up with Assiena and Gertie the house staff and Rafette the gardener, who could only communicate in Zulu. They taught us to recognize what could be eaten from the veld (bush), how to amuse oneself without toys and many other important aspects of life, especially, how to communicate in Zulu. Because of Dad's businesses, and our having to help in the shop and bakery during school holidays, we not only learnt to speak Zulu, but also to read and write Zulu from an early age.

It is because of my fortunate upbringing, and being able to communicate with and understand the Zulu language, that I would like to share just a little bit of the ethnic language that I know with you.

Nelson Mandela was the first democratic president to be elected in South Africa in 1994. He urged the people of South Africa to learn at least one of the ethnic languages. Not only is this a sign of respect for ones' neighbours, but it enriches your knowledge, and opens up a whole new way of life, communication, culture and you get to make new friends.

"Asikhulumeni" is my contribution to the person who wishes to communicate in an ethnic language. The phonetic pronunciation of the Zulu words is unique. I have used a simple system of phonetics, with accents placed on letters where special emphasis is required.

My dictionary & phrase book will serve as a helpful working tool in the classroom, home, business or to the traveller. Illman's English / Zulu phonetic dictionary & phrase book has been written mainly to assist the person who is keen to communicate in Zulu. My dictionary & phrase book is not just a translation, it shows you exactly how to say the words in Zulu.

It is so easy! Anyone can learn! The benefits are numerous!
Speak another language   - so many more people to communicate with.
Broaden your mind   - opens up a new world.
Improve your skills   - expand your business and broaden your market.

The more you know, the more you grow. So let's all grow together – SIMUNYE!

Sala kahle,

Shirley

AuthorHouse™ UK
1663 Liberty Drive
Bloomington, IN 47403 USA
www.authorhouse.co.uk
Phone: 0800.197.4150

This Phonetic Dictionary and Phrase Book is intended for those people who have an urge to learn and to communicate in an ethnic language. This phrase book and dictionary that I have compiled, is only a start to a long and wonderful relationship with a language that is spoken widely in our country, South Africa.

It is to be understood that the phonetic way of writing the Zulu word is as an English speaking person would read/pronounce it, and not, in some cases, as a Zulu person would read or say the word.

Published by AuthorHouse 10/22/2014

ISBN: 978-1-4969-8961-1 (sc)
ISBN: 978-1-4969-8962-8 (hc)
ISBN: 978-1-4969-8963-5 (e)

Library of Congress Control Number: 2014918043

Published by Paddy Illman
E-mail address: paddyi@mweb.co.za
Cellphone number: +27 83 449 2177

2.

ACKNOWLEDGEMENTS

I wish to acknowledge the people mentioned below for their contributions
towards the creation of my Dictionary and Phrase Book.

Ashley Illman of Created by Mouse for the setting and layout of the book.
My very big happy family for all their support. My husband Paddy, and children Marc and Sharon.
A very special thank you to Paddy, my better half, for all his hard work and encouragement
he has given me. Paddy has been a tremendous inspiration to me.

Thank you to you all.

Shirley

DEDICATION

In Memory of Marc Illman

09 October 1972 to 07 June 2004

This dictionary is dedicated to the memory of our late son MARC who had an amazing knowledge of the Zulu language. He had an incredible flair for speaking Zulu. He was an absolute natural and had such talent in communicating with Zulu speaking people, whether it was about everyday matters, sport, or sharing one of his many jokes with them. He also had a great knowledge and love for the outdoors and the wildlife in our country. He could give you any name in zulu for an animal or bird.

May his knowledge of Zulu and the inspiration he gave me to write this dictionary and phrase book assist you in communicating in Zulu with more ease.

Hamba Kahle Marc, till we meet again.

All our love
Mom, Dad and Sharon

CONTENTS

PRONUNCIATION OF VOWELS AND CONSONANTS

A	As in abafana	(boy) similar to a in father
E	As in sebenza	(work) similar to e in egg (e´)
I	As in insimbi	(iron) similar to ee in feel
O	As in inkomo	(cow) similar to oo in door (o´)
U	As in umuntu	(person) similar to oo in too
B	Softer than the English B	
Bh	H is silent but B is more pronounced	
C	Click sound as in TS - put tongue on top of teeth, and pull tongue away Making click sound - eg. Tut tut or sound of a ticking clock	
CH	Ch sound more pronounced as in chair	
DL	Put tongue on teeth and say D & L together	
F	As in F for fat	
G	As in G in anger	
H	As in H in how when is first letter, but like GH when in middle of sentence	
Hh	Very pronounced, as in H in hotel	
HL	Put tongue on teeth and say H & L together - like a goose hissing	
J	As in J for join when is first letter, but when in middle of word, very similar to J in Jew	
K	Similar to English C but sharper	
Kh	H is silent - as in C in call	
KL	Put tongue on teeth and almost hiss the KL out	
L	As in L in lamp	
M	As in M in mom	
N	As in N in none	
Ng	Pronounce both together as in NG in linger	
Ny	Pronounce both together as in NY in Kenya	
P	As in P in pip but sharper	
Ph	H is silent as in P in posh	
Q	Click sound - put tongue on bottom set of teeth, and make click sound by opening mouth leaving tongue on teeth	
R	As in r in rob	
S	As in S in say so	
Sh	As in SH in shore	
T	As in T in into but sharper	
Th	H is silent as in toss	
Ts	Put tongue on teeth and pronounce together as in tsetse fly	
Tsh	As in CH in church	
V	As in V in vein	
W	As in W in wink	
X	Click sound - differs from other two click sounds, as the sound comes from the sides of the mouth, like egging a horse on	
Y	As in Y in yes / yeast	
Z	As in Z in zoo	

NB. The symbol ´ - accent - placed on e´ and o´ - denotes the stressing of preceeding vowel

Eg.	Paper	iphepha eepe´pa = e´ as in the e in egg
	Hall	ihholo eeho´lo´ = o´ as in the oo in door or a in hall

EVERYDAY CONVERSATION - SOME USEFUL PHRASES

ENGLISH GENERAL	ZULU VAMILE	PHONETIC PRONUNCIATION VAAMEELE'
Hello (singular)	Sawubona	Saawoobo'naa
Hello (plural)	Sanibona	Saaneebo'naa
Goodbye (sing.) - stay well	Sala kahle.	Saalaa kaahle'.
Goodbye (pl.) - stay well	Salani kahle.	Saalaanee kaahle'.
Goodbye (sing.) - go well	Hamba kahle.	Haambaa kaahle'.
Goodbye (pl.) - go well	Hambani kahle.	Haambaanee kaahle'.
We welcome you.	Siyanemukela.	Seeyaane'mooke'laa.
Welcome!	Halala!	Haalaalaa!
How are you? Are you fine?	Unjani? / Usaphila na?	Oonjaanee? / Oosaapeelaa naa?
How do you do?	Unjani?	Oonjaanee?
How are you all?	Ninjani?	Neenjaanee?
I am fine thankyou.	Ngisaphila.	Ngeesaapeelaa.
We are fine.	Siyaphila.	Seeyaapeelaa.
I am not well.	Angiphili.	Aangeepeelee.
I am sick.	Ngiyagula.	Ngeeyaagoolaa.
And you how are you?	Wena, usaphila na?	We'naa, oosaapeelaa naa?
I am well.	Ngisaphila.	Ngeesaapeelaa.
I am ill.	Ngiyagula.	Ngeeyaagoolaa.
What is wrong?	Yini na?	Yeenee naa?
I have a cold.	Ngiphethwe ngumkhuhlane.	Ngeepe'twe' ngoomkoohlaane'.
What do you want here?	Ufunani lapha?	Oofoonaanee laapa?
What do you want ?	Ufunani?	Oofoonaanee?
I want . . .	Ngifuna . . .	Ngeefoonaa . . .
Come in.	Ngena.	Nge'naa.
Go away!	Hamba!	Haambaa!
Sit down. (sing.)	Hlala phansi.	Hlaalaa paansee.
Sit down. (pl.)	Hlalani phansi.	Hlaalaanee paansee.
Come closer. (sing. / pl.)	Sondela. / Sondelani.	So'nde'laa. / So'nde'laanee.
Come here. (sing. / pl.)	Woza lapha. / Wozani lapha.	Wo'zaa laapaa. / Wo'zaanee laapaa.
Come back here. (sing. / pl.)	Buya lapha. / Buyani lapha.	Booyaa laapaa. / Booyaanee laapaa.
Stand up. (sing. / pl.)	Sukuma. / Sukumani.	Sookoomaa. / Sookoomaanee.
What is the time?	Sikhathi sini?	Seekaatee seenee?
It is 12 o' clock.	Isikhathi ngu 12.	Eeseekaatee ngoo 12.
How much do you earn per week / month?	Uhola malini ngesonto / ngenyanga?	Ooho'laa maaleenee nge'so'nto' / nge'nyaangaa?
I / me	Mina	Meenaa
We / us	Thina	Teenaa
You (pl)	Nina	Neenaa
You (sing.)	Wena	We'naa
They / them	Bona	Bo'naa
It is cold.	Kumakhaza.	Koomaakaazaa.
It is hot.	Kuyashisa.	Kooyaasheesaa.
It is wet.	Kumanzi.	Koomaanzee.
It is dry.	Komile.	Ko'meele'.
My cat	Ikati lami	Eekaatee laamee

My dog	Inja yami	Eenjaa yaamee
My mother	Umama wami	Oomaamaa waamee
My father	Ubaba wami	Oobaabaa waamee
His / her mother	Umama wakhe	Oomaamaa waake´
His / her father	Ubaba wakhe	Oobaabaa waake´
When are you going?	Uhamba nini?	Oohaambaa neenee?
I am going at 10.	Ngiyahamba ngo 10. /	Ngeeyaahaambaa ngo´ 10. /
	Ngihamba ngo 10.	Ngeehaambaa ngo´ 10.
A lot	Kakhulu	Kaakooloo
A little	Kancane	Kaancaane´
Lots of times	Kaningi	Kaaneengee
Very badly	Kabi	Kaabee
Well done!	Wenze kahle! / Kahle!	We´nze´ kaahle´! / Kaahle´!
Shortly	Kafishane	Kaafeeshaane´
How often?	Kangaki?	Kaangaakee?
twice	kabili	kaabeelee
three times	kathathu	kaataatoo
four times	kane	kaane´
five times	kahlanu	kaahlaanoo
mine (of mine)	lami / yami / wami / sami	laamee / yaamee / waamee / saamee
his / hers	okwakhe	o´kwaake´
himself / herself / he / she	yena	ye´naa
ours	-ethu / ya + kithi	e´too / yaakeetee
their / theirs	-abo / ayo	-aabo´ / aayo´
You build (house)	Uyakha.....	Ooyaakaa.....
You make (tea)	Uyenza.....	Ooye´nzaa....
You roast / braai... / You fry...	Uyosa.../ Uyathosa ...	Ooyo´saa../ Ooyaato´saa...
Beginning of . . .	Ekuqaleni ko.. / -kwe.. / -kuke..	E´kooqaale´nee ko´.. / -kwe´.. /-kooke´..
End of . . .	Ekupheleni ko . . .	E´koope´le´nee ko´ . . .
this year	lo nyaka	lo´ nyaakaa
next month	inyanga ezayo	eenyaangaa e´zaayo´
last month	inyanga edlule	eenyaangaa e´dloole´
this month	le nyanga	le´ nyaangaa
next week	isonto elizayo	eeso´nto´ e´leezaayo´
last week	isonto eledlule	eeso´nto´ e´le´dloole´
During this week	Ngaleli sonto	Ngaale´lee so´nto´
In the afternoon	Ntambama	Ntaambaamaa
In the evening	Kusihlwa / Ebusuku	Kooseehlwaa / E´boosookoo
In the daytime	Emini	E´meenee
In the morning	Ekuseni	E´koose´nee
yesterday	izolo	eezo´lo´
today	namuhla / namhlanje	naamoohlaa / naamhlaanje´
tomorrow	kusasa	koosaasaa
He / She has just arrived.	Usandukufika.	Oosaandoo – koofeekaa.
To air ones views.	Sakaza imiqondo.	Saakaazaa eemeeqo´ndo´.
In view of	Njengoba	Nje´ngo´baa
Point of view	Umqondo	Oomqo´ndo´
My opinion / view	Umbono wami	Oombo´no´ waamee
Give an opinion.	Beka umqondo.	Be´kaa oomqo´ndo´.
In my opinion	Ngokucabanga kwami	Ngo´koocaabaangaa kwaamee

8.

On the matter---	Ngodaba---	Ngo'daabaa---
Drive one mad.	Hlanyisa.	Hlaanyeesaa.
What are you driving at?	Uqondeni?	Ooqo'nde'nee?
Put out of sight / mind.	Thukuza.	Tookoozaa.
Catch sight of.	Shaziza. / Qabuka.	Shaazeezaa. / Qaabookaa.
Lose sight of.	Lahlekela.	Laahle'ke'laa.
At first sight	Ngokuqabukwa	Ngo'kooqaabookwaa
Out of sight	Ngabonakali	Ngaabo'naakaalee
In my eyes, it was wrong	Ngokubona kwami,	Ngo'koobo'naa kwaamee,
/ a mistake.	kwakuyiphutha.	kwaakooyeepootaa.
I did it only to please you.	Ngifane ngakwenza	Ngeefaane' ngaakwe'nzaa
	ukuze ngikujabulise.	ookooze' ngeekoojaabooleese'.
Only just	Njenjenje	Nje'nje'nje'
If only	Uma-nje	Oomaa-nje'
If only I knew.	Uma-nje ngangazile.	Oomaa-nje' ngaangaazeele'.
Only too pleased	Ngokuthokoza-nje	Ngo'kooto'ko'zaa-nje'
I want . . .	Ngifuna ..	Ngeefoonaa ...
I am . . .	Ngiyi.. /Ngi.. /Ngiya../Ngu ..	Ngeeyee./ Ngee./ Ngeeyaa./ Ngoo..
I have . . .	Ngina.. /Ngino.. / Ngine...	Ngeenaa.. / Ngeeno'.. / Ngeene'. .
You are . . .	Uyi . . . / U . . . / Uya . . .	Ooyee . . ./ Oo . . . / Ooyaa . . .
You have . . .	Una . . .	Oonaa . . .
You want . . .	Ufuna . . .	Oofoonaa . . .
We are . . .	Siyi../ Si.. / Siya.. / Singo. .	Seeyee. ./ See. ./ Seeyaa.. / Seengo'..
We have . . .	Sina . . .	Seenaa . . .
We want . . .	Sifuna . . .	Seefoonaa . . .
Here is . . .	Nakhu . . . / Na . . .	Naakoo . . . / Naa . . .
Where is . . .?	Ikuphi . . .?	Ee-koopee . . .?
What is this?	Yini le?	Yeenee le'?
What is that?	Yini leyo?	Yeenee le'yo'?
Why? /	Kungani? / Ngani? /	Koongaanee? / Ngaanee? /
Why?	Yini ndaba?	Yeenee ndaabaa?
Do that.	Yenza lokho. / Kwenze lokho.	Ye'nzaa lo'ko'. / Kwe'nze' lo'ko'.
Don't do that.	Ungakwenzi lokho.	Oongaakwe'nzee lo'ko'.
I know. / I don't know.	Ngiyazi. / Angazi.	Ngeeyaazee. / Aangaazee.
I think so.	Ngicabanga kanjalo.	Ngeecaabaangaa kaanjaalo'.
I don't think so. /	Angisho. /	Aangeesho'. /
I don't think so.	Angicabangi kanjalo.	Aangeecaabaangee kaanjaalo'.
I am tired.	Ngikhathele.	Ngeekaate'le'.
I am glad.	Ngiyajabula.	Ngeeyaajaaboolaa.
I am cross.	Ngithukuthele.	Ngeetookoote'le'.
I am sorry.	Ngiyaxolisa.	Ngeeyaaxo'leesaa.
Listen!	Lalela!	Laale'laa!
Never!	Angeke!	Aange'ke' !
OK - It is all right.	Kulungile.	Kooloongeele'.
All together	Kanye kanye	Kaanye' kaanye'
I don't understand.	Angizwa.	Aangeezwaa.
I understand.	Ngiyezwa.	Ngeeye'zwaa.
Look out for . . .	Qaphela i . . .	Qaape'laa ee...
What do you mean?	Usho ukuthini?	Oosho' ookooteenee?
Can you explain?	Ungachaza na?	Oongaacaazaa naa?

Do you speak . . . ?	Ukhuluma isi . . . ?	Ookooloomaa eesee …?
Do you speak English?	Ukhuluma isiNgisi yini?	Ookoolomaa eeseeNgeesee yeenee?
Speak slowly / softly.	Khuluma kancane / kahle.	Kooloomaa kaancaanee / kaahle′.
Repeat slowly / softly.	Phinda kancane / kahle.	Peendaa kaancaanee / kaahle′.
Please will you write it down?	Ngicela ukubhale phansi?	Ngeece′laa ookoobaale′ paansee?
Yes	Yebo	Ye′bo′
Please	Ngicela	Ngeece′laa
No	Cha	Caa
Thank You.	Ngiyabonga.	Ngeeyaabo′ngaa.
No thank you. / Thankless	Ngabonga. / Ngabongi	Ngaabo′ngaa. / Ngaabo′ngee
I thank you. / Thank you!	Ngiyakubonga!	Ngeeyaakoobo′ngaa!
Thank (v)	Bonga	Bo′ngaa
Thankful	Bongayo	Bo′ngaayo′
Thankless	Ngabongi	Ngaabo′ngee
Excuse me.	Uxolo.	Ooxo′lo′.
Excuse me, what did you say?	Uxolo, utheni? / Uxolo uthini?	Ooxo′lo′, oote′nee? / Ooxo′lo′ ooteenee?
Good morning.	Sawubona.	Saawoobo′naa.
Good evening.	Sawubona.	Saawoobo′naa.
Is he / she at home ?	Ukhona ekhaya?	Ooko′naa e′kaayaa?
Please tell him / her I phoned / called.	Mtshele ukuthi bengimshayele ucingo.	Mtche′le′ ookootee be′ngeemshaaye′le′ ooceengo′.
Please tell him / her I was looking for him / her.	Mtshele ukuthi bengimfuna.	Mtche′le′ ookootee be′ngeemfoonaa.
Send regards to . . .	Khonza ku . . .	Ko′nzaa koo . . .
Who is there?	Ngubani olapho?	Ngoobaanee o′laapo′?
Where do you come from?	Uphumaphi? / Uvelaphi?	Oopoomaapee? / Oove′laapee?
I come from . . .	Ngiphuma e . . .	Ngeepoomaa e′ . . .
I am asking for work.	Ngizocela umsebenzi.	Ngeezo′ce′laa oomse′be′nzee.
What work do you want?	Ufuna ukusebenzani?	Oofoona ookoose′be′nzaanee?
I want to work in . . .	Ngifuna ukusebenza e . . .	Ngeefoonaa ookoose′be′nzaa e′. .
Where do you work?	Usebenzaphi?	Oose′be′nzaapee?
Come in.	Ngena.	Nge′naa.
Sit down.	Hlala phansi.	Hlaalaa paansee.
Stand up.	Sukuma.	Sookoomaa.
Come nearer.	Sondela.	So′nde′laa.
Come here.	Yiza lapha. / Woza lapha.	Yeezaa laapaa. / Wo′zaa laapaa.
Open. / Close. (v)	Vula. / Vala.	Voolaa. / Vaalaa.
Tell him / her to wait.	Mtshele alinde.	Mtche′le′ aaleende′.
Tell him / her to stop.	Mtshele ame.	Mtche′le′ aame′.
What is the matter?	Yini ndaba?	Yeenee ndaabaa?
What is your name? / What is your name?	Ubani igama lakho? / Igama lakho ngubani?	Oobaanee eegaamaa laako′? / Eegaamaa laako′ ngoobaanee?
My name is Sharon.	Igama lami ngu Sharon.	Eegaamaa laamee ngoo Sharon.
How old are you?	Uneminyaka emingaki?	Oone′meenyaakaa e′meengaakee?
I am ten years old.	Ngineminyaka engu 10.	Ngeene′meenyaakaa e′ngoo 10.
Are you engaged?	Uthengisiwe?	Oote′ngeeseewe′?
Are you married?	Ushadile?	Ooshaadeele′?
Do you have any children?	Unabo abantwana?	Oonaabo′ aabaantwaanaa?

English		
Where do you live ?	Uhlalaphi?	Oohlaalaapee?
I live in . . .	Ngihlala e . . .	Ngeehlaalaa e´ . . .
I am working.	Ngiyasebenza.	Ngeeyaase´be´nzaa.
How long must I wait?	Ngizolinda isikhathi esingakanani?	Ngeezo´leendaa eeseekaatee e´seengaakaanaanee?
What is your telephone number?	Ithini inombolo yakho yocingo?	Eeteenee eeno´mbo´lo´ yaako´ yo´ceengo´?
My number is . . .	Inamba yami ithi . . .	Eenaambaa yaamee eetee . . .
Where are you going?	Uyaphi?	Ooyaapee?
I am going to . . . /	Ngiya e . . ./	Ngeeyaa e´... /
I am going to / (place of)	Ngiya kwa .../	Ngeeyaa kwaa .../
I am going to …(person)	Ngiya ku …	Ngyeeyaa koo …
What day is it today?	Ulwesingaki namhlanje?	Oolwe´seengaakee naamhlaanje´?
It is late / Time is up.	Isikhathi sesishayile.	Eeseekaatee se´seeshaayeele´.
It is still early.	Isikhathi sikahle.	Eeseekaatee seekaahle´.
I am in a hurry.	Ngijahile.	Ngeejaagheele´.
He / she is a good sport.	Unenhliziyo enhle.	Oone´nhleezeeyo´ e´nhle´.
Look after the child.	Gada / Bheka umntwana.	Gaada / Be´kaa oomntwaanaa.
I have come from . . .	Ngiphuma e . . .	Ngeepoomaa e´ . . .
Where is the . . .?	Ikuphi i . . .?	Eekoopee ee . . .?
Where is the toilet? /	Likuphi ithoyilethe? /	Leekoopee eeto´yeele´te´? /
Where is the toilet?	Iphi indlu encane?	Eepee eendloo e´ncaane´?
According to these rules --	Ngokwalemithetho ---	Ngo´kwaale´meete´to´ ---
Please be advised ---	Sicela ukukwazisa ---	Seece´laa ookookwaazeesaa ---
Department of health	Umnyango wezempilo	Oomnyaango´ we´ze´mpeelo´
I do want money.	Ngifuna imali.	Ngeefoonaa eemaalee.
I do not want money.	Angifuni imali.	Aangeefoonee eemaalee.
It can be granted.	Ingatholakala.	Eengaato´laakaalaa.
It cannot be granted.	Lingetholakale.	Leenge´to´laakaale´.
I am not alone.	Angingedwa.	Aangeenge´dwaa.
I am alone.	Ngingedwa.	Ngeenge´dwaa.
It did not register.	Akungenanga kahle.	Aakooge´naangaa kaahle´.
electricity consumption	ugesi osebenzile	ooge´see o´se´be´nzeele´
water consumption	amanzi asebenzile	aamaanzee aase´be´nzeele´
water supply /	amanzi athunyelwe /	aamaanzee aatoonye´lwe´ /
water supply	amanzi athunyelwayo	aamaanzee aatoonye´lwaayo´
raw water supply	amanzi emvelo	aamaanzee e´mve´lo´
Smoking is strictly forbidden !	Ukubhema akuvunyelwe nakancane!	Ookoobe´be´maa aakoovoonye´lwe´ naakaancane´!
Do not smoke.	Musa ukubema.	Moosaa ookoobe´maa.
Do not stand up.	Ungasukuma. / Musa ukusukuma.	Oongaasookoomaa. / Moosaa ookoosookoomaa.
My head swims.	Ikhanda lami liyaduma.	Eekaandaa laamee leeyaadoomaa.

HOUSEHOLD	OKWASEKHAYA	O´KWAASE´KAAYAA
Please will you . . .?	Ngicela u . . .?	Ngeece´la oo . . .?
Thankyou.	Ngiyabonga.	Ngeeyaabo´ngaa.
Can you (do) . . .?	Ungakwazi uku . . .?	Oongaakwaazee ookoo . . .?
Please will you help me?	Ngicela ungisize?	Ngeece´laa oongeeseeze´?
Can you help me?	Ungangisiza?	Oongaangeeseezaa?
I shall be glad to help you.	Ngingajabula ukukusiza.	Ngeengaajaaboolaa ookookooseezaa.
How much do you earn?	Uhola malini?	Ooho´laa maaleenee?
Your salary will be R3000.	Iholo lakho lizoba ngu R3000.	Eeho´lo´ laako´ leezo´baa ngoo R3000.
When do you start?	Uqala nini?	Ooqaalaa neenee?
When do you finish? /	Uqeda nini? /	Ooqe´daa neenee? /
When do you knock off?	Ushayisa nini?	Ooshaayeesaaneenee?
Come back at 2 pm.	Ubuye ngo 2.	Oobooye´ ngo´ 2.
You can have Sundays off.	Uzothola isikhathi sokuphumula nge Sonto.	Oozo´to´laa eeseekaatee so´koopoomoolaa nge´ So´nto´.
What time will you leave?	Uzohamba ngasikhathi sini?	Oozo´haambaa ngaaseekaatee senee?
You can have leave /	Ungakwazi ukuthola	Oongaakwaazee ookooto´laa
holiday in December.	ilivu / iholide ngoDisemba.	eeleevoo / eeho´leede´ ngo´ Deese´mbaa.
This is your uniform.	Le inyunifomu yakho.	Le´ eenyooneefo´moo yaako´.
I will make / cook . . .	Ngizopheka . . .	Ngeezo´pe´kaa . . .
lunch	ilantshi	eelaantshee
supper	isapha	eesaapaa
breakfast.	ibhulakufesi.	eeboolaakoofe´see.
I will bake . . .	Ngizobhaka . . .	Ngeezo´baakaa . . .
a cake / bread /	ikhekhe / isinkwa /	eeke´ke´ / eeseeenkwaa /
scones / a scone.	amaskoni / isiskoni.	aamaasko´nee / eeseesko´nee.
I am thirsty.	Ngomile.	Ngo´meele´.
I am hungry.	Ngilambile.	Ngeelaambeele´.
Make tea.	Yenza itiye.	Ye´nzaa eeteeyaa.
Make coffee.	Yenza ikhofi.	Ye´nzaa eeko´fee.
Wash up dishes.	Geza izitsha.	Ge´za eezeetshaa.
I will dry the dishes.	Ngizozesula izitsha.	Ngeezo´ze´soolaa eezeetshaa.
I will dry the dish.	Ngizosula isitsha.	Ngeezo´soolaa eeseetshaa.
I will dry ....(pl)	Ngizozesula ...	Ngeezo´ze´soolaa....
Defrost the fridge.	Ncibilikisa iqhwa efrijini.	Nceebeeleekeesaa eeqwaa e´freejeenee.
in the fridge / fridge	efrijini / ifriji	e´freejeenee / eefreejee
Clean the . . .	Hlanzisa . . .	Hlaanzeesaa. .
oven	uhhavini	oohaaveenee
stove	isitofu	eeseeto´foo
microwave.	imayikhroweyivi.	eemaayeekro´we´yeevee.
Clean / Dust the house.	Hlanza indlu. / Sula indlu.	Hlaanzaa eendloo. / Soola eendloo.
Wash the windows /	Geza amafasitela /	Ge´zaa aamaafaaseete´laa /
bath / toilet /	ubhavu / ithoyilethi /	oobaavoo / eeto´yeele´tee /
basin / carpets.	isitsha / okhaphethi.	eeseetshaa / o´kaape´tee.
Remove the stains.	Susa amabala.	Soosaa aamaabaalaa.
stain / stains	ibala /amabala	eebaalaa / aamaabaalaa
Disinfect. (v)	Bulala amagciwane.	Boolaala aamaagceewaane´.
disinfectant (jik etc.) /	isibulalimagciwane /	eeseeboolaaleemaagceewaane´ /
disinfectant	isihlanzisisi	eeseehlaanzeeseesee

Use handy andy / starch / sta soft.	Sebenzisa ihandy andy / isitashi / ista- softi.	Se'be'nzeesa ee handy andy / eeseetaashee / eestayso'ftee.
Polish the shoes.	Pholisha izicathulo.	Po'leeshaa eezeecaatoolo'.
Sweep. / Polish.	Shanyela. / Pholisha.	Shaanye'laa. / Po'leeshaa.
Clean. / Scrub.	Hlanza. / Khuhla.	Hlaanzaa. / Koohlaa.
Vacuum carpets.	Hlanza okhaphethi.	Hlaanzaa o'kaape'tee.
Make a / the bed.	Endlala / Yendlula umbhede.	E'ndlaalaa / Ye'ndloolaa oombe'de'.
The . . . is dirty.	I . . ingcolile.	Ee ... eengco'leele'.
Please wash (self).	Ngicela ugeze.	Ngeece'laa ooge'ze'.
Please wash (clothes).	Ngicela uwashe.	Ngeece'laa oowaashe'.
Change the sheets.	Shintsha amashidi.	Sheentshaa aamaasheedee .
Air the bed.	Shayisa umbhede ngomoya.	Shaayeesaa oombe'de' ngo'mo'ya.
Leave it to air out.	Shiya kushaya umoya.	Sheeyaa kooshaaya oomo'yaa.
Wash the clothes.	Washa izingubo.	Waashaa eezeengoobo'.
Wash the curtains / blankets / duvet / net curtains.	Washa amakhethini / izingubo / iduvet / amakhethini enethi.	Waashaa aamaake'teenee / eezeengoobo' / eedoove't / aamaake'teenee e'ne'tee.
Will it shrink?	Kuzofinyela yini?	Koozo'feenye'laa yeenee?
Will this shrink?	Kuzofinyela yini lokhu?	Koozo' feenye'laa yeenee lo'koo?
Does the colour run?	Umbala uyaphuma yini?	Oombaalaa ooyaapoomaa yeenee?
The colour will run.	Umbala uzophuma.	Oombaalaa oozo'poomaa.
Hang out the washing to dry. (plural)	Neka izingubo ukuba zome.(pl)	Ne'kaa eezeengoobo' ookoobaa zo'me'. (pl.)
Hang out the washing to dry. (singular)	Neka ingubo ukuba yome. (sing.)	Ne'kaa eengoobo' ookoobaa yo'me'. (sing.)
Bring in washing.	Ngenisa izingubo.	Nge'neesaa eezeengoobo'.
Iron the clothes.	Ayina izingubo.	Aayeenaa eezeengoobo'.
Hang up clothes.	Gaxa / Phanyeka izingubo.	Gaaxaa / Paanye'kaa eezeengoobo'.
Fold the clothes.	Songa / Goqa izingubo.	So'ngaa / Go'qaa eezeengoobo'.
Put the clothes away.	Beka izingubo.	Be'kaa eezeengoobo'.
This needs mending.	Lokhu kudinga ukuchitshiyelwa.	Lo'koo koodeengaa ookoocheetsheeye'lwaa.
The soap is finished.	Insipho iphelile.	Eenseepo' eepe'leele'.
Take out the rubbish.	Khipha izibi.	Keepaa eezeebee.
Take out dirt / garbage.	Khipha udoti.	Keepaa oodo'tee.
Feed the dogs.	Phakela izinja.	Paake'laa eezeenjaa.
Feed the cat.	Phakela ikati.	Paake'laa eekaatee.
Feed the baby.	Phakela / Dlisa umntwana.	Paake'laa / Dleesaa oomntwaanaa.
Take Marc to school at 8.	Hambisa uMark esikoleni ngo 8.	Haambeesaa ooMark e'seeko'le'nee ngo' 8.
Fetch Sharon from . . .	Landa uSharon e . . .	Laandaa ooSharon e' . . .
Where does Marc go to school / university?	UMark, ufunda kusiphi isikole / iyunivesithi?	OoMark, oofoondaa kooseepee eeseeko'le' / eeyooneeve'seetee?
What Grade are you in?	Ufunda liphi ibanga?	Oofoondaa leepee eebaangaa?
I am in Grade 1.	Ngifunda ibanga 1.	Ngeefoonda eebaangaa 1.
Is there anything we need in the house?	Kukhona yini esikudingayo / esikufunayo endlini?	Kooko'naa yeenee e'seekoodeegaayo' / e'seekoofoonaayo' e'ndleenee?
The . . . is finished.	Iphelile i . . .	Eepe'leele' ee . . .

Where is the . . . ?	Ikuphi i . . . ?	Eekoopee ee . . . ?
bathroom	ibhavulumu	eebaavooloomoo
bedroom	ikamelo lokulala	eekaame'lo' lo'koolaalaa
diningroom	ikamelo lokudlela	eekaame'lo' lo'koodle'laa
garage	igalaji	eegaalaajee
kitchen	ikhishi	eekeeshee
lounge	ilawunji	eelaawoonjee
pantry	iphentri	eepe'ntree
study	isitadi	eeseetaadee
verandah	uvulandi / uvulande	oovoolaandee / oovoolaande'
toilet	ithoyilethe	eeto'yeele'te'
The . . . is broken.	Kuphuke i . . .	Koopooke' ee . . .
What is the time?	Sikhathi sini?	Seekaatee seenee?
The time is 10 o' clock.	Isikhathi ngu - 10.	Eeseekaatee ngoo 10.
I am not treated well.	Ngiphatheke kabi.	Ngee paate'ke' kabee.
I am treated well.	Ngiphatheke kahle.	Ngee paate'ke' kaahle'.

When asking for something, always put please / ngicela before the question / request
Please fetch Marc?   Ngicela ulande uMark?   Ngeece'la oolaande' ooMark?

When finished asking for something, always say thankyou / ngiyabonga.
Thank you   Ngiyabonga   Ngeeyaabo'ngaa

EATING / COOKING	UKUDLA / UKUPHEKA	OOKOODLAA / OOKOOPE′KAA
I am hungry. / I am thirsty.	Ngilambile. / Ngomile.	Ngeelaambeele′. / Ngo′meele′.
I would like you to . . .	Ngi cela u . . .	Ngee ce′laa oo . . .
I would / feel like . . .	Ngithanda . . .	Ngeetaandaa....
baked potato	izambane elibhakiwe	eezaambaane′ e′leebaakeewe′
beef	inyama yenkomo	eenyaamaa ye′nko′mo′
biltong	umqwayiba	oomqwaayeebaa
boil (v)	bilisa	beeleesaa
bread and butter	isinkwa nebhotela	eeseenkwa ne′bo′te′laa
chicken -fowl	inkukhu	eenkookoo
chicken - meat of	inyama yenkukhu	eenyaamaa ye′nkookoo
chips	amashipsi	aamaasheepsee
boiled egg	iqanda elibilisiwe	eeqaandaa e′leebeeleeseewe′
egg - fried egg	iqanda elithosiwe	eeqaandaa e′leeto′seewe′
egg - scrambled egg	iqanda eliphehliwe	eeqaandaa e′leepe′hleewe′
egg - poached egg	iqanda eliphoshiwe	eeqaandaa e′leepo′sheewe′
fat / dripping	amafutha	aamaafootaa
fried fish	inhlanzi ethosiwe	eenhlaanzee e′to′seewe′
grilled fish	inhlanzi egriliwe	eenhlaanzee e′greeleewe′
hot water	amanzi ashisayo	amaanzee asheesaayo′
jam	ujamu	oojaamoo
mash potato	izambane elibondiwe	eezaambaane′ e′leebo′ndeewe′
meat / steak	inyama / isiteki	eenyaamaa / eeseete′kee
mince meat	inyama egayiwe	eenyaamaa e′gaayeewe′
mutton	inyama yemvu	eenyaamaa ye′mvoo
omelette	i-omilethe	ee-o′meele′te′
roast (v)	osa	o′saa
roasted meat (n)	inyama eyosiweyo	eenyaamaa e′yo′seewe′yo′
sausage	isosltshi	eeso′seetshee
Serve / Dish up food (v).	Phakela.	Paake′laa.
May I have some water?	Ngicela amanzi?	Ngeece′laa aamaanzee?
May I have the salt	Ngicela usawoti	Ngeece′laa oosaawo′tee
& pepper?	nophepha?	no′pe′paa?
The food is cold.	Ukudla kuyabanda.	Ookoodlaa kooyabaandaa.
The food is warm.	Ukudla kufudumele.	Ookoodlaa koofoodoome′le′.
The food is overdone.	Ukudla kuvuthwe - lushu.	Ookoodlaa koovootwe′ looshoo.
The food is raw.	Ukudla kuse - luhlaza.	Ookoodla koose′ loohlaaza.
The food is not cooked.	Ukudla ngavuthiwe.	Ookodlaa ngaavooteewe′.
The food is nice.	Ukudla kumnandi.	Ookoodlaa koomnaandee.
Boil in water.	Pheka ngamanzi.	Pe′kaa ngaamaanzee.
Boiled water	Amanzi abilisiwe	Aamaanzee aabeeleeseewe′
Boil over.	Chichima.	Cheecheemaa.
Take this away.	Kususe lokhu.	Koosoose′ lo′koo.
This isn't clean.	Akuhlanzekile lokhu.	Aakoohlaanze′keele′ lo′koo.
No thank you.	Ngabonga.	Ngeeyaabo′ngaa.

GARDEN	INGADI	EENGAADEE
dig / plant (v)	yimba / tshala	yeembaa / tshaalaa / tchaalaa
edge trimmer	isiphundli	eeseepoondlee
flowerbed	umbhede wezimbali	oombe´de´ we´zeembaalee
flower / flowers	imbali / izimbali	eembaalee / eezeembaalee
fork	imfologo	eemfo´lo´go´
garden fence	ifensi / ucingo	eefe´nsee / ooceengo´
garden hose /	ithumbu lokuchelela /	eetoomboo lo´kooche´le´laa /
garden hose	ithumbu lokunisela	eetoomboo lo´kooneese´laa
grass / lawn	utshani	ootshaanee
hedge	uthango	ootaango´
lawn	utshani	ootshaanee / ootchaanee
lawnmower	umshini wokugunda /	oomsheenee wo´koogoonda /
	wokusika utshani	wo´koo- seekaa ootshaanee
leaves	amakhasi / amacembe	aamaakaasee / aamaace´mbe´
manure / compost	umquba / umanyolo	oomqoobaa / oomaanyo´lo´
plant . . .(v)	tshala . . .	tshaalaa / tchaalaa . . .
plants (n)	izithombo	eezeeto´mbo´
potplant	ibhodwe lezimbali	eebo´dwe´ le´zeembaalee
rake	ihhala	eehaalaa
rake (v)	hhala	haalaa
secateurs	isikelo semithi	eeseeke´lo´ se´meetee
seed / seeds	imbewu / izimbewu	eembe´woo / eezeembe´woo
shears / scissors	isikelo	eeseeke´lo´
shrub	isihlahlana	eeseehlaahlaanaa
soil / sand (n)	umhlabathi / inhlabathi	oomhlaabaatee / eenhlaabaatee
spade	isipedi / ifosholo	eeseepe´dee / eefo´sho´lo´
sprinkler	isifafazi	eeseefaafaazee
step ladder	isitebhisi	eeseete´beesee
swimming pool	ichibi lokubhukuda	eecheebee lo´koobookoodaa
tractor	ugandaganda	oogaandaagaandaa
tree	umuthi / isihlahla	oomootee / eeseehlaahlaa
trowel	itrofela	eetro´fe´laa
watering can	ikani lokunisela	eekaanee lo´kooneese´laa
weed killer	isibulalikhula	eeseeboolaaleekoolaa
weeds	ukhula	ookoolaa
wheel barrow	ibhala	eebaalaa
Please will you ....?	Ngicela u .....?	Ngeece´laa oo ....?
Mow the lawn.	Gunda / Sika utshani.	Goondaa / Seekaa ootshaanee.
Sweep the yard.	Shanela iyadi.	Shaane´laa eeyaadee.
Rake up the leaves.	Hhala amacembe ngehhala.	Haalaa aamaace´mbe´ nge´haalaa.
Cut the edges.	Sika emaceleni.	Seekaa e´maace´le´nee.
Trim the hedge.	Sika izihlahlana zothango.	Seekaa eezeehlaahlaanaa zo´taango´.
Water the garden.	Chelela / Nisela ingadi.	Che´le´laa / Neese´laa eengaadee.
Weed the flower beds.	Izimbali zidinga	Eezeembaalee zeedeengaa
	ukuhlakulelwa.	ookoohlaakoolelwaa.

16.

RECREATION	UKUDLALA	OOKOODLAALA
Can you swim?	Uyakwazi ukubhukuda?	Ooyaakwaazee ookoobookoodaa?
What sports do you play?	Udlala mdlalo muni?	Oodlaalaa mdlaalo´ moonee?
I play . . .	Ngidlala. . .	Ngeedlaala . . .
rugby (ama bokka bokka)	iragbhi	eeraagbee
soccer (bafana bafana)	ibhola	eebo´laa
hockey (ama stokka stokka)	ihokhi	eeho´kee
tennis (ama smash smash)	ithenisi	eete´neesee
cricket (ama howzat)	ikhilikithi	eekeeleekeetee
cycling	ukugibela ibhayisikili	ookoogeebe´laa eebaayeeseekeelee
I cycle.	Ngigibela ibhayisikili.	Ngeegeebe´laa eebaayeeseekeelee.
I swim.	Ngiyabhukuda.	Ngeeyaabookoodaa.
I catch fish. /	Ngidoba inhlanzi. /	Ngeedo´baa eenhlaanzee. /
I catch fish.	Ngiyadoba.	Ngeeyaado´baa.
I play golf.	Ngidlala igalofu.	Ngeedlaalaa eegaalo´foo.
I play squash.	Ngidlala isikwashi.	Ngeedlaalaa eeseekwaashee.
I race cars. /	Ngijaha izimoto. /	Ngeejaaghaa eezeemo´to´. /
I race cars.	Ngijahisa izimoto.	Ngeejaagheesaa eezeemo´to´.
racing cars	izimoto zomjaho	eezeemo´to´ zo´mjaagho´
I race horses.	Ngigijima ngamahhashi.	Ngeegeejeemaa ngaamaahaashee.
I run.	Ngiyagijima.	Ngeeyaa geejeemaa.
I don't play any sport.	Angidlali umdlalo / mdlalo.	Aangeedlaalee oomdlaalo´/ mdlaalo´.
I want to . . . (play)	Ngifuna ookoo . . .	Ngeefoonaa ookoo . . .
Go to . . . (the beach)	Hamba e . . . / Yiya e . . .	Haambaa e´ . . . / Yeeyaa e´ . . .
Which way to . . .?	Lingakuphi i . . .?	Leengaakoopee ee . . .?
art gallery	i -athigalari	ee-aateegaalaaree
the beach	ibhishi	eebeeshee
cinema - at the cinema	ebhayisikobho	e´baayeeseeko´bo´
cinema	ibhayisikobho	eebaayeeseeko´bo´
museum	imnyuziyamu	eemnyoozeeyaamoo
Join the library.	Joyina ilayibhrari.	Jo´yeenaa eelaayeebraaree.
I want to borrow	Ngifuna ukuboleka	Ngeefoonaa ookoobo´le´kaa
a book.	incwadi / ibhuku.	eencwaadee / eebookoo.
I want my hair cut.	Ngifuna ukugunda.	Ngeefoonaa ookoogoondaa.
I want to perm my hair.	Ngifuna ukuphema.	Ngeefoonaa ookoope´maa.
I want my hair braided.	Ngifuna ukucwalwa izinwele.	Ngeefoonaa ookoocwaalwaa eezeenwe´le´.
I want my hair done.	Ngifuna ukulungisa izinwele.	Ngeefoonaa ookooloongeesaa eezeenwe´le´.
Where is the nearest . . ?	Ikuphi i . . . eseduze?	Eekoopee ee . . . e´se´dooze´?
arena	inkundla	eenkoondlaa
bait	ukudla kokudoba	ookoodlaa ko´koodo´baa
boxer	umshayisibhakela	oomshaayeeseebaake´laa
boxing	isibhakela	eeseebaake´laa
changerooms	izindlu zokushintsha	eezeendloo zo´koosheentshaa
club - tennis	ikilabhu ye - thenisi	eekeelaaboo ye´ te´neesee
cup / trophy	indebe / ilisimula	eende´be´ / eeleeseemoolaa
fish (v)	doba	do´baa
fish (n)	inhlanzi	eenhlaanzee

17.

fisherman	umdobi wezinhlanzi	oomdo'bee we'zeenhlaanzee
golf club / course	egalofini	e'gaalo'feenee
golf clubs	izinduku zegalofu	eezeendookoo ze'gaalo'foo
golfer	umdlali wegalofu	oomdlaalee we'gaalo'foo
hockey stick	induku yehokhi	eendookoo ye'ho'kee
hockey player	umdlali wehoki	oomdlaalee we'ho'kee
horse	ihhashi	eehaashee
horse race	umjaho wamahhashi	oomjaaho' waamaahaashee
lifesavers	ababhekimpilo	aabaabe'keempeelo'
line – side, border	umugqa / umncele	oomoogqaa / oomnce'le'
Lose game. (v)	Hlulwa emdlalweni.	Hloolwaa e'mdlaawe'nee.
race course	indawo yomjaho	eendaawo' yo'mjaagho'
race horse	ihhashi lomjaho	eehaashee lo'mjaagho'
spectator	isibukeli	eeseebooke'lee
sportsmanship	ubudlaba	ooboodlaabaa
swimmer - competitive	ohlambayo / inhlambi	o'hlaambaayo' / eenhlaambee
swimming pool	ichibi lokubhukuda	eecheebee lo'koobookoodaa
tennis racket	irakhethi lethenisi	eeraake'tee le'te'neesee
win (v)	phuma phambili / phumelela	poomaa paambeelee / poome'le'laa
Win a game.	Wina umdlalo.	Weenaa oomdlaalo'.
Win a point.	Thola iqhuzu.	To'laa eeqoozoo.
I won the race.	Ngiphume phambili emjahweni.	Ngeepoome' paambeelee e'mjaahwe'nee.
Win a race.	Phumelela emjahweni.	Poome'le'laa e'mjaahwe'nee.
It was a tie / draw.	Umdlalo waphela ngokulingana.	Oomdlaalo' waape'laa ngo'kooleengaanaa.
I ride horses.	Ngigibela amahhashi.	Ngeegeebe'laa aamaahaashee.
I rode a horse.	Ngagibela ihhashi.	Ngaageebe'laa eehaashee.
He / she came first in the world.	Yena, uphume phambili emhlabeni wonke.	Yena, oopoome' paambeelee emhlaabenee wo'nke'.
world cup	inkomishi womdlalo womhlaba wonke / inkomishi womdlalo womhlaba /	eenko'meeshee wo'mdlaalo' wo'mhlaabaa wo'nke' / eenko'meeshee wo'mdlaalo' wo'mhlaabaa /
world cup	indebe womhlaba wonke	eende'be' wo'mhlaabaa wo'nke'
World cup rugby	Inkomishi yeragbhi womhlaba wonke	Eenko'meeshee ye'raagbee wo'mhlaabaa wo'nke'
World cup soccer	Inkomishi / Indebe yebhola womhlaba wonke	Eenko'meeshee / Eende'be' ye'bo'laa wo'mhlaabaa wo'nke'
World cup cricket	Inkomishi yekhilikithi womhlaba wonke	Eenko'meeshee ye'keeleekeetee wo'mhlaabaa wo'nke'

SPORTING TERMS	AMAGAMA OMDLALO	AAMAAGAAMA O'MDLAALO'
advantage	ilungelo lokwedlula	eeloonge'lo' lo'kwe'dloolaa
appeal (v) in cricket	khalela	kaale'laa
athlete	umdlali	oomdlaalee
attacking	ukuhlasela	ookoohlaase'laa
award a penalty	ukunikezwa iphenalthi	ookooneeke'zwaa eepe'naaltee
backs	abadlala emuva	aabaadlaalaa e'moovaa
bails	amabheyili	aamaabe'yeelee
ball	ibhola	eebo'laa
bat	bhethi	eebe'tee
batsman	umbhethi	oombe'tee
boundary	umngcele	oomngce'le'
bowler	umbhawuli	oombaawoolee
bye (leg bye)	ibhayi	eebaayee
caution / warning	isexwayiso	eese'xwaayeeso'
centre circle	isiyingi sasesenta	eeseeyeengee saase'se'ntaa
centre field	isisu senkundla	eeseesoo se'nkoondlaa
centre	isenta	eese'ntaa
coach	umlolongi / umqeqeshi	oomlo'lo'ngee / oomqe'qe'shee
commentator	umsakazi	oomsaakaazee
conversion	ikhonveshini	eeko'nve'sheenee
convert a try - (v)	ukukhonvetha	ookooko'nve'taa
corner flag	ikhona flegi	eeko'naa fle'gee
corner	ikhona	eko'naa
crossbar	ikhrosibha	eekro'seebaa
cycle (v)	gibela ibhayisikili	geebe'laa eebaayeeseekeelee
cyclist (ama sho'va sho'va)	umgibeli webhayisikili	oomgeebe'lee we'baayeeseekeelee
deadline - on a field	umugqa ongemuva	oomoogqaa o'nge'moovaa
dead heat	ukufika kanyekanye entanjeni	ookoofeekaa kaanye'kaanye' e'ntaanje'nee
declare (v) (cricket)	nquma	nqoomaa
defenders	amadifenda	aamaadeefe'ndaa
disabled sport	umdlalo wezishosha	oomdlaalo' we'zeesho'shaa
disallow	ukungavumeli	ookoongaavoome'lee
dot down (v)	ukugqoma	ookoogqo'maa
draw - a tie	umdlalo uphela ngokulingana	oomdlaalo' oope'laa ngo'kooleengaanaa
drop kick / drop goal	idropikhiki / idrophugoli	eedro'peekeekee / eedro'poogo'lee
duck - go for a duck	iqanda	eeqaandaa
extra time	isikhathi esengeziwe	eeseekaatee e'se'nge'zeewe'
field - on the field	ebaleni / enkundleni	e'baale'nee / e'nkoondle'nee
field (n)	inkundla / ibala	eenkoondlaa / eebaalaa
fielder – on cricket field	umcoshi bhola	oomco'shee bo'laa
fielders	abadlali	aabaadlaalee
flag	iflegi	eefle'gee
formation / formation	iphethini elungile / ukumiswa	eepe'teenee e'loongeele' / ookoomeeswaa
forwards	amafolosi	aamaafo'lo'see

19.

foul (n)	ifawuli	eefaawoolee
foul (v)	ukufonka / ukwenza iphutha	ookoofo'nkaa / ookwe'nzaa eepootaa
free kick	umkhahlela ohlomekile	oomkaahle'laa o'hlo'me'keele'
game- at the game of rugby	emdlalweni weragbhi	e'mdlaalwe'nee we'raagbee
goal area (rugby)	emapalini	e'maapaaleenee
goal area (soccer, hockey)	emagoli / emagolini	e'maago'lee / e'maago'leenee
goal line (rugby)	ulayini wamapali	oolaayeenee waamaapaalee
goal posts	amapali	aamaapaalee
goal	igoli	eego'lee
goalie	unozinti	oono'zeentee
golf stick / club	induku yegalofu	eendookoo ye'gaalo'foo
golf	igalofu	eegaalo'foo
halftime	isikhathi sekhefu	eeseekaatee se'ke'foo
handball	ukulibamba ngesandla	ookooleebaambaa nge'saandlaa
header	ukulishaya ngekhanda	ookooleeshaayaa nge'kaandaa
injury time	isikhathi sokulimala	eeseekaatee so'kooleemaalaa
innings	amangeno	aamaange'no'
kick a goal	khahlela igoli	kaahle'laa eego'lee
kick off /	ukukhahlela kokuqala /	ookookaahle'laa ko'kooqaalaa /
kick off	ukulisusa / ukuqala	ookooleesoosaa / ookooqaalaa
	komdlalo	ko'mdlaalo'
l b w	ukusitha ngomlenze	ookooseetaa ngo'mle'nze'
line out	ilayini - awuthi	eelaayeenee aawootee
linesman	usomugqa	ooso'moogqaa
match	imeshi / umdlalo	eeme'shee / oomdlaalo'
midfielders	abadlali basesiswini	aabaadlaalee baase'seesweenee
net	inethi	eene'tee
no ball (cricket)	ibhola eliyiphutha	eebo'laa e'leeyeepootaa
obstruction	ukuvimbela	ookooveembe'laa
offside	endaweni engavunyelwe	e'ndaawe'nee e'ngaavoonye'lwe'
oval (n) - cricket oval	umbhoxo	oombo'xo'
over - cricket	i - ova	ee - o'vaa
pass (to) (v)	ukuphasa	ookoopaasaa
penalise (v)	ukujezisa	ookooje'zeesaa
penalty area	indawo yephenalthi	eendaawo' ye'pe'naaltee
penalty kick	iphenalthi	eepe'naaltee
pitch / wicket	iwikhethi	eeweeke'tee
players	abadlali	aabaadlaalee
referee	unompempe	oono'mpe'mpe'
rough play	ukudlalisana kabi	ookoodlaaleesaanaa kaabee
rugby, soccer & cricket	iraghbi, ibhola ne	eeraagbee, eebo'laa ne'
	ikhilikithi	eekeeleekeetee
run out (v) (cricket)	ukukhishelwa ngaphandle	ookookeeshe'lwaa ngaapaandle'
runs (n) (cricket)	amarani	aamaaraanee
save (v)	ukuvimba	ookooveembaa
score a try (v)	ukufaka ithrayi	ookoofaakaa eetraayee
score (n)	isikolo	eeseeko'lo'
scrum (n)	iskramu	eeskraamoo
send off (v)	ukukhishwa emdlalweni	ookookeeshwaa e'mdlaalwe'nee
striker	umgadli	oomgaadlee

stumped (v)	ukustampa	ookoostaampaa
stumps (n)	amapali / amastampu	aamaapaalee / aamaastaampoo
substitute (n)	ongena endaweni yomunye	o'nge'naa e'ndaawe'nee yo'moonye'
substitute (v)	ngena endaweni yomunye	nge'naa e'ndaawe'nee yo'moonye'
tackle (n)	ukuhlasela	ookoohlaase'laa
tackle (v)	hlasela	hlaase'laa
team	ithimu / iqembu	eeteemoo / eeqe'mboo
touch kick	ukukhahlela ngaphandle	ookookaahle'laa ngaapaandle'
touch line / boundary	umngcele / uthashi	oomngce'le' / ootaashee
touchline (on side)	ulayini osemaceleni	oolaayeenee o'se'maace'le'nee
touchline (score line)	uthashi layini	ootaashee laayeenee
upright (pole)	ipali elimile	eepaalee e'leemeele'
vuvuzela (bugle used at soccer)	vuvuzela	voovooze'laa
walk over / beat	ahlula kalula	aahloolaa kaaloolaa
warn (v)	xwayisa	xwaayeesaa
warning (n)	isixwayiso	eeseexwaayeeso'
whistle (n)	indweba / impempe	eendwe'baa / eempe'mpe'
whistle (v) blow	shaya indweba / impempe	shaayaa eendwe'baa / eempe'mpe'
wicket	iwikhethi	eeweeke'tee
wicketkeeper	umbheki wamawikhethi	oombe'kee waamaaweeke'tee
wide - cricket	iwayidi	eewaayeedee

SHOSHOLOZA

Shosholoza, shosholoza
Kulezontaba
Stimela siphuma South Africa
Wenu yabaleka, Wenu yabaleka,
Kulezontaba
Stimela siphuma South Africa

Shosholoza was origanally a sad song sung during hard labour, sometimes far away from home.
It has become one of South Africa's most popular songs, especially as an anthem at sporting events.
Shosholoza means " Go forward ".

A rough English translation:
Move faster, you are meandering on the mountains, the train is from South Africa.
"Stimela " is the Zulu word for a train.

Author Unknown

SHOPPING	UKUTHENGA	OOKOOTE'NGAA
Where is the store?	Sikuphi isitolo?	Seekoopee eeseeto'lo'?
Where is the nearest . . .?	Ikuphi i . . . eseduze?	Eekoopee ee . . .e'se'dooze'?
Where is. . ?	Ikuphi i . . .?	Eekoopee ee . . .?
bookshop	isitolo samabhuku	eeseeto'lo' saamaabookoo
I want to buy . . .	Ngifuna ukuthenga . . .	Ngeefoonaa ookoote'ngaa . . .
clothes	izingubo	eezeengoobo'
groceries	igilosa	eegeelo'saa
a car	imoto	eemo'to'
How much is it?	Kubiza malini? / Malini?	Koobeeza maaleenee? / Maaleenee?
It costs . . . R100.	Kubiza . . . R100.	Koobeeza . . . R100.
Do you have change?	Unawo ushintshi?	Oonaawo' oosheentshee?
Pay with . . .	Khokha nge . . .	Ko'kaa nge' . . .
cheque	ngesheke	nge'she'ke'
credit card	ngekhadi	nge'kaadee
cash	imali / ukheshe	eemaalee / ooke'she'
Put on my account.	Faka kuakhawunti yami.	Faakaa kooaakaawoontee yaamee.
What are the instalments?	Malini ekhokhwa ngamanconzunconzu?	Maaleenee e'ko'kwaa ngaamaanco'nzoonco'nzoo?
Pay at the till.	Khokha ethilini.	Ko'kaa e'teeleenee.
laybye (n)	isibambiso	eeseebaambeeso'
This is too small.	Lokhu kuncane.	Lo'koo kooncaanee.
This is too big.	Lokhu kukhulu.	Lo'koo kookooloo.
I want size. . .	Ngifuna usayizi . . .	Ngeefoonaa oosaayeezee . . .
Will this shrink ?	Kuzofinyela yini?	Koozo'feenye'laa yeenee?
Will this stretch ?	Kuzonwebeka?	Koozo'nwe'be'kaa?
Will the colour run?	Umbala uzophuma yini?	Oombaalaa oozo'poomaa yeenee?
How do you wash it? /	Kugezwa kanjani? /	Kooge'zwaa kaanjaanee? /
How do you wash it ?	Kuwashwa kanjani?	Koowaashwaa kaanjaanee?
This needs mending.	Lokhu kudinga ukuchitshiyelwa.	Lo'koo koodeengaa ookoocheetsheeye'lwaa.
dryclean (v)	drayikilina / washa elondolo	draayeekeeleenaa / waasha e'lo'ndo'lo'
drycleaner	idrayikilina	eedraayeekeeleenaa
shopkeeper	umninisitolo	oomneenee-seeto'lo'
shoplifter	umntshontshi wempahla	oomntsho'ntshee we'mpaahlaa
shopping (n)	izimpahla ezithengiwe	eezeempaahlaa e'zeete'ngeewe'
The glass is broken.	Kuphuke ingilazi.	Koopooke' eengeelaazee.
When will it be ready?	Izolunga nini?	Eezo'loongaa neenee?
Do you deliver ?	Uyadiliva?	Ooyaadeeleevaa?
I shall wait for it.	Ngizoyilindela.	Ngeezo'yeeleende'laa.
I will wait for the parcels.	Ngizozilindela izimpahla.	Ngeezo'zeeleende'la eezeempaahlaaa.

22.

BANKING / BANK	EBHANGE	E'BAANGE'
Where is the bank / building society ?	Liphi ibhange / ibhildingi sosayathi?	Leepee eebaange' / eebeeldeengee so'saayaatee?
What is the exchange rate ?	Yini inani loku-shintshisana ngemali?	Yeenee eenaanee lo'koo-sheentsheesaanaa nge'maalee?
Open an account.	Ukuvula i-akhawunti.	Ookoovoolaa ee-aakaawoontee.
Close my account.	Vala i-akhawunti yami.	Vaalaa ee-aakaawoontee yaamee.
I want change.	Ngifuna ushintshi.	Ngeefoonaa oosheentshee.
I want . . .	Ngifuna . . .	Ngeefoonaa . . .
to draw money /	ukukhipha imali /	ookookeepaa eemaalee /
to deposit money /	ukulondoloza imali /	ookoolo'ndo'lo'zaa eemaalee /
a loan /	ukweboleka imali /	ookwe'bo'le'kaa eemaalee /
a bond /	ibhondi /	eebo'ndee /
a cheque book /	ibhuku lamasheke /	eebookoo laamaashe'ke' /
a credit card /	ikhadi lokuthenga ngesikweleti /	eekaadi lo'koote'ngaa nge'seekwe'le'tee /
an overdraft.	i-ovadrafthi.	ee- o'vaadraaftee.
Where do I sign?	Ngisayina kuphi?	Ngeesaayeena koopee?
Join the queue.	Ngena edilesini / ihele.	Nge'naa e'deele'seenee /eehe'le'.
I want to see the manager.	Ngifuna ukubona umphathi.	Ngeefoonaa ookoobo'naa oompaatee.
Save money.	Beka imali.	Be'kaa eemaalee.
What is the balance of my account?	Malini eyibhalansi ku-akhawunti yami?	Maaleenee e'yeebaalaansee koo-aakaawoontee yaamee?
How much would you like to draw ?	Ufuna ukukhipha malini?	Oofoonaa ookookeepaa maaleenee?
I want R100.	Ngifuna u R100.	Ngeefoonaa oo R100.
I want to cash a cheque.	Ngifuna ukukhesha isheki.	Ngeefoonaa ookooke'shaa eeshe'kee.
I want to draw a cheque.	Ngifuna ukukhipha isheki.	Ngeefoonaa ookookeepaa eeshe'kee.
account	akhawunti	aakaawoontee.
accountant	umbhali wamakhawunti	oombaalee waamaakaawoontee
advance (n)	imali enikwa ngaphambili	eemaalee e'neekwaa ngaapaambeelee
advance (v) / advance (v)	nika ngaphambili / nikela phambili	neeka ngaapaambeelee / neeke'laa paambeelee
auction	indali	eendaalee
auto bank	umshini we-autobank	oomsheenee we'- o'to'bank
balance (n)	ibhalense	eebaale'nse'
balance (v)	linganisa amakhawunti	leengaaneesaa aamaakaawoontee
balance sheet	ibhalenseshidi	eebaale'nse'sheedee
bank balance	imali eseleyo ebhange	eemaalee e'se'le'yo' e'baange'
bank charges	izibizo sobhange	eezeebeezo' so'baange'
bank manager / bank manager	umphathi yebhange / imeneja / imenenja	oompaatee ye'baange' / eeme'ne'jaa / eeme'ne'njaa
banker	umnini webhange	oomneenee we'baange'
bargain / cheap	ishibhile	eesheebeele'
cash withdrawal	ukukhipha imali	ookookeepaa eemaalee
cashier	ukheshiya	ooke'sheeyaa
change (n) - small coins	ushintshi / uhlweza	oosheentshee / oohlwe'zaa
change (v) - change money	shintsha	sheentshaa

23.

cost (v)	biza	beezaa
costly	dulile	dooleele'
counter (n)	itafula lasebhange	eetaafoolaa laase'baange'
counterfeit	imalimbumbulu	eemaaleemboombooloo
deposit (v)	bekelela imali	be'ke'le'laa eemaalee
deposit (n)	isibeko	eeseebe'ko'
financial constraint	ukuntuleka kwezimali	ookoontoole'kaa kwe'zeemaalee
gold	igolide	eego'leede'
joint agreement	isivumelano esihlanganyelwe	eeseevoome'laano' e'seehlaangaanye'lwe'
judgement	ukujezisa	ookooje'zeesaa
loan / account	isikweletu	eeseekwe'le'too
loan (n)	ukuboleka imali	ookoobo'le'kaa eemaalee
loan (v)	boleka	bo'le'kaa
money	imali	eemaale
notes - paper money	imali engamaphepha	eemaalee e'ngaamaape'paa
overdraft	imali esiyeqile ebhange	eemaalee e'seeye'qeele' e'baange'
pin number	inombolo eyimfihlo	eeno'mbo'lo' e'yeemfeehlo'
queue up (v)	hlaba ihele	hlaabaa eehe'le'
queue (n)	ihele	eehe'le'
save (v)	londoloza	lo'ndo'lo'zaa
savings	imali elondoloziwe	eemaalee e'lo'ndo'lo'zeewe'
shares (n)	amasheya	aamaashe'yaa
statement	isitetimende	eeseete'teeme'nde'
stock exchange	indlu yokuthengiselana amasheya	eendloo yo'koote'ngeese'laanaa aamaashe'yaa
transaction	umsebenzi wokuvumelana	oomse'be'nzee wo'koovoome'laanaa
transfer money	ukwedlulisela imali	ookwe'dlooleese'laa eemaalee
withdraw money	kipha imali	keepaa eemaalee
witness / testify (v)	fakaza	faakaazaa
witness (n)	ufakazi	oofaakaazee

MONEY MATTERS	IZINDABA ZEMALI	EEZEENDAABAA ZE'MAALEE
cent	isenti	eese'ntee
2 cents	amasenti amabili	aamaase'ntee aamaabeelee
10 cents	amasenti angu 10	aamaase'ntee aangoo 10
50 cents	osheleni abahlanu / isihlanu	o'she'le'nee aabaahlaanoo / eeseehlaanoo
1 Rand / or	Ishumi	Eeshoomee
1 Rand	Irandi	Eeraandee
10 Rand	Amarandi ayi 10 / Amarandi angu 10	Aamaaraandi aayee 10 / Aamraandee aangoo 10
bank notes	imali engamaphepha	eemaalee e'ngaamaape'paa
banker	umnini webhange	oomneenee we'baange'
bankrupt	shonile	sho'neele'
bankrupt person	umshono / isishoni	oomsho'no' / eeseesho'nee
bankruptcy	ukushona	ookoosho'naa
Bequeath.	Abela aba ifa.	Aabe'laa aabaa eefaa.
change (n)	ushintshi	oosheentshee
cheap - It is cheap.	Kushibhile.	Koosheebeele'.
cheap (to be)	ukushibha	ookoosheebaa
coin	uhlamvu lwemali	oohlaamvoo lwe'maalee
coins	uhlwezu / uhlweza	oohlwe'zoo / oohlwe'zaa
change (n) - small coins	ushintshi / uhlweza	oosheentshee / oohlwe'zaa
change (v) - change money	shintsha	sheentshaa
cost (v)	biza	beezaa
costly	dulile	dooleele'
costs (to cost R10)	ukubiza	ookoobeezaa
count (v)	bala	baalaa
debt	isikweleti	eeseekwe'le'tee
excise (v)	nquma	nqoomaa
excise (n)	intelo yempahla ethengiswayo neyenziwayo	eente'lo' ye'mpaahlaa e'te'ngeeswaayo' ne'ye'nzeewaayo'
expensive (to be)	ukubiza / ukudula	ookoobeezaa / ookoodoolaa
expensive - It is expensive.	Kuyabiza. / Kudulile.	Kooyaabeezaa. / Koodooleele'.
foreign	kwezizwe ezinye	kwe'zeezwe' e'zeenye'
forge (v)	bhumbuluza / lingisa ngokwamanga	boombooloozaa / leengeesaa ngo'kwaamaangaa
forgery	ukubhumbuluza	ookooboombooloozaa
gold	igolide	eego'leede'
gold coins	imali ebomvu	eemaalee e'bo'mvoo
notes – paper money	imali engamaphepha	eemaalee e'ngaamaape'paa
receipt	irisidi	eereeseedee
sale	indali	eendaalee
silver coins	uhlamvu lwesiliva	oohlaamvoo lwe'seeleevaa'
will / testament	incwadi yefa / iwili	eencwaadee ye'faa / eeweelee
Make a will.	Loba incwadi yefa.	Lo'baa eencwaadee ye'faa.

25.

COUNTING	UKUBALA	OOKOOBAALAA
one	kunye	koonye´
two	kubili	koobeelee
three	kuthathu	kootaatoo
four	kune	koone´
five	kuhlanu	koohlaanoo
six	isithupha	eeseetoopaa
seven	isikhombisa	eeseeko´mbeesaa
eight	isishiyagalombili	eeseesheeyaagaalo´mbeelee
(means - leaves ten by two)		
nine	isishiyagalolunye	eeseesheeyaagaalo´loonye´
(means - leaves ten by one)		
ten	ishumi	eeshoomee
eleven	yishumi nanye	yeeshoome naanye´
(means - ten plus one)		
twelve	yishumi nambili	yeeshoomee naambeelee
thirteen	ishumi nantathu	eeshoomee naantaatoo
fourteen	ishumi nane	eeshoomee naane´
fifteen	ishumi nesihlanu	eeshoomee ne´seehlaanoo
sixteen	ishumi nesithupha	eeshoomee ne´seetoopaa
seventeen	ishumi nesikhombisa	eeshoomee ne´seeko´mbeesaa
eighteen	ishumi nesishiyagalombili	eeshoomee ne´seesheeyaagaalo´mbeelee
nineteen	ishumi nesishiyagalolunye	eeshoomee ne´seesheeyaagaalo´loonye´
twenty	amashumi amabili	aamaashoomee aamaabeelee
thirty	amashumi amathathu	aamaashoomee aamaataatoo
forty	amashumi amane	aamaashoomee aamaane´
fifty	amashumi amahlanu	amaashoomee aamaahlaanoo
sixty	amashumi ayisithupha	aamaashoomee aayeeseetoopaa
seventy	amashumi ayisikhombisa	aamaashoomee aayeeseeko´mbeesaa
eighty	amashumi ayisishiyagalombili	aamaashoomee aayeeseesheeyaagaalo´mbeelee
ninety	amashumi ayisishiyagalolunye	aamaashoomee aayeeseesheeyaagaalo´loonye´
hundred	ikhulu	eekooloo
two hundred	amakhulu amabili	aamaakooloo aamaabeelee
thousand	inkulungwane	eenkooloongwaane´
million	imiliyoni / isigidi	eemeeleeyo´nee / eeseegeedee
billion	isigidi sezigidi	eeseegeedee se´zeegeedee
trillion	isigididikazi esinamaqanda angu 18	eeseedeedeekaazee e´seenaamaaqaanda aangoo 18
zero	iliqanda	eeleeqaandaa
half	inxenye / uhafu	eenxe´nye´ / oohaafoo
full	gcwele	gcwe´le´

POST OFFICE	EPOSINI	E'PO'SEENEE
Where is the Post Office?	Likuphi iPosi?	Leekoopee eePo'see?
Post / Send to . . .	Thumela ku . . .	Toome'laa koo . . .
Join the queue.	Ngena edilesini.	Nge'naa e'deele'seenee.
Where is the phone?	Lukuphi ucingo?	Lookoopee ooceengo'?
Post a letter.	Ukuposa incwadi.	Ookoopo'saa eencwaadee.
Buy stamps.	Ukuthenga izitembu.	Ookoote'ngaa eezeete'mboo.
How much is the postage to ...?	Kubiza malini ukuposela e ....?	Koobeezaa maaleenee ookoopo'se'laa e'---?
address	ikheli	eeke'lee
airmail	iposi elihamba ngendiza	eepo'see e' leehaambaa nge'ndeezaa
cancel	esula	e'soolaa
cancellation	ukwesula	ookwe'soolaa
counter	ikhawunta	eekaawoontaa
express post	ukuposa nge-ekspresi	ookoopo'sa nge'- e'kspre'see
insure (v - parcel /letter)	ukuposa ngesiqinisekiso	ookoopo'saa nge'seeqeeneese'keeso'
mail (v)	posa / thuma ngeposi	po'saa / toomaa nge'po'see
mail (n)	iposi	eepo'see
parcel	iphasela	eepaase'laa
phone / call (v)	shaya ucingo	shaayaa ooceengo'
postage / cost of	imali yeposi	eemaalee ye'posee
postbox	ibhokisi lokuposa izincwadi	eebo'keesee lo'koopo'saa eezeencwaadee
registered (mail)	incwadi liqinisekisiwe	eencwaadee leeqeeneese'keeseewe'
stamp (n)	isitembu	eeseete'mboo
Telephone directory	Incwadi yezinamba zocingo	Eencwaadee ye'zeenaambaa zo'ceengo'
I will send a fax.	Ngizothumela ifekisi.	Ngeezo'toome'laa eefe'keesee.
Can I send you an e-mail?	Ngingakuthumela i e-mail?	Ngeengaakootoomelaa ee ee-mail?
Apply for phone.	Ukufaka isicelo sokufakelwa ucingo.	Ookoofaakaa eeseece'lo' so'koofaake'lwaa ooceengo'.
Change address.	Shintsha ikheli.	Sheentshaa eeke'lee.
Fetch the post.	Landa iposi.	Laandaa eepo'see.
Put in the post.	Faka eposini.	Faakaa epo'seenee.
Collect parcel.	Landa iphasela.	Laandaa eepaase'laa.
Pay phone account.	Ukukhokhela i-akhawunti yocingo.	Ookooko'ke'laa ee-aakaawoontee yo'ceengo'.
The phone is out of order.	Ucingo lufile.	Ooceengo' loofeele'.
Send telegram.	Thumela ithelegramu.	Toome'laa eete'le'graamoo.
The parcel is fragile.	Leli phasela lingephuka.	Le'lee paase'laa leenge'pookaa.
Transfer account.	Ukwedlulisela i- akhawunti.	Ookwe'dlooleese'laaee-aakawoontee.
Transfer phone.	Ukwedlulisela ithelefoni / ucingo.	Ookwe'dlooleese'laa eete'le'fo'nee / ooceengo'.

OFFICE / WORK	IHHOVISI / UMSEBENZI	EEHO'VEESEE / OOMSE'BE'NZEE
Where do you work?	Usebenzaphi?	Oose'be'nzaapee?
I work at / in . . .	Ngisebenza e . . .	Ngeese'be'nzaa e' . . .
factory	efektri	e'fe'ktree
garden	engadini	e'ngaadeenee
office	ehhovisi	e'ho'veesee
post office	eposini	e'po'seenee
store / shop	esitolo	e'seeto'lo'
What work do you do? /	Wenza msebenzi muni? /	We'nzaa mse'be'nzee moonee? /
What work do you do?	Yini umsebenzi	Yeenee oomse'be'nzee
	owusebenzayo?	o'woose'be'nzaayo'?
I am a . . .	Ngiyi. . . / Ngingu . . .	Ngeeyee. . . / Ngeengoo . . .
builder	umakhi	oomaakee
cook	umpheki	oompe'kee
driver	umshayeli	oomshaaye'lee
farmer	umlimi	oomleemee
inspector	umhloli	oomhlo'lee
manager	umphathi / imenenja	oompaatee / eeme'ne'njaa
owner	umnikazi	oomneekaazee
parson	umfundisi	oomfoondeesee
teacher	uthishela / uthisha	ooteeshe'laa / ooteeshaa
calculator	isibali	eeseebaalee
calendar	ikhalenda	eekaale'ndaa
computer	ikhompiyutha	eeko'mpeeyootaa
cook	umpheki	oompe'kee
counter	ikhawunta	eekaawoontaa
desk	ideski	eede'skee
diary	idayari	eedaayaaree
directory - telephone	incwadi yezinamba	eencwaadee ye'zeenaambaa
	zocingo	zo'ceengo'
fan	ifeni	eefe'nee
file	ifayili	eefaayeelee
filing cabinet	ikhabethe lamafayili	eekaabe'te' laamaafaayeelee
notebook	inothibhuku	eeno'teebookoo
parcel	iphasela	eepaase'laa
pen	ipeni	eepe'nee
pencil	ipensela	eepe'nse'laa
printer	iphrinta	eepreentaa
rubber	irabha	eeraabaa
sharpener /	isilolipensela /	eeseelo'leepe'nse'laa /
sharpener	umshini wokulola ipensela	oomsheenee wo'koolo'laa eepe'nse'laa
stapler	isitephuli	eeseete'poolee
stationery	okokubhala	o'ko'koobaalaa
sticky tape	ithephu-enamathelayo	eete'poo-e'naamaate'laayo'
telephone	ucingo	ooceengo'

EDUCATION	IMFUNDO	EEMFOONDO´
abacus	i-abakhusi	ee-aabaakoosee
absent (to be absent)	akekhu / agekho	aake´koo / aage´koo
application	isicelo	eeseece´lo´
bursary	umklomelo wokusiza	oomklo´me´lo´ wo´kooseezaa
	ukufunda / umfundaze	ookoofoondaa / oomfoondaaze´
calculator	isibali	eeseebaalee
calendar	ikhalenda	eekaale´ndaa
career	inkambo	eenkaambo´
certificate	isitifiketi	eeseteefeeke´tee
class	ikilasi / iklasi	eekeelaasee / eeklaasee
class - top of the class	inhloko yekilasi	eenhlo´ko´ ye´keelaasee
classroom /	ikamelo lokufundela /	eekaame´lo´ lo´koofoonde´laa /
classroom	ikamelo lekilasi	eekaame´lo´ le´keelaasee
clever	hlakaniphile	hlaakaaneepeele´
computer	ikhompiyutha	eeko´mpeeyootaa
count (v)	bala	baalaa
crayons	amakhrayoni	aamaakraayo´nee
desk	ideski	eede´skee
diary	idayari	eedaayaaree
dictionary	isichazimazwi	eeseecaazeemaazwee
discipline /	impatho eqinileyo /	eempaato´ e´qeeneele´yo´ /
discipline	umthetho	oomte´to´
education	imfundo	eemfoondo´
educational	okufunda	o´koofoondaa
educator	umfundisi / uthisha	oomfoondeesee / ooteeshaa
enthusiasm	umdlandla	oomdlaandlaa
exam	isivivinyo / ukuhlolwa /	eeseeveeveenyo´ / ookoohlo´lwaa /
	izamanesheni	eezaamaane´she´nee
exam paper	iphepha lezamanesheni /	eepe´paa le´zaamaane´she´nee /
	iphepha lokuhlolwa	eepe´paa lo´koohlo´lwaa
exam results	imiphumela	eemeepoome´laa
exercise book	incwadi yokubhala	eencwaadee yo´koobaalaa
expel (v)	xosha esikoleni	xo´shaa e´seeko´le´nee
explain (v)	ukuchaza / chaza	ookoocaazaa / chaazaa
fail (exams) (v)	feyila	fe´yeelaa
file	ifayili	eefaayeelee
hall	ihholo	eeho´lo´
headboy / headgirl	ingqwele yesikole	eengqwe´le´ ye´seeko´le´
holiday	iholide	eeho´leede´
homework	umsebenzi wasekhaya	oomse´be´nzee waase´kaayaa
knowledgeable	isazi	eesaazee
learning	ukufunda	ookoofoondaa
lecture (n)	isifundo	eeseefoondo´
lecturer	umfundisi / umqeqeshi	oomfoondeesee / oomqe´qe´shee
lefthanded	inxele	eenxe´le´
lesson	isifundo	eeseefoondo´
meeting	umhlangano	oomhlaangaano´
Miss.	uNkosazana	ooNko´saazaanaa

Mr. - Mister	uMnumzane	ooMnoomzaane´
Mrs.	uNkosikazi	ooNko´seekaazee
notebook	inothibhuku	eeno´teebookoo
paper	iphepha	eepe´paa
parent	umzali	oomzaalee
pass (exams)	ukuphasa	ookoopaasaa
pay attention	ukunaka / ukuqaphela	ookoonaakaa / ookooqaape´laa
pen	ipeni	eepe´nee
pencil	ipensela	eepe´nse´laa
pencil sharpener	isilolipensela	eeseelo´leepe´nse´laa
prefect	iphrifekti	eepreefe´ktee
primary school	isikole sezingane	eeseeko´le´ se´zeengaane´
principal (of school)	uthishomkhulu /	ooteesho´mkooloo /
	uthishanhloko	ooteeshaanhlo´ko´
printer	iphrinta	eepreentaa
professor	umfundisi omkhulu /	oomfoondeesee o´mkooloo /
	uprofesa	oopro´fe´saa
programme	iprogramu / uhlelo	eepro´graamoo / oohle´lo´
project (n)	iprojekthi	eepro´je´ktee
publish (v)	shicilela	sheeceele´laa
question (n)	umbuzo	oomboozo´
question (v)	buza	boozaa
respect (v)	hlonipha	hlo´neepaa
righthanded	isandla sokunene	eesaandlaa so´koone´ne´
ruler	irula	eeroolaa
scholar	umfundi	oomfoondee
scholarship	umfundaze	oomfoondaaze´
school	isikole	eeseeko´le´
school board	ikomiti lesikole /	eeko´meetee le´seeko´le´/
	ikomiti eliphethe isikole	eeko´meetee e´leepe´te´ eeseeko´le´
schoolbook	incwadi yasesikoleni	eencwaadee yaase´seeko´le´nee
scissors	isikelo	eeseeke´lo´
sport	umdlalo	oomdlaalo´
stationery	okokubhala	o´ko´koobaalaa
student	isitshudeni / umfundi	eeseetshoode´nee / oomfoondee
study (n) - office	isitadi	eeseetaadee
study (v)	ukufunda	ookoofoondaa
subjects	izifundo	eezeefoondo´
succeed (v)	phumelela	poome´le´laa
teach (v)	fundisa	foondeesaa
teach well (v)	fundisa kahle	foondeesaa kaahle´
teacher	umfundisi / uthisha	oomfoondeesee / ooteeshaa
team	ithimu / iqembu	eeteemoo / eeqe´mboo
technikon	ithekhnikhoni	eete´kneeko´nee
term (school term)	ithemu	eete´moo
test (n)	ukuhlolwa / isivivinyo	ookoohlo´lwaa / eeseeveeveenyo´
text book	incwadi yokufunda	eencwaadee yo´koofoondaa
train (v) (sch. / gym)	fundisa / treyina	foondeesaa / tre´yeenaa
trainer / coach	umqeqeshi	oomqe´qe´shee
training college	ikholiji lothisha	eeko´leejee lo´teeshaa

English	Zulu	Pronunciation
type (v)	ukuthayipha	ookootaayeepaa
typewriter	umshini wokuthayipha	oomsheenee wo´kootaayeepaa
uniform	inyufomu	eenyoofo´moo
university	iyunivesithi / inyuvesi	eeyooneeve´seetee / eenyoove´see
write	bhala	baalaa
writing (n)	umbhalo	oombaalo´
writing (v)	ukubhala	ookoobaalaa
Do you know	Uyakwazi	Ooyaakwaazee
how to use	ukusebenzisa	ookoose´be´nzeesaa
a computer?	ikhompiyutha ?	eeko´mpeeyootaa ?
Teach one another.	Fundisanani.	Foondeesaanaanee.
Why are you studying?	Ufundelani?	Oofoonde´laanee?
I like to learn / read.	Ngithanda ukufunda.	Ngeetaandaa ookoofoondaa.
I am reading / learning.	Ngiyafunda.	Ngeeyaafoondaa.
They are studying.	Bayafunda.	Baayaafoondaa.
Marc is learning	uMark, ufundela	OoMark, oofoonde´laa
for an exam.	ukuhlolwa.	ookoohlo´lwaa.
They are at school.	Bayafunda esikoleni.	Baayaafoondaa e´seeko´le´nee.
What school do you go to?	Ufundaphi ?	Oofoondaapee ?
I go to Wykeham school.	Ngifunda eWykeham.	Ngeefoondaa e´ Wykeham.
Read the letter.	Funda incwadi.	Foondaa eencwaadee.
The teacher teaches the	Umfundisi ufundisa	Oomfoondeesee oofoondeesaa
children.	abantwana.	aabaantwaanaa.
The children go to school	Abantwana baya	Aabaantwaanaa baayaa
/ are going to school.	esikoleni.	e´seeko´le´nee.
They are writing exams.	Babhala ukuhlolwa.	Baabaalaa ookoohlo´lwaa.
I am still studying.	Ngisafunda.	Ngeesaafoondaa.
I am studying Zulu.	Ngifunda isiZulu.	Ngeefoondaa eeseeZooloo.
We are learning English.	Sifunda iSingisi.	Seefoonda eeSeengeesee.
Are you studying?	Uyafunda?	Ooyaafoondaa?
They are speaking Zulu.	Bakhuluma isiZulu.	Baakooloomaa eeseeZooloo.
Well done!	Kuhle !	Koohle´!
English is easy.	iSingisi silula.	eeSeengeesee seeloolaa.
Zulu is difficult.	IsiZulu sinzima.	EeseeZooloo seenzeemaa.
By yourself.	Ngokwakho.	Ngo´kwaako´.
It does not matter.	Akunalutho. / Akunandaba.	Aakoonaalooto´. / Aakoonaandaabaa.
He / she is absent.	Akekho. / Agekho.	Aake´ko´. / Aage´ko´.
Pass with honours.	Phumelela ngodumo.	Poome´le´laa ngo´doomo´.
He / She is clever.	Uhlakaniphile.	Oohlaakaaneepeele´.
He / She is stupid.	Uyisiphukuphuku.	Ooyeeseepookoopookoo.
He / She is dumb.	Yena, uyisithutha.	Ye´naa, ooyeeseetootaa.
He / She is deaf and dumb.	Uyisithulu nesimungulu.	Ooyeeseetooloo ne´seemoongooloo.
Study medicine.	Fundela imithi.	Foonde´laa eemeetee.
skilled person	uchwepheshe / ingweti	oochwepe´she´ / eengwe´tee

MEDICAL	MAYELANA NEMITHI	MAAYE'LAANAA NE'MEETEE
I want to see the doctor.	Ngifuna ukubona udokotela.	Ngeefoona ookoobo'naa oodo'ko'te'laa.
I want to see the dentist.	Ngifuna ukubona udokotela wamazinyo.	Ngeefoonaa ookoobo'naa oodo'ko'te'laa waamaazeenyo'.
What is the matter?	Yini na?	Yeenee naa?
I have toothache.	Ngiphethwe yizinyo.	Ngeepe'twe' yeezeenyo'.
My tooth is broken.	Izinyo lami liphukile.	Eezeenyo' laamee leepookeele'.
My tooth is rotten.	Izinyo lami libolile.	Eezeenyo' laamee leebo'leele'.
Take a tooth out.	Khipha izinyo.	Keepaa eezeenyo'.
You need a filling.	Udinga isigcwalisa samazinyo.	Oodeenga eeseegcwaleesaa saamaazeenyo'.
I will have to take your tooth out.	Kufanele ngilikhiphe izinyo lakho.	Koofaane'le' ngeeleekeepe' eezeenyo' laako'.
teeth	amazinyo	aamaazeenyo'
dentures	amazinyo afakwayo	aamaazeenyo' aafaakwaayo'
I need glasses.	Ngidinga izibuko.	Ngeedeengaa eezeebooko'.
I want my eyes tested.	Ngifuna ukuhlolwa amehlo ami.	Ngeefoona ookoohlo'lwaa aame'hlo' aamee.
I am sick.	Ngiyagula.	Ngeeyaagoolaa.
I am injured.	Ngilimele.	Ngeeleeme'le'.
Are you hurt?	Ulimele yini?	Ooleeme'le' yeenee?
Where does it hurt?	Kubuhlungu kuphi?	Kooboohloongoo koopee?
I am bleeding.	Ngiyopha.	Ngeeyo'paa.
I have a headache.	Ngiphethwe yikhanda.	Ngeepe'twe' yeekaandaa.
I have a sore throat.	Ngiphethwe umphimbo.	Ngeepe'twe' oompeembo'.
I have a temperature.	Ngizwa ukushisa.	Ngeezwaa ookoosheesaa.
I have . . .	Ngiphethwe . . .	Ngeepe'twe' . . .
chest trouble	yisifuba	yeeseefoobaa
cold / fever	umkhuhlane	oomkoohlaane'
earache	yindlebe	yeendle'be'
dysentry	isisu segazi	eeseesoo se'gaazee
heartburn	isilungulela	eeseeloongoole'laa
indigestion	ukuqumba	ookooqoombaa
sprained	isenyelo	eese'nye'lo'
stomach ache	yisisu	yeeseesoo
wound	inxeba	eenxe'baa
I have been stung . . .	Ngitinyelwe . . .	Ngeeteenye'lwe' . . .
by a - bee	inyosi	eenyo'see
- insect	isinambuzane	eeseenaamboozaane'
- bluebottle	imivi	eemeevee
I have been bitten . . .	Ngilunywe. . .	Ngeeloonywe' . . .
by a - dog	inja	eenjaa
- snake	inyoka	eenyo'kaa
- cat	ikati	eekaatee
I have been scratched.	Ngiklwejiwe.	Ngeeklwe'jeewe'.
I need stitches.	Ngidinga uuthungwa.	Ngeedeenga ookootoongwaa.
I have broken . . .	Ngephuke . . .	Nge'pooke' . . .
an arm	ingalo	eengaalo'

a leg	umlenze	oomle′nze′
nose	ikhala	eekaalaa
a finger	umunwe	oomoonwe′
a nail	uzipho	oozeepo′
a bone	ithambo	eetaambo′
Put plaster of paris on.	Faka ukhonkolo.	Faakaa ooko′nko′lo′.
I have diarrhoea.	Ngiphethwe yisihudo. / Ngiphethwe yisifo sohudo.	Ngeepe′twe′ yeeseehoodo′. / Ngeepe′twe′ yeeseefo′ so′hoodo′.
I am constipated.	Ngiqumbile.	Ngeeqoombeele′.
I have chest problems.	Ngiphethwe yisifuba.	Ngeepe′twe′ yeeseefoobaa.
I am coughing.	Ngiyakhwehlela.	Ngeeyaakwe′hle′laa.
I feel nauseous.	Nginesicanucanu.	Ngeene′seecaanoocaanoo.
I am vomitting.	Ngiyahlanza.	Ngeeyaahlaanzaa.
I am bleeding.	Ngiyopha.	Ngeeyo′paa.
I am limping.	Ngiyaqhuga.	Ngeeyaaqoogaa.
I feel weak.	Anginamandla.	Aangeenaamaandlaa.
I can't breathe.	Angikwazi ukuphefumula.	Aangeekwaazee ookoope′foomoolaa.
I can't sleep.	Angikwazi ukulala.	Aangeekwaazee ookoolaalaa.
I am deaf.	Angizwa.	Aangeezwaa.
Stay in bed.	Hlala embhedeni.	Hlaalaa e′mbe′de′nee.
What is the matter?	Yini ndaba?	Yeenee ndaabaa?
Where is the . . .?	Ikuphi i . . .?	Eekoopee ee . . .?
What is the time?	Sikhathi sini? / Ubani isikhathi?	Seekaatee seenee ? / Oobaanee eeseekaatee?
The time is . . .10.	Isikhathi ngu . . .10.	Eeseekaatee ngoo . . .10.
May I have . . ?	Ngicela . . .?	Ngeece′laa . . . .?
- pills	amaphilisi	aamaapeeleesee
- medicine	-umuthi	-oomootee
- bandage	-ibhandishi / indwangu yokubopha inxeba	-eebaandeeshee / eendwaangoo yo′koobo′paa eenxe′baa
Do you have any allergies?	Unayo i-aleji?	Oonaayo′ ee-aale′jee?
Take this medicine before meals /	Phuza lo muthi ngaphambili / ngaphambi kokudla /	Poozaa lo′ mootee ngaapaambeelee / ngaapaambee ko′koodlaa /
after meals.	emuva kokudla.	e′moovaa ko′koodlaa.
Go to casualty department /	Yiya kumnyango wabalimele /	Yeeyaa koomnyaango′ waabaaleeme′le′ /
out patients ward.	egumbini labagulela ngaphandle.	e′goombeenee laabaagoole′laa ngaapaandle′.
How is the patient today?	Sinjani isiguli namuhla / namhlanje?	Seenjaanee eeseegoolee naamoohlaa / naamhlaanje′?
The nurse is giving the patients medicine.	Unesi upha iziguli umuthi.	Oone′see oopaa eezeegoolee oomootee.
How is he / she walking today?	Uhamba kanjani namuhla / namhlanje?	Oohaambaa kaanjaanee naamoohlaa / naamhlaanje′?
He / she speaks with difficulty because she is ill.	Ukhuluma kalukhuni ngoba uyagula.	Ookooloomaa kaalookoonee ngo′baa ooyaagoolaa.
She walks with difficulty.	Uhamba kalukhuni.	Oohaambaa kaalookoonee.
To be cold.	Ukugodola.	Ookoogo′do′laa.

English	Zulu	Phonetic
She walks with difficulty.	Uhamba kalukhuni.	Oohaambaa kaalookoonee.
To be cold.	Ukugodola.	Ookoogo'do'laa.
To be hot. / To feel hot.	Uzwa ukushisa.	Oozwaa ookoosheesaa.
hospital	isibhedlela	eeseebe'dle'laa
Go to hospital.	Hamba esibhedlela.	Haambaa e'seebe'dle'laa.
Where is the hospital?	Siphi isibhedlela?	Seepee eeseebe'dle'laa?
What killed him ?	Ubulawe yini?	Ooboolaawe' yeenee?
an accident	ingozi	eengo'zee
Murder a person.	Ukubulala umuntu.	Ookooboolaalaa oomoontoo.
His death was a great shock to me.	Ukufa kwakhe kwangihlukumeza kabi.	Ookoofaa kwaakhe' kwaangeehlookoome'zaa kaabee.
My heart bleeds for him.	Inhliziyo yami iyamkhalela.	Eenhleezeeyo' yaamee eeyaamkaale'laa.
My baby is sick.	Umntwana wami uyagula.	Oomntwaana waamee ooyaagoolaa.
Is it safe for babies?	Kuphephile kubantwana yini?	Koope'peele' koobaantwaanaa yenee?
Help!	Ngisize!	Ngeeseeze'!
Please call an ambulance.	Ngicela ubize iambulense.	Ngeecela oobeeze' ee-aamboole'nse'.
Take your medicine until the nurse tells you to stop.	Phuza umuthi wakho uze utshelwe ngunesi ukuthi ungayeka.	Poozaa oomootee waako' ooze' ootshe'lwe' ngoone'see ookootee oongaaye'kaa.
The nurse has a warm heart.	Unesi unenhliziyo enhle.	Oone'see oone'nhleezeeyo' e'nhle'.
He / She did a good deed.	Uyenze okuhle.	Ooye'nze' o'koohle'.
Poison someone.	Faka ubuthi.	Faakaa oobootee.
poison (n)	ushevu	ooshe'voo
poisoning (n)	ukudlisa ngoshevu	ookoodleesaa ngo'she'voo
Infect. (v)	Fakela ubuthu.	Faake'laa oobootoo.
He / She has bedsores.	Unezilonda sokulala.	Oone'zeelondaa so'koolaalaa.

MEDICAL COMMANDS	IZILAYELO	EEZEELAAYE´LO´
anoint (v)	gcoba	gco´baa
bend (v)	goba / khothama	go´baa / ko´taamaa
blink (v)	cwayiza	cwaayeezaa
blow nose (v)	finya	feenyaa
boil (v)	bilisa	beeleesaa
breathe (v)	phefumula	pe´foomoolaa
change sheets (v)	shintsha amashidi	sheentshaa aamaasheedee
chew (v)	hlafuna	hlaafoonaa
close eyes (v)	cimeza	ceeme´zaa
cough (v)	khwehlela	kwe´hle´laa
cough (n)	ukukhwehlela	ookookwe´hle´laa
disinfect (v)	hlanzisisa	hlaanzeeseesaa
drink (v)	phuza	poozaa
finish (v)	qeda	qe´daa
kneel (v)	guqa	gooqaa
lick (v)	khotha	ko´taa
look at (v)	buka	bookaa
open mouth (v)	khamisa	kaameesaa
quiet - to be quiet	ukuthula	ookootoolaa
quiet (v– shh)	thula	toolaa
rest (v)	phumula	poomoolaa
return (v) - come back	buya	booyaa
stitch (v)	thunga	toongaa
swallow (v)	gwinya	gweenyaa
take out (v)	khipha	keepaa
think (v)	cabanga	caabaangaa
undress (v)	khumula	koomoolaa
Wake up. (v)	Vuka.	Vookaa.
wash (v)	geza	ge´zaa
wrap (v)	songa	so´ngaa
bed - Make the bed. (v)	Yendlula umbhede.	Ye´ndloolaa oombe´de´.
Examine the patient.	Popola isiguli. / Hlola isiguli.	Po´po´laa eeseegoolee. / Hlo´la eeseegoolee.
Feed the patient.	Funza isiguli.	Foonzaa eeseegoolee.
Finish your muti.	Qeda umuthi wakho.	Qe´daa oomootee waako´.
How many times?	Kangaki?	Kaangaakee?
Inject the patient.	Jova isiguli.	Jo´vaa eeseegoolee.
Rinse mouth. (v)	Xubha.	Xoobaa.
Stand up. (v)	Sukuma.	Sookoomaa.
Starve (v) – Don't eat.	Musa ukudla. / Ungadli.	Moosaa ookoodlaa. / Oongaadlee.
Take to theatre.	Hambisa etiyetha.	Haambeesaa e´teeye´taa.
Wash the sheets.	Washa amashidi.	Waashaa aamaasheedee.

PARTS OF THE BODY	IZITHO ZOMZIMBA	EEZEETO' ZO'MZEEMBAA
ankle	iqakala	eeqaakaalaa
arm	ingalo	eengaalo'
arm, forearm	umkhono	oomko'no'o
back - small of back	iqolo	eeqo'lo'
back (of person)	umhlane	oomhlaane'
bile	inyongo	eenyo'ngo'
bladder	isinye	eeseenye'
body	umzimba	oomzeembaa
brain	ubuchopho	oobooco'po'
buttock	isinqe	eeseenqe'
cheek	isihlathi	eeseehlaatee
chest	isifuba	eeseefoobaa
chin	isilevu	eeseele'voo
ear	indlebe	eendle'be'
elbow	indololwane	eendo'lo'lwaane'
eye / eyes	iso / amehlo	eeso' / aame'hlo'
eyebrow	ishiya	eesheeyaa
eyelash	ukhophe	ooko'pe'
face	ubuso	oobooso'
finger - small	ucikicane	ooceekeecaane'
finger	umunwe	oomoonwe'
fingernail	uzipho	oozeepo'
foot	unyawo	oonyaawo'
forefinger	ukhombisile	ooko'mbeeseele'
forehead	isiphongo	eeseepo'ngo'
gall bladder	inyongo	eenyo'ngo'
gullet	umminzo	oommeenzo'
hair - sing / plural	unwele / izinwele	oonwe'le' / eezeenwe'le'
hand	isandla	eesaandlaa
head	ikhanda	eekaandaa
heart	inhliziyo	eenhleezeeyo'
heel	isithende	eeseete'nde'
intestine	ithumbu	eetoomboo
jaw	umhlathi	oomhlaatee
kidney	inso	eenso'
knee	idolo	eedo'lo'
leg	umlenze	oomle'nze'
lip	udebe	oode'be'
liver	isibindi	eeseebeendee
lung	iphaphu	eepaapoo
mouth	umlomo	oomlo'mo'
neck	intamo	eentaamo'
nose, nostril	ikhala	eekaalaa
nose	impumulo / ikhala	eempoomoolo' / eekaalaa
rib	ubambo	oobaambo'
ribs	izimbambo	eezeembaambo'
shinbone	umbala	oombaalaa
shoulder	ihlombe	eehlo'mbe'

stomach	isisu	eeseesoo
thigh	ithanga	eetaangaa
throat	umphimbo	oompeembo´
thumb	isithupha	eeseetoopaa
thyroid gland	indlala yegilo	eendlaala ye´geelo´
thyroid	igilo	eegeelo´
toe	uzwane	oozwaane´
tongue	ulimi	ooleemee
tooth	izinyo	eezeenyo´
waist	ukhalo	ookaalo´
windpipe	uqhoqhoqho	ooqo´qo´qo´
wrist	isihlakala	eeseehlaakaalaa

USEFUL WORDS IN MEDICINE SYMPTOMS & DISEASES	AMAGAMA AVAMILE EMUTHINI IZIMPAWU NA IZIFO	AAMAAGAAMAA AAVAAMEELE´ E´MOOTEENEE EEZEEMPAAWOO NAA EEZEEFO´
abortion	ukukhipha isisu	ookookeepaa eeseessoo
abscess	ithumba	eetoombaa
accident	ingozi	eengo´zee
adam's apple	igilo	eegeelo´
adenoids	amankanka	aamaankaankaa
age	ubudala	ooboodaalaa
aids (n) (illness)	ingculazi	eengcoolaazee
alcoholic	isidakwa	eeseedaakwaa
alimentary canal	umgudu wokudla	oomgoodoo wo´koodlaa
amputate (v)	ukugquma	ookoogqoomaa
anaemia	ukuphaphatheka kwegazi	ookoopaapaate´ka kwe´gaazee
anaesthetic	isidikizisa-mizwa	eeseedeekeezeesaa meezwaa
anaethetist	umdikizisa wernizwa	oomdeekeezeesaa we´meezwaa
anaethetize (v)	dikizisa imizwa	deekeezaa eemeezwaa
anatomy	umumo womzimba	oomoomo´ wo´mzeembaa
anoint (v)	gcoba	gco´baa
antibody	inhlayiyana esegazini	eenhlaayeeyaanaa e´se´gaazeenee
antidote	isibiba	eeseebeebaa
antiseptic	isinqandakuvunda	eeseenqaandaakoovoondaa
antitoxin	isinqandabuthi	eeseenqaandaabootee
anus	ingquza	eengqoozaa
artery	umthambo othumelayo	oomtaambo´ o´toome´laayo´
artificial respiration	ukuphefumulisa	ookoope´foomooleesaa
ask (v)	buza	boozaa
asthma	yisifuba somoya / umbefu	yeeseefoobaa so´mo´yaa /oombe´foo
autopsy	ukusika isidumbu	ookooseekaa eeseedoomboo
avoid	xwaya	xwaayaa
bacteria	ibangwa	eebaangwaa
bacterial infection	yisifo yesibangwa	yeeseefo´ ye´seebaangwaa
become thin	zaca	zaacaa
bilharzia	isichenene	eeseece´ne´ne´
birth (v –give)	beletha	be´le´taa
bleed (v)	opha	o´paa
blind person	impumputhe	eempoompoote´
blood	igazi	eegaazee
body	umzimba	oomzeembaa
boil (n)	ithumba	eetoombaa
boil (v- water)	bila (amanzi)	beelaa (aamaanzee)
boil water (v)	bilisa amanzi	beeleesa aamaanzee
boiled water	amanzi abilisiwe	aamaanzi aabeeleeseewe´
carry (v- on back)	beletha	be´le´taa
chemist	ikhemisi	ke´meesee
chiken pox	inqubulunjwana	eenqooboolonjwaanaa
cholera	ikholera	eeko´le´raa
collapse (v)	quleka	qoole´kaa

condom	ijazi lomkhwenyane	eejaazee lo´mkwe´nyaane´
convalesce (v)	lulama	loolaamaa
corpse	isidumbu	eeseedoomboo
cry (v)	khala	kaalaa
diabetes	isifo sikashukela	eeseefo´ seekaashooke´laa
diarrhoea	uhudo	oohoodo´
difficult	lukhuni	lookoonee
difficulty -with	nzima	nzeemaa
dirty (v)	ngcolisa	ngco´leesaa
dirty	ngcolile	ngco´leele´
disease	isifo	eeseefo´
disinfect (v)	hlanzisisa	hlaanzeeseesaa
disinfectant	isihlanzisisi	eeseehlaanzeeseesee
dysentry	isisu segazi	eeseeso´ se´gaazee
epilepsy	isithuthwane	eeseetootwaane´
examine - to be examined	ukupopolwa / ukuhlolwa	ookoopo´po´lwaa / ookoohlo´waa
examine (v)	popola / hlola	po´po´laa / hlo´laa
face	ubuso	oobooso´
faint (v)	quleka	qoole´kaa
fainting fit	isinxi	eeseenxee
fall down (v)	dilika	deeleekaa
fever	umkhuhlane / imfiva	oomkoohlaane´/ eemfeevaa
finish (v)	qeda	qe´daa
germ	igciwane	eegceewaane´
germs /	amagciwane yokufa /	aamaagceewaane´ yo´koofaa /
germs	amagciwane	aamaagceewaane´
heart trouble	isigula senhliziyo	eeseegoolaa se´nhleezeeyo´
hungry	lambile	laambeele´
hygiene	inhlanzeko	eenhlaanze´ko´
incubate (v)	fukamela	fookaame´laa
incurable	ngenakwelashwa / ngelapheki	nge´naakwe´laashwaa / nge´laape´kee
indigestion	ukuqumba	ookooqoombaa
infect – with disease	Esulela ngokufa.	E´soole´laa ngo´koofaa.
infect (v)	thelela ngokufa	te´le´laa ngo´koofaa
infection	umhabalo	oohaabaalo´
infectious	thathelanayo	taate´laanaayo´
inflamed	okuvuvukele / vuvukile	o´koovoovooke´le´ / voovookeele´
injection	umjovo	oomjo´vo´
innoculation	umjovo	oomjo´vo´
inoculate (v)	jova	jo´vaa
limp (v)	qhuga	qoogaa
loose	xega / xegayo	xe´gaa / xe´gaayo´
madman / woman	uhlanya	oohlaanyaa
malaria	uqhuqho / umalaleveva	ooqooqo´ / oomaalaale´ve´vaa
malarial fever	uluqhuqho / imbo	oolooqooqo´ / eembo´
maternity ward	igumbi lokubelethela	eegoombee lo´koobe´le´te´laa
measles	isimungumungwane	eeseemoongoomoongwaane´
medicine	umuthi	oomootee
midwife	umbelethisi	oombe´le´teesee

mucus	amafinyila	aamaafeenyeelaa
mumps	uzagiga	oozaageegaa
nurse	unesi	oone'see
once	kanye	kaanye'
pain	ubuhlungu	ooboohloongoo
painful	buhlungu	boohloongoo
perspire (v)	juluka	joolookaa
plaster of paris	ukhonkolo	ooko'nko'lo'
pleurisy	amahlaba	aamaahlaabaa
poison -from snake bite	isihlungu senyoka	eeseehloongoo se'nyo'kaa
poison (n)	ubuthi	oobootee
polio	uvendle / ipolio	oove'ndle' / eepo'leeo'
pray	thandaza	taandaazaa
pregnant	mithiyo / nesisu / khulelwe	meeteeyo' / ne'seeso' / koole'lwe'
prescription	sithako	seetaako'
prevent (v)	vikela	veeke'laa
prevention	ukuvikela	ookooveeke'laa
sadness	usizi / ukudabuka	ooseezee / ookoodaabookaa
shiver (v)	qhaqhazela	qaaqaaze'laa
smallpox	ingxibongo	eengxeebo'ngo'
snake poison	isihlungu	eeseehloongoo
stab (v)	gwaza	gwaazaa
start (v)	qala	qaalaa
stitch (v)	thunga	toongaa
stitch (n)	umthungo	oomtoongo'
suffer (v) / suffer from (v)	hlupheka / phathwa	hloope'kaa / paatwaa
symptons	izimpawu	eezeempaawoo
theatre	thiyetha	teeye'taa
three times	kathathu	kaataatoo
tick fever	umganda / inkasa	oomgaandaa / eenkaasaa
tooth decay	ukubola kwamazinyo	ookoobo'la kwaamaazeenyo'
treatment	ukuzelapha	ookooze'laapaa
tuberculosis / T.B.	i-T.B.	eeTeeBee
tumour	iqhubu	eeqooboo
twice	kabili	kaabeelee
urinate (v)	chama	caamaa
urine	umchamo	oomcaamo'
vein	umthambo	oomtaambo'
veneral disease / v.d.	ugcusula	oogcoosoolaa
ward - labour	igumbi lokubelethela	eegoombee lo'koobe'le'te'laa
ward - general	igumbi	eegoombee
warm (temp.)	fudumele	foodoome'le'
warm (v) - up	fudumeza	foodoome'zaa
wet (v)	manzisa	maanzeesaa
whooping cough	isankonkonko /	eesaanko'nko'nko' /
	ugonqogonqo	oogo'nqo'go'nqo'
worms (intestinal)	izilo / izikelemu	eezeelo' / eezeeke'le'moo
wound (v)	limaza	leemaazaa
wound - small wound	isilonda	eeseelo'ndaa
wound - big wound	inxeba	eenxe'baa

40.

English	Zulu	Phonetic
I am not feeling well.	Angiphilile kahle.	Aangeepeeleele´ kaahle´.
I got ill during the night.	Kungihlabe ebusuku.	Koongeehlaabe´ e´boosookoo.
I have been ill for a long time.	Kade ngagula.	Kaade´ ngaagoolaa.
I fell ill last week.	Ngiqale ukugula ngesonto eledlule.	Ngeeqaale´ ookoogoolaa nge´so´nto´ e´le´dloole´.
I become breathless.	Ngiphelelwa ngumoya.	Ngeepe´le´lwaa ngoomo´yaa.
I get sharp pains.	Nginamahlaba.	Ngeenaamaahlaabaa.
I vomit.	Ngiyabuyisa.	Ngeeyaabooyeesaa.
I have fits / epilepsy.	Nginesithuthwane.	Ngeene´seetootwaane´.
He is dying from a fever.	Umkhuhlane uhamba naye.	Oomkoohlaane´ oohaambaa naaye´.
Take ill with fever.	Hlatshwa ngumkhuhlane.	Hlaatshwaa ngoomkoohlaane´.
His body was wasted away by hunger.	Umzimba wakhe wadliwa wukulamba.	Oomzeembaa waake´ waadleewaa wookoolaambaa.
Die a natural death.	Zifela nje.	Zeefe´laa nje´.
Cough up food.	Buyisa ukudla.	Booyeesaa ookoodlaa.
He / She is thin.	Uondile. / Uzacile.	Oo-o´ndeele´. / Oozaakeele´.
I am a diabetic.	Ngiphethwe yisifo sikashukela.	Ngeepe´twe´ yeeseefo´ seekaashooke´laa.
I am allergic to penicillin.	Angizwani nephenisilini.	Aangeezwaanee ne´peneeseeleenee.
Do you have wheelchairs?	Unawo izihlalo kwabazekile?	Oonaawo´ eezeehlaalo´ kwaabaaze´keele´?
I have a sore.	Ngiphethwe isilonda.	Ngeepe´twe´ eeseelo´ndaa.
He / She has septicaemia.	Unesifo segazi elinesihlungu.	Oone´seefo´ se´gaazee e´leene´seehloongoo.
He / She is wounded.	Ulimele.	Ooleeme´le´.

HYGIENE	UKUHLANZEKA	OOKOOHLAANZE´KAA
aids	ingculazi	eengcoolaazee
cholera	ikholera	eeko´le´raa
dehydrate (v)	omisa / mukisa amanzi	o´meesaa / mookeesaa aamaanzee
dehydration	ukulahlekelwa amanzi	ookoolaahle´ke´lwaa aamaanzee
diarrohea	uhudo	oohoodo´
dysentery	isihudo esinegazi	eeseehoodo´ e´seene´gaazee
germs	amagciwane	aamaagceewaane´
gonorrhea	isipatsholo	eeseepaatsho´lo´
hygiene	ukuhlanzeka	ookoohlaanze´kaa
leprosy	ubhadeka /uchoko	oobaade´kaa / oocho´ko´
prevent (v)	vimba	veembaa
prevention	ukuvimbela	ookooveembe´laa
prostitute	isifebe	eeseefe´be´
protect (v)	vikela	veeke´laa
protection	ukuvikelwa	ookooveeke´lwaa
symptoms	izimpawu	eezeempaawoo
treat (v)	elapha	e´laapaa
treatment	ukwelapha	ookwe´laapaa
tuberculosis –T.B.	isifuba sexhwala	eeseefoobaa se´xhwaalaa
typhoid	entelika	e´nte´leekaa
veneral disease – V.D.	ugcusula	oogcoosoolaa
vomit (v)	hlanza	hlaanzaa
vomiting	ukuhlanza	ookoohlaanzaa
Infect with disease.	Esulela ngokufa.	E´soole´laa ngo´koofaa.
Hygiene helps to ---	Ukuhlanzeka kuyasiza ...	Ookoohlaanze´kaa kooyaaseezaa ...
prevent disease /	vikela isifo /	veeke´laa eeseefo´ /
prevent the spread	vikela ukwanda	veeke´laa ookwaandaa
of germs /	kwamagciwane /	kwaamaagceewaane´ /
fight disease.	ilwa isifo.	eelwaa eeseefo´.
Prevent an outbreak of	Vikela ukuqala	Veeke´laa ookooqaalaa
disease.	kwesifo.	kwe´seefo´.
Hygiene also helps in	Ukuhlanzeka kusiza	Ookoohlaanze´ka kooseezaa
stopping the spreading	ekwandiseni	e´kwaandeese´nee
and in the prevention of	nasekuvikeleni	naase´kooveeke´le´nee
the following ailments ---	lezizifo ezilandelayo ---	le´zeezeefo´ e´zeelaande´laayo´---
cholera	ikholera	eeko´le´raa
aids	ingculazi	eengcoolaazee
tuberculosis / TB	isifuba sexhwala / iTB	eeseefoobaa se´xhwaalaa / eeTB
typhoid	entelika	e´nte´leekaa
veneral disease / VD.	ugcusula.	oogcoosoola.
Wash your hands before	Geza izandla zakho	Ge´za eezaandlaa zaako´
handling or eating food.	ngaphambi kokuphatha	ngaapaambee ko´koopaataa
	ukudla.	ookoodlaa.
Wash all raw food	Geza zonke izitshalo	Ge´za zo´nke´ eezeetshaalo´
with clean, treated	eziluhlaza ngamanzi	e´zeeloohlaaza ngaamaanzee
or boiled water.	ahlanzekile noma abilisiwe.	aahlaanze´keele´ no´maa aabeeleeseewe´.

42.

CHOLERA

What is cholera?
Cholera is a bacterial infection contracted by drinking contaminated water, or by eating food which has been in contact with contaminated water, flies or dirty hands. Cholera germs are found in the faeces of cholera infected people. Cholera spreads when the water we drink is contaminated with faeces. This happens when sanitation is poor.

People go to the toilet in or near the river or other water sources. People wash infected nappies in the water.

Faeces infected with cholera contaminates the water we drink. These germs multiply rapidly in water. Prevent cholera. Dispose of human faeces far away from water sources. Keep household water safe and clean. Wash hands - - - after going to the toilet / before preparing food /

or eating food / after changing a baby's nappy. Only use water that is safe and germ free. Use only clean treated or boiled water.

IKHOLERA

Iyini ikholera?
Ikholera yisifo esibangwa yigciwane elitholakala ngokuphuza amanzi anukubezekile, noma ngokudla ukudla okunukubezwe ngamanzi, izimpukane, noma izandla ezingahlanzekile. Amagciwane ekholera atholakala endleni yabantu abanalesisifo. Ikholera iyanda ngesikhathi siphuza amanzi anukubezwe indle. Lokho kwenzeka lapho indlela yokulahlwa kwendle kungaphephile. Abantu bazikhululela emfuleni noma eduze nemithombo yamanzi. Abantu bahlanzela amanabukeni emfuleni anamakaka esezihlabekile. Indle yasebeguliswa ikholera iyawanukubeza amanzi okuphuza. Lamagciwane anda ngokukhulu ukushesha emanzini. Vimbela ikholera. Lahla indle yabantu kude nezindawo zokukha amanzi. Gcina amanzi omndeni ephephile futhi ehlanzekile. Geza izandla - - - emuva kokuzikhulula / ngaphambi kokulungisa ukudla / noma ngaphambi kokudla / emuva kokushintsha inabukeni yengane. Sebenzisa amanzi ahlanzekile kuphela. Sebenzisa amanzi ahlanzekile noma abilisiwe.

EEKO'LE'RAA

Eeyeenee ee-ko'le'raa?
Eeko'le'raa yeeseefo' e'seebaangwaa yeegceewaane' e'leeto'laakaalaa ngo'koopoozaa aamaanzee aanookoobe'ze'keele', no'maa ngo'koodlaa ookoodlaa okoonookoobe'zwe' ngaamaanzee, eezeempookaane', no'maa eezaandlaa e'zeengaahlaanze'keele'. Aamaagceewaane' e'ko'le'raa aato'laakaalaa e'ndle'nee yaabaantoo aabaanaale'seeseefo'. Eeko'le'raa eeyaandaa nge'seekaatee seepoozaa aamaanzee aanookoobe'zwe' eendle'. Lo'ko' kwe'nze'kaa laapo' eendle'laa yo'koolaahlwaa kwe'ndle' koongaape'peele'. Aabaantoo baazeekooloole'laa e'meefoole'nee no'maa e'dooze' ne'meeto'mbo' yaamaanzee. Aabaantoo baahlaanze'laa aamaanaabooke'nee e'mfoole'nee aanaamaakaaka e'se'zeehlaabe'keele'. Eendle' yaase'be'gooleeswaa eeko'le'raa eeyaawaanookoobe'zaa aamaanzee o'koopoozaa. Laamaagceewaane' aandaa ngo'kookooloo ookooshe'shaa e'maanzeenee. Veembe'laa eeko'le'raa. Laahlaa eendle' yaabaantoo koode' ne'zeendaawo' zo'kookaa aamaanzee. Gceenaa aamaanzee o'mnde'nee e'pe'peele' footee e'hlaanze'keele'. Ge'zaa eezaandlaa - - - e'moovaa ko'koozeekooloolaa / ngaapaambee ko'kooloongeesaa ookoodlaa / no'maa ngaapaambee ko'koodlaa / e'moovaa ko'koosheentshaa eenaabooke'nee ye'ngaane'. Se'be'nzeesaa aamaanzee aahlaanze'keele' koope'laa. Sebe'nzeesaa aamaanzee aahlaanze'keele' no'maa aabeeleeseewe'.

43.

Wash all raw food with clean treated or boiled water.	Geza zonke izitshalo eziluhlaza ngamanzi ahlanzekile noma abilisiwe.	Ge'zaa zo'nke' eezeetshaalo' e'zeeloohlaazaa ngaamaanzee aahlaanze'keele' no'maa aabeeleeseewe'.
Protect food from flies.	Vikela ukudla ezimpukaneni.	Veeke'laa ookoodlaa e'zeempookaane'nee.
Use proper toilet facilities.	Sebenzisa indlu efanele yangasese njalo.	Se'be'nzeesaa eendloo e'faanele' yaangaase'se' njaalo'.
Do not allow children to play in dirty water.	Abantwana mabanqatshelwe ukudlala emaxhaphozini angcolile.	Aabaantwaanaa maabaanqaatshwe'le' ookoodlaalaa e'maaxaapo'zeenee aangco'leele'.
Boil water thoroughly.	Bilisa amanzi.	Beeleesaa aamaanzee.
Put one teaspoon of jik in 25 litres of water.	Faka ithisipuni kajikhi emanzini alingana namalitha angu 25.	Faakaa eeteeseepoonee kaajeekee e'maanzeenee aaleengaanaa naamaaleetaa aangoo 25.
Let water stand for two hours before use.	Wayeke amanzi amahora amabili ngaphambi kokuwasebenzisa.	Waaye'ke' aamaanzee aamaaho'raa aamaabeelee ngaapaambee ko'koowaase'be'nzeesaa.
Will not spread.	Ngeke ukufafaze.	Nge'ke' ookoofaafaaze'.
The water is clean.	Amanzi ahlanzekile.	Aamaanzee aahlaanze'keele'.
Hygiene helps prevent cholera.	Ukuhlanzeka kuyasiza ekuvikeleni kwekholera.	Ookoohlaanze'kaa kooyaaseezaa e'koovee ke'le'nee kwe'ko'le'raa.
Symptoms of cholera --- diarrhoea / vomitting / dehydration	Izimpawu zekholera --- uhudo / ukuhlanza / ukulahlekelwa ngamanzi emzimbeni	Eezeempaawoo ze'ko'le'raa --- oohoodo' / ookoohlaanzaa / ookoolaahle'ke'lwaa ngaamaanzee e'mzeembe'nee
Give extra fluids.	Nikeza amanzi amaningi.	Neeke'zaa aamaanzee aamaaneengee.
We must work together to make sure that cholera is prevented.	Kufanele sisebenzisane ukuze siqinisekise ukuthi ikholera iyavinjelwa.	Koofaane'le' seese'be'nzeesaane' ookooze' seeqeeneese'keese' ookootee eeko'le'raa eeyaaveenje'lwaa.
Hygiene helps you to prevent desease.	Ukuhlanzeka kuyasiza ekuvikeleni isifo.	Ookoohlaanze'kaa kooyaaseezaa e'koovee ke'le'nee eeseefo'
Use only clean, treated or boiled water.	Sebenzisa amanzi ahlanzekile noma abilisiwe.	Se'be'nzeesaa aamaanzee aahlaanze'keele' no'maa aabeeleeseewe'.
Protect food and inside your homes from fly contamination.	Vikela ukudla nekhaya lakho ezimpukaneni uzixwaye.	Veeke'laa ookoodlaa ne'kaayaa laako' e'zeempookaane'nee oozeexwaaye'.

AIDS	INGCULAZI	EENGCOOLAAZEE
Managing aids.	Ukuphathwa kwengculazi.	Ookoopaatwaa kwe'ngcoolaazee.
Unite against aids.	Hlanganyela ngengculazi.	Hlaangaanye'laa nge'ngcoolaazee.
What is aids?	Yini ingculazi?	Yeenee eengcoolaazee?
Aids is a disease.	Ingculazi yisifo.	Eengcoolaazee yeeseefo'.
It is caused by a virus	Yisifo esibangelwa	Yeeseefo' e'seebaange'lwaa
called HIV.	yigciwane / ivayirasi	yeegceewaane' / eevaayeeraasee
	ebizwa ngeHIV.	e'beezwaa nge' HIV.
Aids slowly weakens	Ingculazi ibulala	Eengcoolaazee eeboolaalaa
a person's ability to	amasosha omzimba	aamaaso'shaa o'mzeembaa
fight off other diseases.	alwa nezifo.	aalwaa ne'zeefo'.
HIV test	Ukuhlolelwa i HIV.	Ookoohlo'le'lwaa eeHIV.
HIV positive	Une ngculazi.	Oone' ngcoolaazee.
Medical treatment and care.	Ukwelapha nokunakekela.	Ookwe'laapa no'koonaake'ke'laa.
Terminate pregnancy.	Khipha isisu.	Keepaa eeseesoo.
A person with HIV has	Umuntu onengculazi	Oomoontoo o'ne'ngcoolaazee
a right to confidentiality.	unelungelo lwemfihlo.	oone'loonge'lo' lwe'mfeehlo'.
People with aids have the	Abantu abanengculazi	Aabaantoo aabaane'ncgoolaazee
right to live	banelungelo lokuphila	baane'loonge'lo' lo'koopeelaa
their lives	impilo yabo ngendlela	eempeelo' yaabo' nge'ndle'laa
with respect, dignity and	ehloniphekile,	e'hlo'neepe'keele',
freedom from	enesithunzi nokuba	e'ne'seetoonzee no'koobaa
discrimination	nenkululeko, nokuthi	ne'nkooloole'ko', no'kootee
and blame.	bangabandlululwa	baangaabaandlooloolwaa
	bangabekwa icala.	baangaabe'kwaa eecaalaa.
Aids can be passed from	Ingculazi ithelelana	Eengcoolaazee eete'le'laanaa
one person to another---	ngokusuka komunye	ngo'koosookaa ko'moonye'
	umuntu ingene	oomoontoo eenge'ne'
	komunye ngesikhathi--	ko'moonye' nge'seekaatee---
during sex /	sokulalana /	so'koolaalaanaa /
blood transfusion /	ukuthasiselwa igazi /	ookootaaseese'lwaa eegaazee /
giving / donating blood /	kuthekelisa ngegazi /	koote'ke'leesa nge'gaazee /
infected wounds.	izilonda ezithathelanayo.	eezeelo'ndaa e'zeetaate'laanaayo'.
Talk about the risk of HIV	Xoxisanani nophathina	Xo'xeesaanaanee no'paateenaa
and dangers of infection	wakho kwezokulalana	waako' kwe'zo'koolaalaanaa
with your partner.	ngezingozi ze HIV.	nge'zeengo'zee ze'HIV.
There are a number	Kunezindlela eziningi	Koone' zeendle'laa e'zeeneengee
of ways to have safe sex ---	zokuya ocansini	zo'kooyaa o'caanseenee
	ngendlela ephephile ---	nge'ndle'laa e'pe'peele' ---
including using condoms /	ukusebenzisa	ookoose'be'nzeesa
	amakhondomu /	aamaako'ndo'moo /
or having sex with no	ukungalalani	ookoongaalaalaanee
penetration /	nomhlobo wakho /	no'mhlo'bo' waako' /
or contact with body fluids.	nizidlalele nje ngaphandle	neezeedlaale'le' nje' ngaapaandle'
	kokungenelana.	ko'koonge'ne'laanaa.
If infected with HIV	Uma ungenwe yi HIV	Oomaa oonge'nwe' yee HIV
you can still lead a	ungakwazi ukuphila	oongaakwaazee ookoopeelaa
normal healthy life	impilo ekahle	eempeelo' e'kaahle'
for many years by ----	iminyaka eminingi----	eemeenyaakaa e'meeneengee ----

Taking care of your health.

Being positive about life.

Getting support from those around you.

Practising safer sex.

Couples in a serious relationship choose to have an HIV test.

This helps them make choices about their sexual practices and their future.

A baby can be infected with the HIV virus during pregnancy,

or while being breastfed. You have the right to say "NO". Respect your partner. Practise safe sex.

Work together to prevent aids. To rape a child does not cure aids. Taking care of your health includes: eating properly / getting exercise / get enough rest.

Ngokunakekela impilo yakho.

Ngokuba nombono omuhle ngempilo.

Ngokusekelwa yilabo ophilisana nabo.

Ngokuya ocansini ngendlela ephephile.

Izithandani ezizimisele kakhulu zikhetha ukuthi zihlolelwe i HIV.

Lokhu kusiza ukuthi bakwazi ukukhetha kwezokulalana kanye nekusasa lwabo.

Ingane ingangenwa yigciwane le HIV ngesikhathi unina ekhulelwe,

noma ngokuncelisa. Ilungelo lakho ukusho "ANGIFUNI". Hlonipha uphathina wakho Yiya ocansini ngendlela ephephile. Sebenzisanani ndawonye ukuvimbela ingculazi. Ukudlwengula umntwana akuyivikeli ingculazi. Ukunakekela impilo yakho kubandakanya lokhu: idla ukudla okunomsoco / ukwelula umzimba / ukuphumula ngokwanele.

Ngo'koonaake'ke'laa eempeelo' yaako'.

Ngo'koobaa no'mbo'no' o'moohle' nge'mpeelo'.

Ngo'koose'ke'lwaa yeelaabo' o'peeleesaanaa naabo'.

Ngo'kooyaa o'caanseenee nge'ndle'laa e'pe'peele'.

Eezeetaandaanaa e'zeezeemeese'le' kaakooloo zeeke'taa ookootee zeehlo'le'lwe' ee HIV.

Lo'koo kooseezaa ookootee baakwaazee ookooke'taa kwe'zo'koolaalaanaa kaanye' ne'koosaasaa lwaabo.'

Eengaane' eengaange'nwaa yeegceewaane' le' HIV nge'seekaatee ooneenaa e'koole'lwe',

no'maa ngo'koonce'leesaa. Eeleeloonge'lo' laako' ookoosho' "AANGEEFOONEE". Hlo'neepaa oopaateenaa waako'. Yeeyaa o'caanseenee nge'ndle'laa e'pe'peele'. Se'be'nzeesaanaanee ndaawo'nye' ookooveembe'laa eengcoolaazee. Ookoodwle'ngoolaa oomntwaanaa aakooyeeveeke'lee eengcoolaazee. Ookoonaake'ke'laa eempeelo' yaako' koobaandaakaanyaa lo'koo: eedlaa ookoodlaa o'koono'mso'co' / ookwe'loolaa oomzeembaa / ookoopoomoolaa ngo'kwaane'le'.

46.

TUBERCULOSIS / TB

TB is a major problem in South Africa. Some people believe you can only get TB if you are poor or are an alcoholic. This is not true. Anyone can get TB. TB is one of the leading causes of death in South Africa.

It is a curable disease. TB of the lungs is the most common. The main sign of TB is an ongoing cough. Without treatment TB can spread from one person to to another. With the correct treatment TB can be cured. As soon as a person is on treatment, a person is no longer at risk to their family and the community.

These are the symptoms of TB:
An ongoing cough. /
Coughing up blood. /
Loss of weight. /
and loss of appetite. /

Sweating at night. /
To feel tired and weak. /

Pain in the chest. You should see a health worker at your local clinic to be checked for TB. Treatment at all public clinics is free. It is very important to complete your TB treatment.

ISIFUBA SEXHWALA / TB

I-TB iyinkinga enkulu kabi eNingizimu Africa. Kunabantu abakholwa wukuthi i-TB uyithola ngoba uyahlupheka noma uyisidakwa. Akulona iliqiniso. Noma ubani angayithola iTB. I-TB ingesinye sezifo esiphuma phambili ngokubala abantu e South Africa.

I-TB iyisifo eselaphekayo. I-TB yamaphaphu iyona egcwele kakhulu. Izimpawu zeTB ezisemqoka wokukhwehlela okungapheli. Uma ingelashwa, i-TB inganda yedlulele nakwabanye. Kepha, uma yelashwa ngendlela efanele, iyaphela. Uma oguliswa yiyo eseqalile ukudla imithi yokwelashwa, akabe esaba yingozi emndenini nasemphakathini.

Nazi izimpawu ze TB:

Ukukhwehlela okungapheli. /
Ukukhwehlela igazi. /
Ukwehla komzimba. /
nokuphelelwa wuthando lokudhla. /

Ukujuluka ebusuku. /
Ukukhathala futhi ukuphela amandla. /

Ubuhlungu esifubeni. Kudingeka ubone unesi ekliniki eseduze akubheke ukuthi awunayo yini i-TB. Ukwelashwa emakliniki kahulumeni kumahhala. Kubaluleke kabi ukuba uyidle yonke imithi yokwelashwa.

EESEEFOOBAA SE'XHWAALAA / TB

Ee-Teebee eeyeenkeengaa e'nkooloo kaabee e'Neengeezeemoo Aafreekaa. Koonaabaantoo aabaako'lwaa wookootee ee-Teebee ooyeeto'laa ngo'baa ooyaahloope'kaa no'maa ooyeeseedaakwaa. Aakoolo'naa eeleeqeeneeso'. No'maa oobaanee aangaayeeto'laa eeTB. Ee-TB eenge'seenye' se'zeefo' e'seepoomaa paambeelee ngo'koobaalaa aabaantoo e' South Africa.

Ee-TB eeyeeseefo'e'se'laape'kaayo'. Ee-TB yaamaapaapoo eeyo'naa e'gcwe'le' kaakooloo. Eezeempaawoo ze' TB e'zeese'mqo'kaa wo'kookwe'hle'laa o'koongaape'lee. Oomaa eenge'laashwaa, ee-TB eengaandaa ye'dloole'le' naakwaabaanye'. Ke'paa, oomaa ye'laashwaa nge'ndle'laa e'faane'le', eeyaape'laa. Oomaa o'gooleeswaa yeeyo' e'se'qaaleele' ookoodlaa eemeetee yo'kwe'laashwaa aakaabe' e'saabaa yeengo'zee e'mnde'neenee naase'mpaakaateenee.

Naazee eezeempaawoo ze' TB:

Ookookwe'hle'laa o'koongaape'lee. /
Ookookwe'hle'laa eegaazee. /
Ookwe'hlaa ko'mzeembaa. /
no'koope'le'lwaa wootaando' lo'koodlaa. /

Ookojoolookaa e'boosookoo./
Ookookaataalaa footee ookoope'laa aamaandlaa. /

Ooboohloongoo e'seefoobe'nee. Koodeenge'kaa oobo'ne' oone' e'kleeneekee e'se'dooze' aakoobe'ke' ookootee aawoonaayo' yeenee ee-TB. Ookwe'laashwaa e'maakleeneekee kaahooloome'nee koomaahaalaa. Koobaaloole'ke' kaabee ookoobaa ooyeedle' yo'nke' eemeetee yo'kwe'laashwaa.

EMERGENCIES	IZINGOZI	EEZEENGO'ZEE
There has been an accident.	Kuvele ingozi.	Koove'le' eengo'zee.
I am hurt.	Ngilimele.	Ngeeleeme'le'.
Are you hurt ?	Ulimele na?	Ooleeme'le' naa?
He is seriously hurt.	Ulimele kakhulu.	Ooleeme'le' kaakooloo.
This person is injured.	Lo muntu ulimele.	Lo' moontoo ooleeme'le'.
No one is seriously hurt.	Abekho abalimele kakhulu.	Aabe'koo aabaaleeme'le' kaakooloo.
Do not move the person.	Ningamsusi lo muntu.	Neengaamsoosee lo' moontoo.
Is anyone dead ?	Ukhona oshonile?	Ooko'naa o'sho'neele'?
Can we help ?	Singasiza na?	Seengaaseezaa naa?
Can you help me please ?	Ngicela ungisize?	Ngeece'laa oongeeseeze'?
Please call a . . .	Ngicela ubize . . .	Ngeece'laa oobeeze' . . .
doctor	udokotela	oodo'ko'te'laa
an ambulance	i-ambulense	ee-aamboole'nse'
the police	amaphoyisa	aamaapo'yeesaa
Come as soon as	Yiza / Woza lapha	Yee'zaa / Wo'zaa laapaa
possible.	ngokushesha.	ngo'kooshe'shaa.
This is an emergency.	Lokhu yingozi. / Le yingozi.	Lo'koo yeengo'zee. / Le' yeengo'zee.
Report an accident.	Ngizobika ingozi.	Ngeezo'beekaa eengo'zee.
Where is the nearest . . .?	Sikuphi i . . .siseduze?	Sekoopee ee . . .seese'dooze'?
hospital	isibhedlela	eeseebe'dle'laa
garage	igalaji	eegaalaajee
Do you have a first aid kit?	Unawo yini umgodla wezinto zosizo lokuqala?	Oonaawo' yeenee oomgo' dlaa we'zeento' zo'seezo' lo'kooqaalaa?
Please call a	Ngicela ungibizele	Ngeece'laa oongeebeeze'le'
breakdown service.	imoto ezongidonsa.	eemo'to' e'zo'ngeedo'nsaa.
I have been robbed of	Imali yami nezingubo	Eemaali yaami ne'zeengooboo
my money and clothes.	kwebiwe ngamasela.	kwe'beewe' ngaamaase'laa.
robber	umphangi	oompaangee
The house is on fire.	Indlu iyasha.	Eendloo eeyaashaa.
The river is in flood.	Umfula usudla izindwani.	Oomfoolaa oosoodlaa eezeendwaanee.

VIOLENCE / CRIME	ISIDLAKADLA / ICALA ELINZIMA	EESEEDLAAKAADLAA / EECAALA E´LEENZEEMAA
accident	ingozi	eengo´zee
act recklessly (v)	ngokuhlambalaza	ngo´koohlaambaalaazaa
admitted guilt	vumile icala	voomeele´ eecaalaa
advisor	umeluleki	oome´loole´kee
aids (n) - sickness	ingculazi	eengcoolaazee
annoy (v)	hlupha / casula	hloopaa / caasoolaa
appeal (v) in court	dlulisa	dlooleesaa
arrest (v)	bamba / boshwa	baambaa / bo´shwaa
arrested	boshiwe	bo´sheewe´
arrived - We arrived in time.	Sifike ngesikhathi.	Seefeeke´ nge´seekaatee.
assault (v)	dumela / sukela	doome´laa / sooke´laa
assault (n)	ukudumela / ukusukela	ookoodoome´laa / ookoosooke´laa
assegai / spear	umkhonto	oomko´nto´
attack (v)	sukela	sooke´laa
attack (n)	ukusukela	ookoosooke´laa
attack - with a vengeance	Sukela / Vukela.	Sooke´laa / Vooke´laa.
attack – on one's life	Ukulinga Ukumbulala.	Ookooleengaa Ookoomboolaalaa.
authority (n)	izikhulu	eezeekooloo
batter (v)	mbungqa / shaya	mboongqaa / shaayaa
beat (v) hit hard /	hlukumeza /	hlookoome´zaa /
beat (v) hit hard	shaya ngamandla	shaayaa ngaamaandlaa
beat up	shaya / dovadova	shaayaa / do´vaado´vaa
blame (n)	umsolwa	oomso´lwaa
blame (v)	jezisa / sola	je´zeesaa / so´laa
bomb (n)	ibhomu	eebo´moo
bomb (v) - to bomb	ukubhomba	ookoobo´mbaa
brave - to be brave	unesibindi	oone´seebeendee
break down (house)	diliza	deeleezaa
breathalyser test	ukuhlola umoya	ookoohlo´laa oomo´yaa
burn (v)	shisa	sheesaa
care (v)	naka	naakaa
catch fire	okheleka	o´khe´le´kaa
catch (v)	bamba	baambaa
charge (v) - accuse / blame	beka icala	be´kaa eecaalaa
charge (v) - falsely	phoqa	po´qaa
charge (v) - sue	mangala	maangaalaa
chief	inkosi	eenko´see
commit – (v) a crime	lelesa / gebenga	le´le´saa / ge´be´ngaa
commit (n) a crime	ukulelesa	ookoole´le´saa
commit - adultery	phinga / ukuphinga	peengaa / ookoopeengaa
commit - high treason	ukuvukela umbuso	ookoovooke´laa oombooso´
commotion	isidumo	eeseedoomo´
conflict (n)	ukuphambana	ookoopaambaanaa
conflict (v) - with	phambana na	paambaanaa naa
conflict (v)	phambana	paambaanaa
confuse (v)	dida	deedaa
console (v)	duduza	doodoozaa

49.

contract (v) - disease (aids)	habula	haaboolaa
contract (n)	isivumelwano	eeseevoome'lwaano'
contract (v)	vumelana	voome'laanaa
control (v)	ukuzibamba	ookoozeebaambaa
cover - cover up (v)	mboza / gqiba	mbo'zaa / gqeebaa
coward	igwala	eegwaalaa
crack shot	umnembi	oomne'mbee
crime	icala / ubugebengu	eecaalaa / oobooge'be'ngoo
criminal	isigebengu	eeseege'be'ngoo
crowd (n)	isixuku	eeseexookoo
damage (n)	umonakalo / ukulimaza	oomo'naakaalo' / ookooleemaazaa
damage (v)	ona / limaza	o'naa / leemaazaa
danger - His life is in danger.	Impilo yakhe isengozini.	Eempeelo' yaake' eese'ngo'zeenee.
danger	ingozi	eengo'zee
deceive (v)	khohlisa	ko'hleesaa
defend (v)	vikela	veeke'laa
deliberate	ngamabomu	ngaamaabo'moo
demand (n)	ukudingeka	ookoodeenge'kaa
demand (v)	dinga	deengaa
demolish (v)	diliza	deeleezaa
deny (v)	phika	peekaa
destroy (v) - property	bulala / chitha	boolaalaa / ceetaa
destroy (v) - utterly	shabalalisa	shaabaalaaleesaa
detective	ufokisi	oofo'keesee
detention - place of	isitokisi	eeseeto'keesee
detention - eg. to be in jail	toka	to'kaa
disappoint (v)	dumaza	doomaazaa
dispute(v)	banga	baangaa
dispute (n)	umbango	oombaango'
each & everyone	yilowo nalawo	yeelo'wo' naalaawo'
election	ukhetho	ooke'to'
employ (v) (use / employ)	sebenzisa / qasha	se'be'nzeesaa / qaashaa
end (v)	phela	pe'laa
enemy	isitha	eeseetaa
escape (v) - from capture	dlibula	dleeboolaa
escape (v) - from danger	sinda engozini	seendaa e'ngo'zeenee
escape (v) /	baleka /	baale'kaa /
escape (v)	dlubulundela	dloobooloonde'laa
escape (v) - from jail	eqa etilongweni	e'qaa e'teelo'ngwe'nee
evidence (v) - give evidence	fakaza	faakaazaa
evidence (n) - witness	ubufakazi	ooboofaakaazee
evidence (n) – proof	isiqiniseko	eeseeqeeneese'ko'
example - bad example	yisibonelo esibi	yeeseebo'ne'lo' e'seebee
example	isibonelo	eeseebo'ne'lo'
exhume (v)	umbulula / ukumbulula	oombooloolaa / ookoombooloolaa
expose (v)	veza	ve'zaa
faction fight	ukulwa kwezigodi ezimbili ezalanayo	ookoolwaa kwe'zeego'dee e'zeembeelee e'zaalaanaayo'
faction	isixexelegu	eeseexe'xe'le'goo
famine	indlala	eendlaalaa

50.

fight - with assegais (v)	hlabana / gwazana	hlaabaanaa / gwaazaanaa
fight - with sticks (v)	shayana	shaayaanaa
fight (n)	ukulwa	ookoolwaa
fight savagely (v)	maklazana	maaklaazaanaa
fight war (v)	ilwa impi	eelwaa eempee
fight (v)	ilwa	eelwaa
fine (money) (v)	ukuhlawulisa	ookoohlaawooleesaa
flock / swarm (v)	ubhuzane	ooboozaane′
followers	abalandeli	aabaalaande′lee
freedom	inkululeko	eenkooloole′ko′
frighten (v)	thusa	toosaa
gang - up against (v)	vukelana	vooke′laanaa
gang of youths	injisuthi / umgengane	eenjeesootee / oomge′ngaane′
gang	iqembu / iviyo	eeqe′mboo / eeveeyo′
gangster	isigebengu	eeseege′be′ngoo
gangsterism	ubugebengu	oobooge′be′ngoo
Go! (v)	Hamba!	Haambaa!
Go away!!	Suka!	Sookaa!
government	uhulumeni	oohooloome′nee
gun	isibhamu	eeseebaamoo
handcuff (n)	uzankosi	oozaanko′see
handcuff (v)	Faka uzankosi.	Faakaa oozaanko′see.
hang (v)	lengisa	le′ngeesaa
Help them.	Basize.	Baaseeze′.
Help one another.	Sizana / Sizanani.	Seezaanaa / Seezaanaanee.
help (v)	siza	seezaa
helper	umsizi	oomseezee
hide (v) (something)	fihla	feehlaa
hide (v)	bhaca / casha	baacaa / caashaa
hijack (v)	ukubamba inkunzi	ookoobaambaa eenkoonzee
Hold a meeting.	Bamba umhlangano.	Baambaa oomhlaangaano′.
Hold an election.	Senza ukhetho.	Se′nzaa ooke′to′.
Hold responsible.	Ubekwe icala.	Oobe′kwe′ eecaalaa.
Hold up bank.	Vimbezela ibhange.	Veembe′ze′laa eebaange′.
honest / They are honest.	Bathembekile.	Baate′mbe′keele′.
honest	qotho / neqiniso	qo′to′ / ne′qeeneeso′
honest people	abaqotho	aabaaqo′to′
hostage (n)	umthunjwa	oomtoonjwaa
hostage (v) - Take as hostage	Thumba.	Toombaa.
hurt (v) - get hurt	limala	leemaalaa
hurt (v) - make sore/damage	limaza	leemaazaa
hurt (v)	limaza	leemaazaa
immoral person	ongenambeko	o′nge′naambe′ko′
incident	isehlakalo	eese′hlaakaalo′
inform (v)	azisa	aazeesaa
initiate (v)	sungula	soongoolaa
injure (v)	limaza	leemaazaa
justice	ukwenza komthetho	ookwe′nzaa ko′mte′to′
killers	ababulali	aabaaboolaalee
law / regulation / rule	umthetho	oomte′to′

lawyer	ummeli	oome'lee
legislate (v)	shaya umthetho	shaayaa oomte'to'
lies	amanga	aamaangaa
life / health	impilo	eempeelo'
magistrate court	inkantolo	eenkaanto'lo'
magistrate	imantshi	eemaantshee
march - forced march	Ukuhambisisa indlela ende.	Ookoohaambeeseesaa eendle'la e'nde'.
march - peaceful	Ukuhamba uthulile / uthule.	Ookoohaambaa ootooleele'/ ootoole'.
march - on the march	endleleni	endle'le'nee
matter - Does not matter.	Akunandaba.	Aakoonaandaabaa.
matter (n)	udaba	oodaabaa
meet with (v)	hlangana no	hlaangaanaa no'
meet with demands	anelisa	aane'leesaa
meeting (v)	hlangana	hlaangaanaa
meeting place	isidlanga / isidlangala	eeseedlaangaa / eeseedlaangaalaa
meeting /	ukuhlangana /	ookoohlaangaanaa /
meeting	umhlangano	oomhlaangaano'
member	ilungu	eeloongoo
mock (v)	bhuqa	booqaa
molest (v)	nukubeza / hlupha	nookoobe'zaa / hloopaa
murder (v)	bulala umuntu	boolaalaa oomoontoo
nation	isizwe	eeseezwe'
negotiate (v)	vumelana	voome'laanaa
nervous (to be)	kuba novalo	koobaa no'vaalo'
numbers - in large numbers	ngezinqwaba	nge'zeenqwaabaa
out - of control (mind)	ngaphethwe	ngaape'twe'
pardon (v) - ask for pardon	shweleza / shwelezisa	shwe'le'zaa / shwe'le'zeesaa
patrol (v)	gada	gaadaa
patrol (n)	iqembu lamaphoyisa	eeqe'mboo laamaapo'yeesaa
pay fine	hlawula	hlaawoolaa
peace - Be at peace with.	Hlalisana ngokuthula na.	Hlaaleesaanaa ngo'kootoolaa naa.
peace – (v) be at peace	thula	toolaa
peace – (v) make peace	xolisa	xo'leesaa
peace - peace of mind	ukuba noxolo	ookoobaa no'xo'lo'
peace - stop the peace	- gcina ukuthula	- gceenaa ookootoolaa
peace	uxolo / lu-xolo	ooxo'lo' / loo-xo'lo'
peaceful march /	ukuhamba uthulile /	ookoohaambaa ootooleele' /
peaceful march	ukuhamba uthule	ookoohaambaa ootoole'
peaceful	thulile / thule	tooleele' / toole'
peacemaker /	umthulisazwe /	oomtooleesaazwe' /
peacemaker	umthiwoxolo	oomteewo'xo'lo'
perjury	icala lokufungela amanga	eecaala lo'koofoonge'laa aamaangaa
permission	imvume	eemvoome'
petrol bomb	ibhomu kaphethroli	eebo'moo kaape'tro'lee
plan / plot (v)	ceba	ce'baa
plan / plot (n)	icebo	eece'bo'
plot (n)	isigungu / uzungu	eeseegoongoo / oozoongoo
plot (v)	enza isigungu / uzungu	e'nzaa eeseegoongoo / oozoongoo
prevent (v)	vimba	veembaa
prison	ijele	eeje'le'

prisoner	isiboshwa	eeseebo'shwaa
prisoners	iziboshwa	eezeebo'shwaa
problems	izinkinga	eezeenkeengaa
prosecutor	umshushisi	oomshoosheesee
protest (v)	ukubhikisha	ookoobeekeeshaa
protest march /	hamba ezwini lokunqaba /	haamba e'zweenee lo'koonqaabaa /
protest march	nqaba	nqaabaa
protestors	ababhikishi	aabaabeekeeshee
Punish the enemy.	Shaya isitha.	Shaayaa eeseetaa.
punish (v)	shaya / jezisa	shaayaa / je'zeesaa
question (n)	umbuzo	oomboozo'
question (v)	buza	boozaa
quickly (hurry)	masinya	maaseenyaa
quickly - go quickly	ngokushesha	ngo'kooshe'shaa
rage (n)	ulaka olukhulu	oolaakaa o'lookooloo
rage (v)	dlanga	dlaangaa
rampage (n)	ukudlovunga	ookoodlo'voongaa
rampage (v)	dlovunga	dlo'voongaa
rape (n)	ukudlwengula	ookoodlwe'ngoolaa
rape (v)	dlwengula	dlwe'ngoolaa
refuse (v)	ala / ukwala	aalaa / ookwaalaa
relatives	izihlobo	eezeehlo'bo'
request (n)	isicelo	eeseece'lo'
revolver	ivolovolo	eevo'lo'vo'lo'
reward (v)	klomela / vuza	klo'me'laa / voozaa
reward (n)	umvuzo	oomvoozo'
riot - run riot	banga isidumo	baangaa eeseedoomo'
riot (n)	isidumo	eeseedoomo'
riot (v)	banga isidumo	baangaa eeseedoomo'
rioter /	umbangi /	oombaangee /
rioter	umsusi wesidumo	oomsoosee we'seedoomo'
ritual	isimo senkonzo	eeseemo' se'nko'nzo'
rob (v) (a bank)	ukuphanga ibhange	ookoopaangaa eebaange'
robber	umphangi	oompaangee
robbery	ukweba	ookwe'baa
rule - Break a rule.	Phula umthetho.	Poolaa oomte'to'.
rule (law & order)	umthetho	oomte'to'
rule (v)	phatha	paataa
ruler	inkosi	eenko'see
rules & regulations	imithetho nezimiso	eemeete'to' ne'zeemeeso'
Run away from jail.	Eqa etilongweni.	E'qaa e'teelo'ngwe'nee.
run away (v)	baleka	baale'kaa
run (v)	gijima	geejeemaa
rural areas	emaphandleni	e'maapaandle'nee
savagery	ubulwane	ooboolwaane'
set alight (v)	okheleka	o'khe'le'kaa
shield (n)	isihlangu	eeseehlaangoo
shoot (v)	dubula	dooboolaa
shot - be shot (v)	dutshulwa	dootshoolwaa
soldier	isosha	eeso'shaa

solution	isixazululo	eeseexaazooloolo'
spear	umkhonto	oomko'nto'
stab (v)	gwaza	gwaazaa
stampede (v)	gulukudela	goolookoode'laa
statement	isitetimende	eeseete'teeme'nde'
stick (n)	uthi / induku	ootee / eendookoo
stone (v) - throw a stone	phonsa	po'nsaa
stoning	shaya ngamatshe	shaayaa ngaamaatshe'
strength	amandla	aamaandle'
strike (n)	isiteleka	eeseete'le'kaa
strike - Go on strike.	Duba umsebenzi. / Teleka.	Doobaa oomse'be'nzee. / Te'le'kaa.
strike - against work	ngqubuza / strayika	ngqooboozaa / straayeekaa
sue (v)	ukumangalela	ookoomaangaale'laa
take away (v)	susa	soosaa
tease (v)	sukela / hlupha	sooke'laa / hloopaa
thief	isela	eese'laa
thieving	ubusela	ooboose'laa
throw (v)	phosa	po'saa
tie up (v)	bopha	bo'paa
track (n)	unyawo	oonyaawo'
track down / follow	landela	laande'laa
trade union /	inyunyana yabasebenzi /	eenyoonyaanaa yaabaase'be'nzee /
trade union	inyunyana	eenyoonyaanaa
tradition /	indaba ethathwe kokhokho /	eendaabaa e'taatwe' ko'ko'ko' /
tradition	imvelo / isiko	eemve'lo' / eeseeko'
traditional	phathelene nesiko lemvelo	paate'le'ne' ne'seeko' le'mve'lo'
tragedy / misfortune	umshophi / ishwa	oomsho'pee / eeshwaa
tragic	sabekayo ngosizi	saabe'kaayo' ngo'seezee
train of events	ukulandelana kwezehlakalo	ookoolaande'laanaa kwe'ze'hlaakaalo'
traitor	ixoki / imbuka	eexo'kee / eembookaa
trap (v) – entrap	bamba ngecebo	baambaa nge'ce'bo'
trap - police trap (n)	umcuphi	oomcoopee
treaty	inhlangano	eenhlaangaano'
trial (n)	icala	eecaalaa
tribal – name	isibongo	eeseebo'ngo'
tribal	isizwe	ee'seezwe'
tribe	uhlobo	oohlo'bo'
trouble (n)	inhlupheko	eenhloope'ko'
trouble - Cause trouble.	Banga amacala.	Baangaa aamaacaalaa.
truth - It is the truth.	Yiqiniso.	Yeeqeeneeso'.
truth - They speak the truth.	Baqinisile.	Baaqeeneeseele'.
truth – Speak the truth.	Khuluma iqiniso.	Kooloomaa eeqeeneeso'.
truth	iqiniso	eeqeeneeso'
try - Try a case.	Thetha icala.	Te'taa eecaalaa.
uncover (v)	ambula	aamboolaa
under discussion	saxoxwayo	saaxo'xwaayo'
under oath	fungile	foongeele'
under orders	phansi kwemiyalo	paansee kwe'meeyaalo'
undercover (v) - to go	ngokucasha ebumnyameni	ngo'koocaashaa e'boomnyaame'nee
undercover agent	umshoshaphansi	oomsho'shaapaansee

verdict	isigwebo	eeseegwe´bo´
victim	umhlukunyezwa	oomhlookoonye´zwaa
violence	udlame	oodlaame´
violent	nodlame	no´dlaame´
violently / violently	ngamandla / ngendlakadla / ngobudlova	ngaamaandlaa / nge´ndlaakaadlaa / ngo´boodlo´vaa
walk unarmed (v)	bhungcazela	boongcaaze´laa
war	impi	eempee
warn (v)	azisa / exwayisa	aazeesaa / e´xwaayeesaa
warning	isixwayiso	eeseexwaayeeso´
warshield	isihlangu	eeseehlaangoo
welfare	inhlalakahle	eenhlaalaakaahle´
witness (v)	fakaza	faakaazaa
witness (n)	ubufakazi	ooboofaakaazee
worry / tease / annoy (v)	hlupha	hloopaa
He / She was raped twice.	Bamdlwengule kabili. / Bamdlwengula kabili.	Baamdlwe´ngoole´ kaabeelee. / Baamdlwe´ngoolaa kaabeelee.
He / She has got aids.	Unengculazi. / Uphethwe yingculazi.	Oone´ngcoolaazee. / Oope´twe´ yeengcoolaazee.
It is me who took your books.	Yimi othathe izincwadi zakho.	Yeemee o´taate´ eezeencwaadee zaako´.
It is not me who . . .	Akumina o . . .	Aakoomeenaa o´ . . .
It is them who . . .	Yibona aba . . .	Yeebo´naa aabaa . . .
Charged with burglary .	Bekwe icala lokugqekeza.	Be´kwe´ eecaalaa lo´koogqe´ke´zaa.
What is your complaint?	Umangaleleni?	Oomaangaale´le´nee?
He owes me money.	Ungikweleta imali.	Oongeekwe´le´taa eemaalee.
You are telling lies.	Uqamba amanga.	Ooqaambaa aamaangaa.
Who killed that person?	Ubani obulele lowo muntu?	Oobaanee o´boole´le´ lo´wo´ moonto?
Follow that man.	Landela leya ndoda.	Laande´laa le´yaa ndo´daa.
Call that person.	Biza / Memeza lowa muntu.	Beezaa / Me´me´zaa lo´waa moontoo.
Fetch my gun.	Landa isibhamu sami.	Laandaa eeseebaamoo saamee.
Have you ever been in jail?	Wake waboshwa?	Waake´ waabo´shwaa?
Try a case.	Ukuqulwa icala. / Ukuthethwa kwecala.	Ookooqoolwaa eecaalaa. / Ookoote´twaa kwe´caalaa.
The men shot them.	Amadoda abadubulile.	Aamaado´daa aabaadoobooleele´.
The money is stolen by thieves.	Imali yebiwa ngamasela.	Eemaalee ye´beewaa ngaamaase´laa.
The person is dead.	Umuntu ushonile.	Oomoontoo oosho´neele´.
The people have gone.	Abantu bahambile.	Aabaantoo baahaambeele´.
The house has been burnt down.	Umuzi ushisiwe.	Oomoozee oosheeseewe´.
The house is burning.	Indlu iyasha.	Eendloo eeyaashaa.
The people ran away.	Abantu babalekile.	Aabaantoo baabaale´keele´.
The thieves ran away.	Amasela abalekile.	Aamaase´laa aabaale´keele´.
Do not fight.	Musa ukulwa. / Ungalwi.	Moosaa ookoolwaa. / Oongaalwee.
To go to war.	Hlasela.	Hlaase´laa.
To rush out in anger.	Dumela.	Doome´laa.
Lay a trap.	Cupha.	Coopaa.
Try a criminal. (v)	Thetha icala lesigebengu.	Te´taa eecaalaa le´seege´be´ngoo.
This person is wicked.	Lo muntu mubi.	Lo´ moontoo moobee.

English		
He / She tells lies.	Ukhuluma amanga.	Ookooloomaa aamaangaa.
Accuse falsely.	Bekwa icala ngephutha.	Be'kwaa eecaalaa nge'pootaa.
How many people are there?	Abantu bangaki lapho?	Aabaantoo baangaakee laapo'?
There are lots of people.	Baningi abantu.	Baaneengee aabaantoo.
Where is the . . .?	Uphi . . . / Ukuphi . . .?	Oopee . . . / Ookoopee . . .?
At my house	Kwami.	Kwaamee.
At your house	Kwakho.	Kwaako'.
At our house	Kwethu.	Kwe'too.
It is necessary to go.	Kufanele sihambe.	Koofaane'le' seehaambe'.
It is not necessary to go.	Akufanele sihambe.	Aakoofaane'le' seehaambe'.
The soldiers are dead.	Amabutho ashonile. / Amasosha ashonile.	Aamaabooto' aasho'neele'. / Aamaaso'shaa aasho'neele'.
What did they hit you with?	Bakushaye ngani?	Baakooshaaye' ngaanee?
The man hit him with a stone.	Indoda imshaye ngetshe.	Eendo'daa eemshaaye' nge'tshe'.
Hit with a stick.	Shaya ngenduku.	Shaayaa nge'ndookoo.
Assault with a stick.	Galela.	Gaale'laa.
I did not hit him.	Angimshayanga.	Aangeemshaayaangaa.
They have returned.	Abantu babuyile.	Aabaantoo baabooyeele'.
They went by foot.	Bahambe ngezinyawo.	Baahaambe' nge'zeenyaawo'.
They went by car.	Bahambe ngemoto.	Baahaambe' nge'mo'to'.
This is a hold up!	Kubanjwa inkunzi!	Koobaanjwaa eenkoonzee!
I want money.	Ngifuna imali.	Ngeefoonaa eemaalee.
Wait a bit.	Ima kancane. / Mana kancane.	Eemaa kaancaane'. / Maanaa kaancaane'.
Behave respectfully.	Ubohlonipha.	Oobo'hlo'neepaa.
It is the truth.	Yiqiniso.	Yeeqeeneeso'.
Who killed this child?	Ubani obulele lomntwana?	Oobaanee o'boole'le' lo'mntwaanaa?
Call that person.	Biza lowa muntu.	Beezaa lo'waa moontoo.
Fetch my gun.	Landa isibhamu sami.	Laandaa eeseebaamoo saamee.
What tribe is he from?	Lo muntu uluhlobo luni ?	Lo' moontoo ooloohlo'bo' loonee?
They marched to town.	Babhikishele edolobheni.	Baabeekeeshe'le' e'do'lo'be'nee.
They ran down the streets with weapons.	Bagijime nezikhali esitaladini.	Baageejeeme' ne'zeekaalee e'seetaalaadeenee.
They threw petrol bombs into the buildings.	Baphonse amabhomu kaphethroli kwizakhiwo.	Baapo'nse' aamaabo'moo kaape'tro'lee kweezaakeewo'.
They shot the people with rubber bullets.	Badubule abantu ngezinhlamvu zenjoloba.	Baadoobole' aabaantoo nge'zeenhlaamvoo ze'njo'lo'baa .
The police threw tear gas at the crowd.	Amaphoyisa aphonse isisi esikhalisa unyembezi kusixukwini.	Aamaapo'yeesaa aapo'nse' eeseesee e'seekaaleesaa oonye'mbe'zee kooseexookweenee.
They used smoke bombs on the mob.	Basebenzise ibhomu lentuthu kuntukazana.	Baase'be'nzeese' eebo'moo le'ntootoo koontookaazaanaa.
The law has no hold on him.	Umthetho awumcindezeli nakancane.	Oomte'to' aawoomceende'ze'lee naakaancaane'.
Go in peace.	Hamba ngoxolo.	Haambaa ngo'xo'lo'.
He is a thief.	Unesandla.	Oone'saandlaa.
Make a noise.	Banga umsindo.	Baangaa oomseendo'.
Let us meet.	Asihlangane.	Aaseehlaangaane'.
It does not matter.	Akunalutho.	Aakoonaalooto'.

56.

English		
The laws are changing.	Imithetho iyashintsha.	Eemeete'to' eeyaasheentshaa.
The police help the boy.	Amaphoyisa asiza umfana.	Aamaapo'yeesaa aaseezaa oomfaanaa.
Do not go.	Musa ukuhamba.	Moosaa ookoohaambaa.
At what time? (When)	Ngasikhathi sini?	Ngaaseekaatee seenee?
I am sorry.	Ngiyaxolisa.	Ngeeyaaxo'leesaa.
The men and women are fighting.	Amadoda namakhosikazi ayalwa.	Aamaado'daa naamaako'seekaazee aayaalwaa.
Can you help me?	Ungangisiza?	Oongaangeeseezaa?
There is no work.	Akukho umsebenzi.	Aakooko' oomse'be'nzee.
There is nothing wrong.	Akukho lutho olubi.	Aakooko' looto' o'loobee.
I am not scared.	Angisabi.	Aangeesaabee.
I was not scared.	Angesabi.	Aange'saabee.
We do not have time.	Asinasikhathi.	Aaseenaaseekaatee.
He / She is naughty.	Akezwa.	Aake'zwaa.
There is no way out.	Ayikho indlela.	Aayeeko' eendle'laa.
Speak the truth.	Khuluma iqiniso.	Kooloomaa eeqeeneeso'.
It is the truth.	Liqiniso. / Yiqiniso.	Leeqeeneeso'. / Yeeqeeneeso'.
It is important.	Kubalulekile.	Koobaloole'keele'.
Make a noise.	Banga umsindo.	Baangaa oomseendo'.
Peaceful march	Hlaba uhele bekhononda. / Ukumasha ngoxolo.	Hlaabaa oohe'le' be'ko'no'ndaa. / Ookoomaashaa ngo'xo'lo'.
They robbed a bank.	Baphange ibhange.	Baapaange' eebaange'.
Walk out of work.	Ukushiya umsebenzi.	Ookoosheeyaa oomse'be'nzee.
They want more money.	Bafuna kwengezwe imali.	Baafoonaa kwe'nge'zwe' eemaalee .
They went on strike.	Batelekile.	Baate'le'keele'.
Take as hostage.	Thumba.	Toombaa.
They held him hostage.	Bamthumbile.	Baamtoombeele'.
An attack on his life.	Ukulinga ukumbulala.	Ookooleengaa ookoomboolaalaa.
Bring to justice.	Letha emthethweni.	Le'taa e'mte'twe'nee.
Fight crime.	Yilwa nobugebengu.	Yeelwaa no'booge'be'ngoo.
Reported crimes.	Amacala abikiwe.	Aamaacaalaa aabeekeewe'.
I will report you.	Ngizokuceba.	Ngeezo'kooce'baa.
Every day ----	Zonke izinsuku ----	Zo'nke' eezeensookoo ----
20 children are reported raped.	Izingane ezingu 20 kubikwa ukuthi zidlwenguliwe.	Eezeengaane' e'zeengoo 20 koobeekwaa ookootsee zeedlwe'ngooleewe'.
40 women are raped.	Abesifazane abangu 40 badlwenguliwe.	Aabe'seefaazaane' aabaangoo 40 baadlwe'ngooleewe'.
66 people are murdered.	Abantu abangu 66 babulewe.	Aabaantoo aabaangoo 66 baaboole'we'.
600 houses are broken into.	Izindlu ezingu 600 zigqekeziwe.	Eezeendloo e'zeengoo 600 zeegqe'ke'zeewe'.
Scared to death.	Saba / Sabela impilo yakho.	Saabaa / Saabe'laa eempeelo' yaako.'
We can beat the criminals.	Singazehlula izigebengu.	Seengaaze'hloolaa eezeege'be'ngoo.
Safety of property.	Ukuphepha kwempahla.	Ookoope'paa kwe'mpaahlaa.
On the streets where you live.	Emigwaqeni lapho uhlala khona.	E'meegwaaqe'nee laapo' oohlaalaa ko'naa.
You are under arrest.	Uboshiwe.	Oobo'sheewe'.
I want an interpreter.	Ngifuna umhumushi.	Ngeefoonaa oomhoomooshee.
You can call a lawyer.	Ungabiza ummeli.	Oongaabeezaa oomme'lee.
You must appear in court.	Kumele uze enkantolo.	Koome'le' ooze' e'nkanto'lo'.

I want to report an --- accident / fire / burglary.	Ngizobika --- ingozi / umlilo / ukweba.	Ngeezo'beekaa --- eengo'zee / oomleelo' / ookwe'baa.
It is his / her right.	Ilungelo lakhe.	Eeloonge'lo' laake'.
The ruffians pushed him down and broke his bone.	Izigebengu zamwisa phansi nazamephula ithambo.	Eezeege'be'ngoo zaamweesaa paansee naazaame'poolaa eetaambo'.
It is not right to steal.	Akulungile ukweba.	Aakooloongeele' ookwe'baa.
To blame someone else.	Esulela ngecala.	E'soole'laa nge'caalaa.
Blame someone.	Sola omunye.	So'laa o'moonye'.
Take action.	Thatha isinyathelo.	Taataa eeseenyaate'lo'.

58.

WEATHER	IZULU	EEZOOLOO
SEASONS OF THE YEAR	ISIKHATHI SONYAKA	EESEEKAATEE SO'NYAAKAA
The weather is fine.	Ilanga libalele.	Eelaanga leebaale'le'.
The sun is hot.	Ilanga liyashisa.	Eelaangaa leeyaasheesaa.
The day is cool.	Ilanga lipholile.	Eelaangaa leepo'leele'.
It is cloudy.	Liguqubele.	Leegooqoobe'le'.
It is thundering.	Liyaduma.	Leeyaadoomaa.
It is lightening.	Liyabaneka.	Leeyaabaane'kaa.
It is drizzling.	Liyakhiza.	Leeyaakeezaa.
It is raining.	Liyana.	Leeyaanaa.
It is snowing.	Liyakhithika.	Leeyaakeeteekaa.
There is frost.	Kulele isithwathwa.	Koole'le' eeseetwaatwaa.
There is snow.	Kuneqhwa.	Koone'qwaa.
There is dew.	Kulele amazolo.	Koole'le' aamaazo'lo'.
There is mist.	Kunenkungu.	Koone'nkoongoo.
The wind is blowing.	Kuvunguza umoya.	Koovoongoozaa oomo'yaa.
It is windy.	Kunomoya.	Koono'mo'yaa.
It is dusty.	Kunothuli.	Koono'toolee.
There is moonlight.	Kunonyezi.	Koono'nye'zee.
It is dry.	Komile.	Ko'meele'.
It is wet.	Kumanzi.	Koomaanzee.
It is overcast.	Kubuyisile.	Koobooyeeseele'.
It is hot.	Kufudumele.	Koofoodoome'le'.
The weather is cold.	Izulu limakhaza.	Eezooloo leemaakaazaa.
Summer	Ihlobo	Eehlo'bo'
Autumn	Ukwindla	Ookweendlaa
Winter	Ubusika	Oobooseekaa
Spring	Intwasahlobo	Eentwaasaahlo'bo'
bitterly cold	-qandayo mo	-qaandaayo' mo'
chilliness	amakaza	aamaakaazaa
cloudy	-guqubele	-gooqoobe'le'
cold - feel cold / shiver	godola	go'do'laa
crack of thunder	ukuklaklabula	ookooklaaklaaboolaa
cyclone (n)	isikhwishikwishi	eeseekweesheekweeshee
drizzle (n)	umkhizo	oomkeezo'
drizzle (v)	khiza	keezaa
duststorm	isiphepho sothuli	eeseepe'po' se'toolee
earthquake	indudumela	eendoodoome'laa
flood (v)	ngenisa amanzi	nge'neesaa aamaanzee
flood (n)	isikhukhula	eeseekookoolaa
full moon	inyanga igcwele	eenyaangaa eegcwe'le'
flood – The river is in flood.	Umfula udla izindwani.	Oomfoolaa oodlaa eezeendwaanee.
half moon	inyanga elucezu	eenyaangaa elooce'zoo
hot - very hot	-haza	-haazaa
hot spring	ushushu	ooshooshoo
hurricane	isiphepho	eeseepe'po'
lightning (n)	umbani	oombaanee
mist (n)	inkunga	eenkoongaa
mist - thick mist	umlalamvubu	oomlaalaamvooboo

59.

rain (n)	imvula / izulu	eemvoolaa / eezooloo
rain (v) It is raining.	Liyana.	Leeyaanaa.
sandstorm	isivunguvungu sesihlabathi	eeseevoongoovoongoo se'seehlaabaatee
scattered showers (n)	umkhemezelo	oomke'me'ze'lo'
scattered showers (v)	khemezela	ke'me'ze'laa
snowstorm (v)	ukukhithika kweqhwa	ookookeeteekaa kwe'qhwaa
storm (n)	isivunguvungu	eeseevoongoovoongoo
thunder (v)	duma	doomaa
thunderclap	umklaklabulo	oomklaaklaaboolo'
thunder cloud	ifu elitetha ukuduma kwezulu	eefoo e'leete'taa ookoodoomaa kwe'zooloo
thunder storm	ukuduma kwezulu	ookoodoomaa kwe'zooloo
tidal wave	igagasi elikhulu elibangwa olwandle	eegaagaasee e'leekooloo e'leebaangwaa o'lwaandle'
tornado	isiphepho esinamandla amakhulu	eeseepe'po' e'seenaamaandlaa aamaakooloo
tsunami (v)	amandlambi aselwandle ayakhukhula	aamaandlaambee aase'lwaandle' aayaakookoolaa
tsunami (n)	udlambi elikhukhulayo	oodlaambee e'leekookoolaayo'
wave (n) - ocean /	ilidlambi / idlambi /	eeleedlaambee / eedlaambee /
wave (n) - ocean	igagasi / iligagasi	eegaagaasee / eeleegaagaasee
weather (n)	isimo sezulu	eeseemo' se'zooloo
weather – The weather is clearing.	Liyaphenya.	Leeyaape'nyaa.
wind	umoya	oomo'yaa
wind - biting cold wind	umshazo	oomshaazo'
wind - gale force	isivunguvungu	eeseevoongoovoongoo
whirlpool	isishingishane samanzi / umsinga	eeseesheengeeshaane' saamaanzee / oomseengaa
whirlwind	isishingishane somoya / isikhwishikazana	eeseesheengeeshaane' so'mo'yaa / eeseekweesheekaazaanaa
windstorm	isiphepho	eeseepe'po'

DIRECTIONS	IZINKOMBA	EEZEENKO'MBA
East	Impumalanga	Eempoomaalaangaa
West	Intshonalanga	Eentsho'naalaangaa
North	Inyakatho	Eenyaakaato'
South	Iningizimu	Eeneengeezeemoo

TRAVEL	UHAMBO	OOHAAMBO´
Where is the . . . ?	Ikuphi i. . .?	Eekoopee ee . . . ?
airport	inkundla yezindiza	eenkoondlaa ye´zeendeezaa
boat	umkhumbi	oomkoombee
bus	ibhasi	eebaasee
bus stop	isitobhi sebhasi	eeseeto´bee se´baasee
dining car	inqola yokudla	inqo´laa yo´koodlaa
hotel	ihhotela	eeho´te´laa
luggage office	ihhovisi lezimpahla	eeho´veesee le´zeempaahlaa
platform	ipulatfomu	eepoolaatfo´moo
police	amaphoyisa	aamaapo´yeesaa
station	isiteshi	eeseete´shee
taxi	itekisi	eete´keesee / eete´ksee
toilet	ilavathi / ithoyilethe	eelaavaatee / eeto´yeele´te´
train	isitimela	eeseeteeme´laa
What time does the ... leave?	Isi. . .sihamba ngasikhathi sini?	Eesee. . .seehaamba ngaaseekaatee seenee?
What time does the. . . arrive?	Isi. . .sifika ngasikhathi sini?	Eesee. . . seefeekaa ngaaseekaatee seenee?
driver's licence	ilayisense yokushayela	eelaayeese´nse´ yo´kooshaaye´laa
How much?	Kumalini?	Koomaaleenee?
How much is it?	Kubiza malini?	Koobeezaa maaleenee?
How far is it?	Kukude kangakanani?	Kookoode´ kaangaakaanaanee?
How long ? (time)	Isikhathi esingakanani?	Eeseekaatee e´seengaakaanaanee?
I am lost.	Ngidukile.	Ngeedookeele´.
Please show me the way to . . .?	Ngicela indlela eya e. . .?	Ngeece´laa eendle´laa e´yaa e´ . . .?
Is this the right way to. . .?	Yiyo indlela eya . . .?	Yeeyo´ eendle´laa e´yaa . . .?
Where does this road go to?	Iyaphi le ndlela?	Eeyaapee le´ ndle´laa?
Straight on.	Uqonde phambili.	Ooqo´nde´ paambeelee.
left - on the left	ngakwesokunxele	ngaakwe´so´koonxe´le´
right - on the right	ngakwesokudla	ngaakwe´so´koodla
I have lost my car.	Ngilahlekelwe imoto yami.	Ngeelaahle´ke´lwe´ eemo´to´ yami.
I have lost my car keys.	Ngilahlekelwe izikhiye zemoto yami.	Ngeelaahle´ke´lwe´ eezeekeeyaa ze´mo´to´ yaamee.
My car has been stolen.	Imoto yami yebiwe.	Eemo´to´ yaamee ye´beewe´.
My car has broken down.	Imoto yami ifile.	Eemo´to´ yaamee eefeele´.
The petrol is finished.	Uphelile uphethroli.	Oope´leele´ oope´tro´lee.
The tyre is punctured.	Liphantshile isondo.	Leepaantsheele´ eeso´ndo´.
lift (n)	umgibeli	oomgeebe´lee
lift (v)	gibela	geebe´laa
Can I have a lift?	Ngicela ukugibela?	Ngeece´laa ookoogeebe´laa?
Where is the garage?	Likuphi igalaji?	Leekoopee eegaalaajee?
Please fill the car.	Ngicela ugcwalise imoto.	Ngeece´laa oogcwaaleese´eemo´to´.
Check the oil.	Ubheke u-oyela.	Oobe´kaa oo-o´ye´laa.
Please wash the car.	Ngicela ugeze imoto.	Ngeece´laa ooge´zaa eemo´to´.
There has been an accident.	Kuvele ingozi.	Koove´le´ eengo´zee.
Are you hurt?	Ulimele na?	Ooleeme´le´ naa?
Can I help?	Ngingasiza na?	Ngeengaaseezaa naa?

61.

Write down.	Bhala phansi.	Baalaa paansee.
Do you have a map?	Unayo imephu?	Oonaayo´ eeme´poo?
detour	indlela ephambukayo	eendle´laa e´paambookaayo´
Please help me.	Ngicela ungisize.	Ngeece´laa oongeeseeze´.
How do you get to work?	Uhamba ngani ukuya emsebenzini?	Oohaambaa ngaanee ookooyaa e´mse´be´nzeenee?
How will you be travelling?	Uhamba ngani ? / Uzohamba ngani?	Oohaambaa ngaanee? / Oozo´haambaa ngaanee?
by car	ngemoto	nge´mo´to´
by bus	ngebhasi	nge´baasee
by taxi	ngethekisi	ngete´keesee
by bicycle	ngebhayisikili	nge´baayeeseekeelee
by train	ngesitimela	nge´seeteeme´laa
by motorbike	ngesithuthuthu	nge´seetootootoo
by aeroplane (flying)	ngebhanoyi	nge´baano´yee
by ship (sailing)	ngomkhumbi	ngo´mkoombee
by foot (walking)	ngezinyawo	nge´zeenyaawo´
Put R500 petrol in.	Thela uphethroli ka R500.	Te´laa oope´tro´lee kaa R500.
Pump the wheels / tyres.	Futha amasondo.	Footaa aamaaso´ndo´.
How is the oil?	Unjani u-oyela?	Oonjaanee oo- o´ye´laa?
Check oil & water.	Sheka u-oyela namanzi.	She´kaa oo-o´ye´laa naamaanzee.
Petrol is expensive.	Uphethroli uyadula.	Oopeetro´lee ooyaadoolaa.
The windows are dirty.	Amafasitela angcolile.	Aamaafaaseete´laa aangco´leele´.
Please wash the windows.	Ngicela ugeze amafasitela.	Ngeece´laa ooge´ze´ aamaafaaseete´laa.
Have you been there before?	Waze wa fika lapha nga phambili?	Waaze´ waa feekaa laapaa ngaa paambeelee?
Stop the car!	Misa imoto!	Meesaa eemo´to´!
The car is dirty.	Imoto ingcolile.	Eemo´to´ eengco´leele´.
Please wash the car.	Ngicela ugeze imoto.	Ngeece´laa ooge´ze´ eemoto´.

ACCOMODATION HOLIDAY	INDAWO YO'KOOHLAALA NOKULALA / IHOLIDE	INDAAWO' YOKUHLALA NO'KOOLAALA / EEHO'LEEDE'
Where is the hotel?	Likuphi ihhotela?	Leekoopee eeho'te'laa?
Where is the . . (place)?	Ikuphi indawo ye . .?	Eekoopee eendaawo'. .?
ablution block	indawo yokugeza	eendaawo' yo'kooge'zaa
beach	ulwandle	oolwaandle'
braai area	indawo yokosa	eendaawo' yo'ko'saa
campsite	indawo yokukhempa	eendaawo' yo'kooke'mpaa
caravan park	ipaki yekharaveni	eepaakee ye' kaaraave'nee
chalet / cottage	indlwana	eendlwaana
game / nature reserve	isiqiwi	eeseeqeewee
office	ihhovisi	eeho'veesee
toilets	amathoyilethi	aamaato'yeele'tee
Did you see any game?	Uzibonile izilwane?	Oozeebo'neele' eezeelwaane'?
I saw a lion.	Ngibone ibhubesi.	Ngeebo'ne' eeboobe'see.
I saw a buck.	Ngibone inyamazane.	Ngeebo'ne' eenyaamaazaane'.
Did you swim?	Ubhukudile yini?	Oobookoodeele' yeenee?
Do / Can you swim?	Uyabhukuda yini?	Ooyaabookoodaa yeenee?
Where can I . . .?	Nginga . . .?	Ngeengaa . . .?
dispose of the rubbish?	Nginga lahlaphi izibi?	Ngeengaa laahlaapee eezeebee?
empty the toilet?	Nginga lithululela kuphi ithoyilethe? /	Ngeengaa leetooloole'laa koopee eeto'yeele'te'? /
fill the gas bottle?	Nginga ligcwaliswa kuphi ibhodlela legesi?	Ngeengaa leegcwaaleeswaa koopee eebo'dle'laa le'ge'see?
To light a fire.	Ukubasa umlilo.	Ookoobaasaa oomleelo'.
Is there electricity?	Ukhona ugesi?	Ooko'naa ooge'see?
Is there a shop?	Sikhona isitolo?	Seeko'naa eeseeto'lo'?
May I have a receipt?	Ngicela irisidi?	Ngeece'laa eereeseedee?
How much do you charge?	Ubiza malini?	Oobeezaa maaleenee?
I have a booking.	Ngibhukhile.	Ngeebookeele'.
Sign the register.	Sayina irejista.	Saayeenaa eere'jeestaa.
Is there a message?	Ukhona umlayezo?	Ooko'naa oomlaaye'zo'?
luggage	izimpahla yendlela / izimpahla	eezeempaahlaa ye'ndle'laa / eezeempaahlaa
I want a room.	Ngifuna ikamelo.	Ngeefoonaa eekaame'lo'.
Where is . . ?	Ikuphi . . .?	Eekoopee . . .?
the bar	inkantini	eenkaanteenee
the toilet	ithoyilethe	eeto'yeele'te'
the dining room	ikamelo lokudlela	eekaame'lo' lo'koodle'laa
May I have the key?	Ngicela isikhiye?	Ngeece'laa eeseekeeye'?
May I have the bill?	Ngicela i-akhawunti yami?	Ngeece'laa ee-aakaawoontee yaamee?
Where is the manager? /	Ukuphi umphathi? /	Ookoopee oompaatee ? /
Where is the manager?	Iphi imenenja?	Eepee eeme'ne'njaa?
Can I have a drink?	Ngicela isiphuzo?	Ngeece'laa eeseepoozo'?
How many beds are there?	Mingaki imibhede ekhona?	Meengaakee eemeebe'de' e'ko'na?
Is there television?	Ikhona ithelevishini?	Eeko'naa eete'le'veesheenee?
binoculars	isibonakude	eeseebo'naakoode'
bathroom	ibhavulumu / indlu yokugezela	eebaavooloomoo / eendloo yo'kooge'ze'laa

63.

shower	ishawa	eeshaawaa
air conditioning	i-ekhondishini	ee-e'ko'ndeesheenee
Please sign.	Ngicela usayine.	Ngeece'laa oosaayeene'.
Park the car.	Paka imoto. / Beka imoto.	Paakaa eemo'to'. / Be'kaa eemo'to'.
Please call me a taxi.	Ngicela ungibizele ithekisi.	Ngeece'laa oongeebeeze'le' eete'keesee.
I shall be leaving at 8.	Ngizohamba ngo 8.	Ngeezo'haambaa ngo' 8.
I will be arriving at 8.	Ngizofika ngo 8.	Ngeezo'feekaa ngo' 8.
Enjoy yourself.	Uhambe kahle. / Uzijabulise.	Oohaambe' kaahle'. / Oozeejaabooleese'.
Enjoy yourselves.	Hambani kahle.	Haambaanee kaahle'.
Our guests will be	Abavakashi bethu bazo	Aabaavaakaashee be'too baazo'
leaving ---	hamba ---	haambaa ---
at 6 o'clock /	ngo 6 /	ngo' 6 /
at crack of dawn.	entathakusa.	e'ntaataakoosaa.
The visitors ---	Izivakashi ---	Eezeevaakaashee ---
will be arriving / leaving	zizofika / zizohamba	zeezo'feekaa / zeezo'haambaa
tonight /	namuhla ebusuku /	naamoohlaa e'boosookoo /
in the morning /	ekuseni /	e'koose'nee /
this afternoon /	ntambana /	ntaambaanaa /
this evening /	ebusuku /	e'boosookoo /
today / tomorrow	namuhla / kusasa	naamoohlaa / koosaasaa /
at the weekend /	ngempelasonto /	nge'mpe'laaso'nto' /
at the beginning / end	ekuqaleni / ekupheleni	e'kooqaale'nee / e'koope'le'nee
of the week /	kwesonto /	kwe'so'nto' /
on Saturday /	ngoMgqibelo /	ngo'Mqeebe'lo' /
next week /	ngesonto elizayo /	nge'so'nto' e'leezaayo' /
in two weeks time /	emasontweni amabili ezayo /	e'maaso'ntwe'nee aamaabeelee e'zaayo' /
at the end of the month /	ekupheleni kwenyanga /	e'koope'le'nee kwe'nyaangaa /
at Christmas /	ngoKhisimusi /	ngo'Keeseemoosee /
at Easter /	ngePhakisa /	nge'- Paakeesaa /
for the July holidays /	ngamaholide kaJulayi /	ngaamaaho'leede' kaaJoolaayee /
in October.	ngo-Okthoba.	ngo' – O'kto'baa.
There will be place for	Kuzobakhona izindawo	Koozo'baako'naa eezeendaawo'
two bookings.	ezimbili zokubhuka.	e'zeembeelee zo'koobookaa.
There will be	Kuzobakhona izindawo	Koozo'baako'naa eezeendaawo'
accommodation	ezimbili zokulala.	e'zeembeelee zo'koolaalaa.
for two people.		
Dinner bed and breakfast.	Idina indawo yokulala nebhulakufesi.	Eedeenaa eendaawo' yo'koolaalaa ne'boolaakoofe'see.
Bed and breakfast.	Indawo yokulala nebhulakukufesi.	Eendaawo' yo'koolaalaa ne'boolaakoofe'see.
Self-catering	Ukuziphakela.	Ookoozeepaake'laa.
Bed only	Indawo yokulala kuphela.	Eendaawo' yo'koolaalaa koope'laa.
Accommodation only	Indawo yokulala kuphela.	Eendaawo' yo'koolaalaa koope'laa.
We have room for one	Sinendawo yokulala	Seene'ndaawo' yo'kooolaalaa
couple only.	yabantu ababili kuphela.	yaabaantoo aabaabeelee koope'laa.
We are fully booked.	Ayikho indawo.	Aayeeko' eendaawo'.
We have room for one	Sinendawo yokulala	Seene'ndaawo' yo'koolaalaa
person only.	umuntu oyedwa.	oomoontoo o'ye'dwaa.

There is only a single room available.	Kunekamelo lokulala umuntu oyedwa kuphela.	Koone'kaamelo' lo'koolaalaa oomoontoo o'ye'dwaa koope'laa.
We have one room.	Sinekamelo elilodwa.	Seene'kaame'lo' e'leelo'dwaa.
We have two double rooms.	Sinamakamelo amabili amakhulu.	Seenaamaakaame'lo' aamaabeelee aamaakooloo.
How long will you be staying for?	Uzohlala isikhathi esingakanani?	Oozo'hlaalaa eeseekaatee e'seengaakaanaanee?
When will you be leaving?	Uzohamba nini?	Oozo'haambaa neenee?
On which day will you arrive?	Uzobuya ngaliphi ilanga?	Oozo'booyaa ngaaleepee eelaangaa?
On which day will you leave / depart?	Uzohamba ngaliphi ilanga?	Oozo'haambaa ngaaleepee eelaangaa?
What date will they be arriving ?	Bazobuya ngaliphi ilanga?	Baazo'booyaa ngaaleepee eelaangaa?
What date will they be going?	Bazohamba ngaliphi ilanga?	Baazo'haambaa ngaaleepee eelaangaa?
I want a --- single room / double room.	Ngifuna ikamelo eliyisingili / eliyidabuli.	Ngeefoonaa eekaame'lo' e'leeyeeseengeelee / e'leeyeedaaboolee.
There will be three empty rooms available.	Kuzobakhona amakamelo amathathu angenabantu.	Koozo'baako'naa aamaakaame'lo' aamaataatoo aange'naabaantoo.
There will be five full rooms.	Kuzobakhona amakamelo amahlanu agcwele.	Koozo'baako'naa aamaakaame'lo' aamaahlaanoo aagcwe'le'.
We have ten rooms available.	Sinamakamelo ayishumi atholakalayo.	Seenaamaakaame'lo' aayeeshoomee aato'laakaalaayo'.
There are four rooms available--	Kunamakamelo amane atholakalayo---	Koonaamaakaame'lo' aamaane' aato'laakaalaayo'---
one from 5th,	elilodwa kusukela ngomhlaka 5,	e'leelo'dwaa koosooke'laa ngo'mhlaakaa 5,
and one from the 6th.	nelilodwa kusukela ngomhlaka 6.	ne'leelo'dwaa koosooke'laa ngo'mhlaakaa 6.
When would you like to come?	Ungathanda ukufika nini?	Oongaataandaa ookoofeekaa neenee?
Have a good trip.	Ube nohambo oluhle.	Oobe' no'haambo' o'loohle'.
We hope you enjoyed your stay / visit.	Siyethemba ukujabulele ukuhlala / ukuvakasha.	Seeye'te'mbaa ookoojaaboole'le' ookoohlaalaa / ookoovaakaashaa.
I hope you enjoyed yourselves.	Ngiyethemba nizijabulisile.	Ngeeye'te'mbaa neezeejaabooleeseele'.
We hope you enjoy yourself.	Siyethemba uzijabulisile.	Seeye'te'mbaa oozeejaabooleeseele'.
Please come again.	Ngicela ubuye futhi.	Ngeece'laa oobooye' footee.
We hope you come again.	Siyathemba uzobuya futhi.	Seeyaate'mbaa oozo'booyaa footee.
Sorry the weather is / was so bad.	Siyaxolisa isimo sezulu libi / besisibi.	Seeyaaxo'leesaa eeseemo' se'zooloo leebee / be'seebee.
The weather is / has been fantastic.	Isimo sezulu sihle / besisihle.	Eeseemo' se'zooloo seehle' / be'seeseehle'.
Go for a walk.	Elula imilenze.	E'loolaa eemeele'nze'.

English	Zulu	Pronunciation
Go for a game drive.	Hamba uyobuka izilwane ngemoto.	Haambaa ooyo'bookaa eezeelwaane' nge'mo'to'.
Go for a game drive with a game warden / guide.	Hamba uyobuka izilwane nombheki wezilwane.	Haambaa ooyo'bookaa eezeelwaane' no'mbe'kee we'zeelwaane'.
Go for a --- guided tour of the village / guided tour of the sights.	Hamba u --- vakashiswa edolobhaneni / vakashiswa ezindaweni ezibonakalayo.	Haambaa oo --- vaakaasheeswaa e'do'lo'baane'nee / vaakaasheeswaa e'zeendaawe'nee e'zeebo'naakaalaayo'.
Visit the flea market.	Vakashela imakethe yezimpahla.	Vaakaashe'laa eemaake'te' ye'zeempaahlaa.
Walk on the beach.	Vakashela umngcele wolwandle. / Hamba ebishi.	Vaakaashe'laa oomngce'le' wo'lwaandle'. / Haamba e'beeshee.
Walk next to the sea.	Hamba ngezinyawo eceleni kolwandle.	Haambaa nge'zeenyaawo' e'ce'le'nee ko'lwaandle'.
Do a bit of sight seeing---	Vakashela izindawo ezibonakalayo---	Vaakaashe'laa eezeendaawo' e'zeebo'naakaalaayo'---
at the local village /	edolobhaneni /	e'do'lo'baane'nee /
around the country side /	izwe langaphandle /	eezwe' laangaapaandle' /
in the country /	ezweni /	e'zwe'nee /
in the neighbourhood /	komakhelwane /	ko'maake'lwaane' /
in the vicinity / area.	ezindaweni ezihlukene.	e'zeendaawe'nee e'zeehlooke'ne'.
We will have drinks at sunset / on the verandah.	Sizophuza iziphuzo ngokushona kwelanga / emphemeni.	Seezo'poozaa eezeepoozo' ngo'koosho'naa kwe'laangaa / e'mpe'me'nee.
I will meet you at the pub for drinks and snacks.	Ngizohlangana nawe enkantini, siphuze iziphuzo nezidlo ezimnandi.	Ngeezo'hlaangaanaa naawe' e'nkaanteenee, seepooze' eezeepooso' ne'zeedlo' e'zeemnaandee.
Go for guided walk.	Vakasha ngomkhaphi ngezinyawo.	Vaakaashaa ngo'mkaapee nge'zeenyaawo'.
Go for guided tour ----	Vakasha nomkhaphi endaweni yokuvakasha ---	Vaakaashaa no'mkaapee e'ndaawe'nee yo'koovaakaashaa ---
in an open vehicle /	ngemoto evuleke phezulu /	nge'mo'to' e'voole'ke' pe'zooloo /
in the early morning /	ekuseni kakhulu /	e'koose'nee kaakooloo /
at night /	ebusuku /	e'boosookoo /
when the sun sets /	ngokushona kwelanga /	ngo'koosho'naa kwe'laangaa /
at sunrise.	ngokuphuma kwelanga.	ngo'koopoomaa kwe'laangaa.
The service in the hotel is bad.	Impatho ehotela yimbi.	Eempaato' e'ho'te'laa yeembee.
The service in the hotel is good.	Impatho ehotela ilungile / yinhle.	Eempaato' e' ho'te'laa eeloongeele' / yeenhle'.
We expect him / her today.	Simbhekile namhlanje.	Seembe'keele' naamhlaanje'.

WILD LIFE ANIMALS	IZILWANE ZASENDLE	EEZEELWAANE´ ZAASE´NDLE´
INSECTS	IZINAMBUZANE	EEZEENAAMBOOZAANE´
REPTILES	IZILWANE ESIHUQUZELA NGESISU	EEZEELWAANE´ E´SEEHOOQOOZE´LAA NGE´SEESOO
BIRDS	IZINYONI	EEZEENYO´NEE
FISH	INHLANZI	EENHLAANZEE

ant	intuthwane	eentootwaane´
ant bear	isambane	eesaambane´
ape	imfene / inkawu	eemfe´ne´ / eenkaawoo
baboon	imfene	eemfe´ne´
bear	ibhele	eebe´le´
bee	inyosi	eenyo´see
beetle	ibhungane	eeboongaane´
bird	inyoni	eenyo´nee
blue	imvimvi	eemveemvee
bottle	uxukazana	ooxookaazaanaa
buck	inyamazane	eenyaamaazaane´
buffalo	inyathi	eenyaatee
bug	imbungulu	eemboongooloo
bull	inkunzi	eenkoonzee
bush pig	ingulube yasendle	eengooloobe´ yaase´ndle´
bushbaby	isinkwe	eeseenkwe´
bushbuck	unkonka	oonko´nkaa
camel	ikameli	eekaame´lee
cane rat	imbuzimeshe	eemboozeeme´she´
cat fish / barbel	ingwane	eengwaane´
caracal	indabushe	eendaabooshe´
centipede	inkuma	eenkoomaa
cerval cat	indlozi	eendlo´zee
chameleon	unwabu	oonwaaboo
cheetah	ingulule	eengooloole´
cockroach	iphela	eepe´laa
crab	inkalankala	eenkaalaankaalaa
cricket	inyendle	eenye´ndle´
crocodile	ingwenya	eengwe´nyaa
crow	igwababa	eegwaabaabaa
cuttlefish	isifu	eeseefoo
dolphin	uhlobo lwehlengethwa	oohlo´bo´ lwe´hle´nge´twaa
donkey	imbongolo	eembo´ngo´lo´
dove	ijuba	eejoobaa
dragonfly	uzekamanzi	ooze´kaamaanzee
duiker	impunzi	eempoonzee
eagle	ukhozi	ooko´zee
earthworm	umsundu	oomsoondoo
eel	umbokwane	oombo´kwaane´
eland	impofu	eempo´foo
elephant	indlovu	eendlo´voo
feral / wild	asendle	aase´ndle´
firefly	ukhanyikhanyi	ookaanyeekaanyee

67.

fish	inhlanzi	eenhlaanzee
fish eagle	inkwazi	eenkwaazee
fish moth	inyundu	eenyoondoo
flamingo	umakholwane	oomaako´lwaane´
fly	impukane	oompookaane´
flying ant	inhlwa	eenhlwaa
frog	isele	eese´le´
giraffe	indlulamithi	eendloolaameetee
goat	imbuzi	eemboozee
grasshopper	intethe	eente´te´
guinea fowl	impangele	eempaange´le´
hawk	uklebe	ookle´be´
hippopotamus	imvubu	eemvooboo
hoopoe	uziningweni	oozeeneengwe´nee
hornbill	umkholwane	oomko´lwaane´
hyena	impisi	eempeesee
ibis – common ibis	inkankane	eenkaankaane´
jackal	impungushe	eempoongooshe´
jelly fish	itheketheke	eete´ke´te´ke´
kingfisher	isixula	eeseexoolaa
kudu	umgankla	oomgaanklaa
ladybird	umanqulwana	oomaanqoolwaanaa
lark	inqomfi	eenqo´mfee
leopard	ingwe	eengwe´
lice	izintwala	eezeentwaalaa
lice - on fowl	ubukhuphe	oobookoope´
lion	ingonyama / ibhubesi	eengo´nyaama / eeboobe´see
lizard	isibankwa	eeseebaankwaa
loerie	igwala	eegwaalaa
lobster	isikhupashe	eeseekoopaashe´
locust	isikhonyane	eeseeko´nyaane´
lynx	indabushe	eendaabooshe´
maggot	imphetu	eempe´too
maggot fly	ubomi	oobo´mee
mamba	imamba	eemaaambaa
millipede	isongololo / ishongololo	eeso´ngo´lo´lo´/ eesho´ngo´lo´lo´
mole	imvukuzane	eemvookoozaane´
monitor lizard	uxamu	ooxaamoo
monkey	inkawu	eenkaawoo
mosquito	umiyane	oomeeyaane´
moth	ibhu	eeboo
octopus	imbambela	eembaambe´laa
ostrich	intshe	eentshe´
owl	isikhova	eeseeko´vaa
pigeon	ivukutha / ijuba	eevookootaa / eejoobaa
polecat	iqaqa	eeqaaqaa
porcupine	ingungumbane	eengoongoombaane´
porcupine quill	inungu	eenoongoo
porpoise	inhlengethwa	eenhle´nge´twaa
puffadder	ibululu	eeboolooloo

python	inhlwathi	eenhlwaatee
rabbit	unogwaja	oono´gwaajaa
rat	ibuzi / iligundane	eeboozee / eeleegoondaane´
reed buck	umziki / inhlangu	oomzeekee / eenhlaangoo
rhinoceros – white	umkhombe	oomko´mbe´
rhinoceros - black	ubhejane	oobe´jaane´
rock lizard	imbulu	eembooloo
rock rabbit	imbila	eembeelaa
salmon	usalimoni	oosaaleemo´nee
sardine	usadinsi	oosaadeensee
scorpion	ufezela	oofe´ze´laa
sea lice	imfanzi	eemfaanzee
serval cat	indlozi	eendlo´zee
shark – ama Sharks!	ushaka / imfingo	ooshaaka / eemfeengo´
spider	isicabucabu / ulwembu	eeseecaaboocaaboo / oolwe´mboo
springbok	insephe	eense´pe´
(ama bokka-bokka)		
stork	unogolantethe	oono´go´laante´te´
swallow	inkonjane	eenko´njaane´
termite	umuhlwa	oomoohlwaa
tick	umkhaza / umkhizane	oomkaazaa / oomkeezaane´
tick bird	ihlalanyathi	eehlaalaanyaatee
tiger	ithayiga	eetaayeegaa
tortoise	ufudu	oofoodoo
tsetse fly	isibawu / impukuvane	eeseebaawoo / eempookoovaane´
vulture	inqe	eenqe´
wart hog	indlovudawana	eendlo´voodaawaanaa
water rat	ilidwele	eeleedwe´le´
whale	umkhomo	oomko´mo´
wild animal	isilwane yasendle	eeseelwaane´ yaase´ndle´
wild boar	ingulube yasendle	eengooloobe´ yaase´ndle´
wild cat	imbodla	eembo´dlaa
wild dog	inkentshane	eenke´ntshaane´
wild pig	ingulube yehlathi	eengooloobe´ ye´hlaatee
wildebeest	inkonkoni	eenko´nko´nee
zebra	idube	eedoobe´
bush camp	inkambu sahlathi	eenkaamboo saahlaatee
fence (v)	vika / akhela uthango	veekaa / aake´laa ootaango´
fence (n)	uthango	ootaango´
game – animals	izilwane	eezeelwaane´
gamekeeper	umbheki wezilwane	oombe´kee we´zeelwaane´
game reserve	isiqiwi	eeseeqeewee
malaria	uqhuqho	ooqhooqho´
malarial fever	uluqhuqho / imbo	oolooqhooqho´ / eembo´
protective fencing	intendemuzi	eente´nde´moozee
sight / view	umbukiso / imboniso	oombookeeso´ / eembo´neeso´
sight seeing	ukubukabuka	ookoobookaabookaa
sightseer	umbukwaze	oombookwaaze´
tick fever	umganda / inkasa	oomgaandaa / eenkaasaa

tsetse fly	impukuvane	eempookoovaane´
view (v)	buka / bheka	bookaa / be´kaa
view / sight	isibonakaliso	eeseebo´naakaaleeso´
view point	imboniso	eembo´neeso´

See the sights.	Bukabuka okuboniswayo.	Bookaabookaa o´koobo´neeswaayo´.
We saw baboons &	Sibone izimfene	Seebo´ne´ eezeemfe´ne´
leopards yesterday.	nezingwe izolo.	ne´zeengwe´ eezo´lo´.
Two snakes appeared	Kuqhamuke izinyoka	Kooqaamooke´ eezeenyo´kaa
from the stones.	ezimbili ematsheni.	e´zeembeelee e´maatshe´nee.
Leopards and lions live	Izingwe nezingonyama	Eezeengwe´ ne´zeengo´nyaamaa
in the forests / trees.	zihlala emahlathini.	zeehlaalaa e´maahlaateenee.
Out in the open.	Endle.	E´ndle´.
To sleep out in the open.	Ukulala endle.	Ookoolaalaa e´ndle´.
A lion roars.	Ibhubesi liyabhodla.	Eeboobe´see leeyaabo´dlaa.
The lions were chasing	Amabhubesi abexosha	Aamaaboobe´see aabe´xo´shaa
the buck / buck (plural).	inyamazane /	eenyaamaazaane´ /
	izinyamazane.	eezeenyaamaazaane´.
We saw lions.	Sibone amabhubesi.	Seebo´ne´ aamaaboobe´see.
The lions sit under	Amabhubesi ahlala	Aamaaboobe´see aahlaalaa
the trees.	phansi kwemithi.	paansee kwe´meetee.
Lions like meat	Amabhubesi athanda	Aamaaboobe´see aataandaa
and bones.	inyama namathambo.	eenyaamaa naamaataambo´.
The lions kill the children.	Amabhubesi abulala	Aamaaboobe´see aaboolaalaa
	abantwana.	aabaantwaanaa.
The animals are	Izilwane	Eezeelwaane´
running away.	ziyabaleka.	zeeyaabaale´kaa.
The animals are	Izilwane ziphuza	Eezeelwaane´ zeepoozaa
drinking water.	amanzi.	aamaanzee.
The animals are eating.	Izilwane ziyadla.	Eezeelwaane´ zeeyaadlaa.
The hippos are swimming.	Izimvubu ziyabhukuda /	Eezeemvooboo zeeyaabookoodaa /
	ziyahlamba.	zeeyahlaambaa.
The animals are grazing.	Izilwane zidla utshani.	Eezeelwaane´ zeedlaa ootshaanee.
The zebra is mating.	Idube liyakhwela.	Eedoobe´ leeyaakwe´laa.
The monkeys like to	Izinkawu zithanda	Eezeenkaawoo zeetaandaa
imitate / mimic people.	ukulingisa abantu.	ookooleengeesaa aabaantoo.

FARMING	UKULIMA	OOKOOLEEMAA
abattoir	isilaha	eeseelaaghaa
agriculture	ezokulima	e'zo'kooleemaa
agriculturist	umlimi	oomleemee
antheap	isiduli	eeseedoolee
anthrax	undicosho / umbendeni	oondeeco'sho' / oombe'nde'nee
arable	limekayo	leeme'kaayo'
arid	omile	o'meele'
army worm	umcwangubane	oomcwaangoobaane'
bull	inkunzi	eenkoonzee
bull calf	inxabi	eenxaabee
castrate (v)	phakula / thena	paakoolaa / te'naa
castration	ukuthena	ookoote'naa
cattle farming	ukufuya izinkomo	ookoofooyaa eezeenko'mo'
corn – grain	izinhlamvu	eezeenhlaamvoo
corn (variety of)	amabele	aamaabe'le'
cow / ox / bull	inkomo	eenko'mo'
cow	inkomazi	eenko'maazee
cow – milking cow	insengwakazi	eense'ngwaakaazee
cow – recently calved	indlezane	eendle'zaane'
cream (n)	ulaza	oolaazaa
crop	isithelo	eeseete'lo'
crop – poor crop	inkwico	eenkweeco'
crop – bumper crop	inala	eenaalaa
cross grain – hybrid	inhlobo exubanise	eenhlo'bo' e'xoobaaneese'
crushed mealies	umgqakazo	oomgqaakaazo'
cultivate (v)	lima / tshala	leemaa / tshaalaa
cultivated lands / land	amasimu / insimu	aamaaseemoo / eenseemoo
cultivating machine	umsheshane	oomshe'shaane'
cultivation	ukulima / umlimo	ookooleemaa / oomleemo'
cultivator (n)	umlimi	oomleemee
dagga	insangu	eensaangoo
dairy	ideli	eede'lee
dairy farming	ukufuyela ubisi	ookoofooye'laa oobeesee
dam	idamu / ichibi	eedaamoo / eecheebee
dam (v)	enza idamu	e'nzaa eedaamoo
damage	ukonakala	ooko'naakaalaa
damage (v)	ona	o'naa
damp	ubumanzi	ooboomaanzee
dig (v)	imba	eembaa
dig a hole	imba umgodi	eembaa oomgo'dee'
dig up /	lima /	leemaa /
dig up	phanda / vumbulula	paandaa / voombooloolaa
dip (v)	dipha / cwilisa	deepaa / cweeleesaa
dip (n) /	ukucwila /	ookoocweelaa /
dip (n)	ukucwilisa	ookoocweeleesaa
dipping tank	idiphu	eedeepoo
disaster	ingozi enkulu	eengo'zee e'nkooloo
eradicate (v)	siphula	seepoolaa

71.

eradication	ukusiphula	ookooseepoolaa
erosion – soil	ukuguguleka komhlabathi	ookoogoogoole'kaa ko'mhlaabaatee
farm (v)	lima / phatha ipulazi	leemaa / paataa eepoolaazee
farm (n)	ipulazi	eepoolaazee
farmer	umlimi	oomleemee
farming	ukulima	ookooleemaa
fatten	khuluphalisa	kooloopaaleesaa
feed (v)	fuya	fooyaa
fertilize (v)	thela umquba / vundisa	te'laa oomqoobaa / voondeesa
fertilizer	umquba	omqoobaa
field	insimu	eenseemoo
fierce bull	inkunzi enolaka	eenkoonzee e'no'laakaa
fence	uthango	ootaango'
fence (v)	vika	veekaa
flock – of sheep	umhlambi	oomhlaambee
forest	ihlathi elikhulu	eehlaatee e'leekooloo
forester	umgadi wamahlathi	oomgaadee waamaahlaatee
forestry	umsebenzi wokutshala amahlathi	oomse'be'nzee wo'kootshaalaa aamaahlaatee
graze (v)	idla utshani	eedlaa ootshaanee
grazing (n)	idlelo	eedle'lo'
harrow	ihala	eehaalaa
harrow (v)	hala	haalaa
harvest – season	isikhathi sokuvuna	eeseekaatee so'koovoonaa
harvest (v)	vuna	voonaa
harvest (n)– crop	umvuno	oomvoono'
harvested field	ihlanga	eehlaangaa
harvester (n) –person	umvuni	oomvoonee
harvester (n) - machine	umshini wokuvuna	oomsheenee wo'koovoonaa
hatch – eggs	chamusela	chaamoose'laa
hatchery	indawo yokuchamusela amaqanda	eendaawo' yo'koochaamoose'laa aamaaqaandaa
hay	utshani obomile	ootshaanee o'bo'meele'
haystack	inqwaba yotshani obomileyo	eenqwaabaa yo'tshaanee o'bo'meele'yo'
heifer	isithole / ilithokazi	eeseeto'le' / eeleeto'kaazee
herd – of cattle	umhlambi	oomhlaambee
lake	ichibi elikhulu	eecheebee e'leekooloo
lay (eggs) (v)	zalela / zala	zaale'laa / zaalaa
layer – of eggs	ezalelayo	e'zaale'laayo'
lick (v)	khotha	ko'taa
locust	inkasa	eenkaasaa
log – of wood	isigodo	eeseego'do'
lucerne	ilusene	eeloose'ne'
machine	umshini	oomsheenee
machine (v)	enza ngomshini	e'nzaa ngo'msheenee
mealie	ummbila	oom-mbeelaa
mielie field	isimbila	eeseembeelaa
milk (n)	ubisi	oobeesee

milk (v)	senga	se'ngaa
milkcow	insengwakazi	eense'ngwaakaazee
ox	inkabi	eenkaabee
paddock	inkambu	eenkaamboo
pasture	idlelo	eedle'lo'
pig	ingulube	eengooloobe'
pig farming	ukufuya izingulube	ookoofooyaa eezeengooloobe'
pitchfork	imfologo yotshani	eemfo'lo'go' yo'tshaanee
plough (n)	igeja	eege'jaa
plough (n)– many disced	umagejageja	oomaage'jaage'jaa
plough (v)	lima	leemaa
plough furrows (v)	dweba	dwe'baa
ploughed land	umqatho	oomqaato'
plough over / up (v)	senula	se'noolaa
sheep sing. / pl.	imvu / izimvu	eemvoo / eezeemvoo
sheep farm	ipulazi lezimvu	eepoolaazee le'zeemvoo
shelling machine	umhlululo	omhlooloolo'
sileage	ukudla kwezinkomo	ookoodlaa kwe'zeenko'mo'
silo	isayilo	eesaayeelo'
soil	umhlabathi	oomhlaabaatee
sour milk	amasi	aamaasee
subsoil	umhlabathi ongaphansi	oomhlaabaatee o'ngaapaansee
sugar cane	umoba	oomo'baa
sugar cane field	isimoba	eeseemo'baa
termite	umuhlwa	oomoohlwaa
treeless / open veld	inkangala	eenkaangaalaa
wheat	ukolo	ooko'lo'

The cattle are in the pastures.	Izinkomo zisedlelweni.	Eezeenko'mo' zeese'dle'lwe'nee.
The sheep ---	Izimvu ---	Eezeemvoo ---
The goats ---	Izimbuzi ---	Eezeemboozee ---
The herdman is in the pastures.	Umelusi usedlelweni.	Oome'loosee oose'dle'lwe'nee.
The horses are in the stable.	Amahhashi asesitebeleni.	Aamaahaashee aase'seete'be'le'nee.
The sheep are eating grass in the paddock.	Izimvu zidla utshani enkanjini.	Eezeemvoo zeedlaa ootshaanee e'nkaanjeenee.
The farmer will plant potatoes and beans.	Umlimi uzotshala amazambane nobhontshisi.	Oomleemee oozo'tshaalaa aamaazaambaane' no'bo'ntsheesee.
It is time for milking.	Sekuyisikhathi sokusenga.	Se'kooyeeseekaatee so'koose'ngaa.
Wash the milk-pails.	Geza amathunga.	Ge'zaa aamaatoongaa.
Wash the milk machine.	Geza umshini wokusenga.	Ge'zaa oomsheenee wo'koose'ngaa.
Let the cattle out.	Vulelani izinkomo.	Voole'laanee eezeenko'mo'.
Separate the calves from the mothers.	Khetha amankonyane konina.	Ke'taa aamaanko'nyaane' ko'neenaa.
Let the calves suck.	Nikela amankonyane ancele.	Neeke'laa aamaanko'nyaane' aance'le'.
Wash your hands.	Geza izandla.	Ge'zaa eezaandlaa.
The boy is milking.	Umfana uyasenga.	Oomfaanaa ooyaase'ngaa.
Give the cattle some fodder.	Fakela izinkomo imfulo.	Faake'laa eezeenko'mo' eemfoolo'.
The cattle are grazing.	Izinkomo zidla utshani.	Eezeenko'mo' zeedlaa ootshaanee.

73.

English		
The cow is about to calve.	Lenkomazi isizozala.	Le´ nko´maazee eeseezo´zaalaa.
The cow has gone dry.	Lenkomazi yephusile.	Le´ nko´maazee ye´pooseele´.
The cow's teats are cracked.	Imibele yalenkomazi igazukile.	Eemeebe´le´ yaale´nko´maazee eegaazookeele´.
Smear the teats with fat / ointment.	Gcoba imibele ngamafutha.	Gco´baa eemeebe´le´ ngaamaafootaa.
This cow is a good milk cow.	Lenkomazi iyinsengwakazi.	Le´nko´maazee eeyeense´ngwaakaazee.
The farmer is planting early crops.	Umlimi uyandulelisa.	Oomleemee ooyaandoole´leesaa.
Cut the lucerne.	Sika uluseni.	Seekaa ooloose´nee.
The firewood and coal is finished.	Izinkuni namalahle aphelile.	Eezeenkoonee naamaalaahle´ aape´leele´.
They will fetch coal and firewood tomorrow.	Bazowalanda kusasa amalahle nezinkuni.	Baazo´waalaandaa koosaasaa aamaalaahle´ ne´zeenkoonee.
On the edge of the forest.	Ogwini lwehlathi.	O´gweenee lwe´hlaatee.
A lion roars.	Ibhubesi liyabhodla.	Eeboobe´see leeyaabo´dhlaa.
A dog barks.	Inja iyakhonkotha.	Eenjaa eeyaako´nko´taa.
A frog croaks.	Isele liyakhala.	Eese´le´ leeyaakaalaa.
Bees make honey.	Izinyosi zenza uju.	Eezeenyo´see ze´nzaa oojoo.
Beware of the dog.	Qaphela inja.	Qaape´laa eenjaa.
Feed the fowls.	Yipha izinkukhu.	Yeepaa eezeenkookoo.
Flock of sheep	Umhlambi wezimvu	Oomhlaambee we´zeemvoo
Shear the sheep.	Gunda izimvu.	Goondaa eezeemvoo.
The hens lay eggs.	Izinkhukhukazi zizalela amaqanda.	Eezeenkookookaazee zeezaale´laa aamaaqaandaa.
The hens sit on the eggs.	Izinkhukhukazi zifukamela amaqanda.	Eezeenkookookaazee zeefookaame´laa aamaaqaandaa.
Herd of cattle	Umhlambi wezinkomo	Oomhlaambee we´zeenko´mo´
Milk the cows.	Senga izinkomo.	Se´ngaa eezeenko´mo´.
Slaughter the oxen.	Hlaba izinkabi.	Hlaabaa eezeenkaabee.
Make biltong.	Enza umqwayiba.	E´nzaa oomqwaayeebaa.
Kill the snake.	Bulala inyoka.	Boolaalaa eenyo´kaa.
Spray the flies.	Futha izimpukane.	Footaa eezeempookaane´.

DAYS OF THE WEEK TIME	IZINSUKU ZESONTO ISIKHATHI	EEZEENSOOKOO ZE'SO'NTO' EESEEKAATEE
Monday	uMsombuluko	ooMso'mboolooko'
Tuesday	uLwesibili	ooLwe'seebeelee
Wednesday	uLwesithathu	ooLwe'Seetaatoo
Thursday	uLwesine	ooLwe'Seene'
Friday	uLwesihlanu	ooLwe'seehlaanoo
Saturday	uMgqibelo	ooMgqeebe'lo'
Sunday	iSonto	eeSo'nto'
today	namuhla / namhlanje	naamoohla / naamhlaanje'
Today is . . . (Monday)	Namuhla ngu . . .	Naamoohlaa ngoo . . .
tomorrow	kusasa	koosaasaa
Tomorrow is . . . (Monday)	Kusasa ngu . . .	Koosaasaa ngoo . . .
day after tomorrow	ngomhlomunye	ngo'mhlo'moonye'
yesterday	izolo / izo	eezo'lo' / eezo'
day before yesterday	kuthangi	kootaangee
last week	ngesonto elidlule	nge'so'nto' e'leedloole'
this week	leli sonto	le'lee so'nto'
during this week	ngaleli sonto	ngaale'lee so'nto'
month	inyanga	eenyaangaa
this year	lonyaka	lo' nyaakaa
last year	ngonyaka odlule	ngo'nyaakaa o'dloole'
next year	ngonyaka ozayo	ngo'nyaakaa o'zaayo'
During this year / In a year	Ngonyaka / Kulo nyaka	Ngo'nyaakaa / Kooloo' nyaakaa
During last year	Ngonyaka odlule / Ngalonyaka odlule	Ngo'nyaakaa o'dloole' / Ngaalo'nyaakaa o'dlooleele'
During this coming year	Ngonyaka ozayo / Ngalonyaka ozayo	Ngo'nyaakaa o'zaayo' / Ngaalo'nyaakaa o'zaayo'
On Monday, Tues, Wed. etc.	NgomSombuluko	Ngo'Mso'mboolooko'
On Sunday	NgeSonto	Nge'So'nto'
Last Tuesday	NgolweSibili olwedlule / oludlule	Ngo'lwe'Seebeelee o'lwe'dloole' / o'loodloole'
Last Sunday	NgeSonto eledlule	Nge'So'nto' e'le'dloole'
Next Sunday	NgeSonto elizayo	Nge'So'nto' e'leezaayo'
Next Wednesday	NgolweSithathu oluzayo	Ngo'lwe'Seetaatoo o'loozaayo'
On the same / one day	Ngalanga linye	Ngaalaangaa leenye'
In the same / one week	Ngasonto linye	Ngaaso'nto' leenye'
In the same / one month	Nganyanga linye	Ngaanyaangaa leenye'
In the same / one year	Nganyaka munye	Ngaanyaakaa moonye'
In the same / one hour	Ngahora linye	Ngaaho'raa leenye'
At the same time	Ngasikhathi sinye	Ngaaseekaatee seenye'
At the same moment	Ngamzuzu munye	Ngaamzoozoo moonye'
On a certain day	Ngasuku luthize	Ngaasookoo looteeze'
On that day	Ngalolo suku	Ngaalo'lo' sookoo
On the following day	Ngomuso	Ngo'mooso'
On the previous day	Ngayizolo	Ngaayeezo'lo'
On the next day	Ngakusasa	Ngaakoosaasaa
What day of the week is it?	Namuhla ngulwesingaki?	Naamoohlaa ngoolwe'seengaakee?
Today is Saturday.	Namuhla nguMgqibelo.	Naamoohlaa ngooMgqeebe'lo'.

English	Zulu	Pronunciation
Yesterday was Friday.	Izolo bekungoLwesihlanu.	Eezo'lo' be'koongo'- Lwe'seehlaanoo.
Tomorrow is Thursday.	Kusasa ngolweSine.	Koosaasaa ngo'lwe'Seene'.
today	namuhla	naamoohlaa
tomorrow	kusasa / ngomuso	koosaasaa / ngo'mooso'
Day after	Ngomhlo munye	Ngo'mhlo' moonye'
Day after tomorrow is --	Ngomhlomunye ---	Ngo'mhlo'moonye' ---
Monday	ngumSombuluko	ngoomSo'mboolooko'
yesterday	izolo	eezo'lo'
day before	kuthangi	kootaangee
Day before was Friday.	Kuthangi bekungu Lwesihlanu.	Kootaangee be'koongoo Lwe'seehlaanoo.
During this month	Ngale nyanga	Ngaale' nyaangaa
During July	NgoJulayi	Ngo'Joolaayee
During last month	Ngalenyanga edlule	Ngaale' nyaangaa e'dloole'
During next month	Ngalenyanga ezayo	Ngaale' nyaangaa e'zaayo'
In the month of May	Ngenyanga kaMeyi	Nge'nyaagaa kaaMe'yee
First year etc.	Ngonyaka wokuqala	Ngo'nyaakaa wo'kooqaalaa
second	--- wesibili	--- we'seebeelee
third	--- wesithathu	--- we'seetaatoo
fourth	--- wesine	--- we'seene'
fifth	--- wesihlanu	--- we'seehlaanoo
sixth	--- wesithupha	--- we'seetoopaa
seventh	--- wesikhombisa	--- we'seeko'mbeesaa
eight	--- wesishiyagalombili	--- we'seesheeyaagaalo'mbeelee
ninth	--- wesishiyagalolunye	--- we'seesheeyaagaalo'loonye'
tenth	--- weshumi	--- we'shoomee
At 12 etc.	Ngo 12	Ngo' 12
in the morning	ekuseni	e'koose'nee
at noon	emini	e'meenee
in the afternoon	ntambama	ntaambaamaa
in the evening	kusihlwa	kooseehlwaa
at night	ebusuku	e'boosookoo
The meeting will begin at 10 in the morning.	Umhlangano uzoqala ngo 10 ekuseni.	Oomhlaangaano' oozo'qaalaa ngo' 10 e'koose'nee.
School comes out at 3 in the afternoon.	Isikole siphuma ngo 3 ntambama.	Eeseeko'le' seepoomaa ngo' 3 ntaambaama.
The church service starts at 8 in the evening.	Isonto lingena ngo 8 ebusuku.	Eeso'nto' leenge'naa ngo' 8 e'boosookoo.

MONTHS OF THE YEAR	IZINYANGA ZONYAKA	EEZEENYAANGA ZO'NYAAKA
January	uJanuwari	ooJaanoowaaree
February	uFebhruwari	ooFe'broowaaree
March	uMashi	ooMaashee
April	u-Ephreli / u-April	oo-E'pre'lee / oo-April
May	uMeyi	ooMayi / ooMe'yee
June	uJuni	ooJoonee
July	uJulayi	ooJoolaayee
August	u-Agasti	oo-Aagaastee
September	uSepthemba	ooSe'pte'mbaa
October	u-Okthoba	oo-O'kto'baa
November	uNovemba	ooNo've'mbaa
December	uDisemba	ooDeese'mbaa

PROVERBS	IZAGA	EEZAAGAA
Crack a joke.	Yenza ihlaya.	Ye'nzaa eehlaayaa.
Rome wasn't built in a day.	Ubude abuphangwa.	Ooboode' aaboopaangwaa.
Green with envy.	Umhawu usuka esweni.	Oomhaawoo oosaakaa e'swe'nee.
Whatever one does has its outcome.	Akundlela ingayi ekhaya.	Aakoondle'laa eengaayee e'kaayaa.
Your turn will come.	Elisina muva liyabukwa.	E'leeseenaa moovaa leeyaabookwaa.
The heart has no boundaries.	Iso liwela umfula ugcwele.	Eeso' leewe'laa oomfoolaa oogcwe'le'.
Look / think before you leap / decide.	Igeja lithengwa ngokubonwa.	Eege'jaa leete'ngwaa ngo'koobo'nwaa.
We are not happy / The shoe doesn't fit.	Ucu kalulingani entanyeni.	Oocoo kaalooleengaanee eentaanye'nee.
One can't compete.	Akumbethe waphika nelanga.	Aakoombe'te' waapeekaa ne'laangaa.
No task is too much or difficult.	Kakundlovu yasindwa ngumboko wayo.	Kaakoondlo'voo yaaseendwaa ngoombo'ko' waayo'.
You must face the truth.	Akundlela ingayi ekhaya.	Aakoondle'laa eengaayee e'kaayaa.
One never knows when ones' day will come.	Elokufa alitsheli.	E'lo'koofaa aaleetshe'lee.
He must face his own music.	Uzenzile kakhalelwa.	Ooze'nzeele' kaakaale'lwaa.
Don't cry over spilt milk.	Kukhalelwa uzumekile.	Kookaale'lwaa oozoome'keele'.
Don't laugh at someone elses misfortune, it could be your turn next.	Inxeba lendoda alihlekwa, kungawe ngomuso.	Eenxe'baa le'ndo'daa aaleehle'kwaa, koongaawe' ngo'mooso'.
Don't procrastinate.	Umthente uhlaba usamila.	Oomte'nte' oohlaabaa oosaameelaa.
If you don't know, ask.	Indlela ibuzwa kwabaphambili.	Eendle'laa eeboozwaa kwaabaapaambeelee.
Don't judge a person from the outside.	Ayihlabi ngakumisa.	Aayeehlaabee ngaakoomeesaa.
Think twice before you leap.	Inyoka kayishaywa isibili ikhanda lingabonwa.	Eenyo'kaa kaayeeshaaywaa eeseebeelee eekaandaa leengaabo'nwaa.
Careful, danger is lurking.	Itshe limi ngothi.	Eetshe' leemee ngo'tee.
Look before you leap.	Isiziba siziwa ngodondolo.	Eeseezeebaa seezeewaa ngo'do'ndo'lo'.
All talk and no action.	Wande ngomlomo njengembenge.	Waande' ngo'mlo'mo' nje'nge'mbe'nge'.
Learn from experience, or suffer the consequences.	Isalakutshelwa sibona ngomopho.	Eesaalaakootshe'lwaa seebo'naa ngo'mo'po'.
Do things for yourself.	Imbila yeswela umsila ngokuyalezela.	Eembeelaa ye'swe'laa oomseelaa ngo'kooyaale'ze'laa.
Too many cooks spoil the broth.	Iningi liyabona ububende.	Eeneengee leeyaabo'naa ooboobe'nde'.
Got a memory like an elephant, never forgets.	Umenziwa akakhohlwa, kukhohlwa umenzi.	Oome'nzeewaa aakaako'hlwaa, kooko'hlwaa oome'nzee.
Puts the blame onto someone else.	Insimba yesulela ngegqumusha.	Eenseembaa ye'soole'laa nge'qoomooshaa.
He discriminates against others.	Ukhetha iphela emasini.	Ooke'taa eepe'laa e'maaseenee.

78.

Set a thief to catch a thief.	Iqili lidliwa ngamanye amaqili.	Eeqeelee leedleewaa ngaamaanye′ aamaaqeelee.
There is no hope for recovery.	Izinhlanga zimuka nomoya.	Eezeenhlaangaa zeemookaa no′mo′yaa.
It will / can never happen.	Kungawa ilanga licoshwe zinkukhu.	Koongaawaa eelaangaa leeco′shwe′ zeenkookoo.
He is at a loss for words.	Amathe abuyele kwasifuba.	Aamaate′ aabooye′le′ kwaaseefoobaa.
He has nothing to show for all the hard work.	Isithukuthuku senja siphelela eboyeni.	Eeseetookootookoo se′njaa seepe′le′laa e′bo′ye′nee.
Thank your lucky stars.	Ukubonga amadlozi.	Ookoobo′ngaa aamaadlo′zee.
One knows not what the future will bring.	Kuhlwile phambili kusile emuva.	Koohlweele′ paambeelee kooseele′ e′moovaa.
Tomorrow is another day. / Every day is different.	Kusa kusa. / Kusa kusa.	Koosaa koosaa. / Koosaa koosaa.
He does not reap the benefits of is hard work.	Yeka amandla esambane sona simba umgodi singawulali.	Ye′kaa aamaandlaa e′saambaane′ so′naa seembaa oomgo′dee seengaawoolaalee.
We all make mistakes, even experts.	Induku ishaya imviki.	Eendookoo eeshaayaa eemveekee.
Once bitten twice shy.	Lixhoshwa kanye lesabe.	Leexo′shwaa kaanye′ le′saabe′.
Goes wrong at the last minute.	Buchitheka bugayiwe.	Boocheete′kaa boogaayeewe′.
Suffer the after effects.	Udle ukudla kwamudla.	Oodle′ ookoodlaa kwaamoodlaa.
Escape by the skin of your teeth.	Iqhina liphuma embizeni.	Eeqeenaa leepoomaa e′mbeeze′nee.
The person that was there for you during hard times, is often forgotten when the times are good.	Umbeki wenkosi kabusi nayo.	Oombe′kee we′nko′see kaaboosee naayo′.
Help the poor, they could be in a position to help you some day.	Ukupha ukuziphakela.	Ookoopaa ookoozeepaake′laa.
Beauty is skin deep.	Ikhiwane elihle ligcwala izimpethu.	Eekeewaane′ e′leehle′ leegcwaalaa eezeempe′too.
A case of the kettle calling the pot black.	Usifumbu ubona uqhaqhazela.	Ooseefoomboo oobo′naa ooqaaqaaze′laa.
Pull together / maintain a good relationship.	Igugu liyadonsiswana.	Eegoogoo leeyaado′nseeswaanaa.
He does not show his true colours.	Unonele phakathi njengendlazi.	Oono′ne′le′ paakaatee nje′nge′ndlaazee.
He can't keep a secret.	Wakhahlelwa yihhashi esifubeni.	Waakaahle′lwaa yeehaashee e′seefoobe′nee.
He is unreliable.	Uyishaya emuva ayishaye phambili.	Ooyeeshaayaa e′moovaa aayeeshaaye′ paambeelee.
He says one thing but means another.	Ubika imbiba abike ibuzi.	Oobeekaa eembeebaa aabeeke′ eeboozee.
He / she takes after the parents.	Ukhamba lufuze imbiza.	Ookhaambaa loofooze′ eembeezaa.
They are bosom pals.	Amathe nolimi.	Aamaate′ no′leemee.
No matter what happens.	Nakanjani.	Naakaanjaanee.

TITLES & FAMILY	AMAGAMA NA ABAZALWE	AAMAAGAAMAA NAA AABAAZAALWE´
aunt	ubabekazi	oobaabe´kaazee
baby	ingane / umntwana	eengaane´ / oomntwaanaa
bachelor	impohlo	eempo´hlo´
bestman	impelesi kamyeni	eempe´le´see kaamye´nee
boy	umfana	oomfaanaa
bride / newly married	umakoti	oomaako´tee
bridegroom	umyeni	oomye´nee
bridesmaid	impelesi kamakoti	eempe´le´see kaamaako´tee
brother	umfowethu	oomfo´we´too
brother-in-law	umkhwenyana / usibali	oomkwe´nyaanaa / ooseebaalee
chief	inkosi	eenko´see
child	ingane	eengaane´
clan	isizalo	eeseezaalo´
cousin	lwakini umzala	lwaakeenee oomzaalaa
daughter	indodakazi	eendo´daakaazee
daughter-in-law	umakoti	oomaako´tee
divorce (n)	idivosi / ukwehlukanisa	eedeevo´see /ookwe´hlookaaneesaa
divorce (v)	divosa / hlukanisa	deevo´saa / hlookaaneesaa
enemy	isitha	eeseetaa
engaged	thenjisiwe umshado	te´njeeseewe´ oomshaado´
engagement	ukuthenjiswa umshado	ookoote´njeeswaa oomshaado´
family	umndeni / inzalo	oomnde´nee / eenzaalo´
family – one of our ---	owakithi	o´waakeetee
family tree	ukwelamana kwabosendo	ookwe´laamaanaa kwaabo´se´ndo´
father	ubaba / umzali wesilisa	oobaabaa / oomzaalee we´seeleesa
father-in-law	ubabezala	oobaabe´zaalaa
friend	umngane	oomngaane´
girl	intombazana	eento´mbaazaanaa
grandchild	umzukulu	oomzookooloo
granddaughter	umzukulu wesifazane	oomzookooloo we´seefaazaane´
grandfather	umkhulu / ubabamkhulu	oomkooloo / oobaabaamkooloo
grandmother	ugogo / umakhulu	oogo´go´ / oomaakooloo
grandson	umzukulu wesilisa	oomzookooloo we´seeleesa
great aunt	umamekazi womzali	oomaame´kaazee wo´mzaalee
great grandchild	umzukulwana	oomzookoolwaanaa
great grandmother	ugogo omdala	oogo´go´ o´mdaalaa
great uncle	umalume womzali	oomaaloome´ wo´mzaalee
husband	umyeni / indoda	oomye´nee / eendo´daa
king	inkosi / ukhingi	eenko´see / ookeengee
lady	inenekazi / inkosikazi	eene´ne´kaazee / eenko´seekaazee
man / men	indoda / amadoda	eendo´daa / aamaado´daa
marriage	umshado	oomshaado´
married	shadile / ganile	shaadeele´ / gaaneele´
married man	indoda eshadileyo	eendo´daa e´shaadeele´yo´
married women	inkosikazi / umfazi	eenko´seekaazee / oomfaazee
marry (v)	shada	shaadaa
master – one in charge	induna	eendoonaa

Miss	NKosazana	NKo'saazaanaa
Mister / Mr.	uMnumzane	ooMnoomzaane'
Mistress / Mrs.	iNkosikazi / uMesisi	eeNko'seekaazee / ooMe'seesee
mother – my ---	umama wami	oomaamaa waamee
mother – your ---	unina - wako	ooneenaa - waako'
mother-in-law – your ---	uninazala -wako	ooneenaazaalaa - waako'
mother-in-law – my ---	umamezala - wami	oomaame'zaalaa - waamee
Mrs. / Mistress	uMesisi	ooMe'seesee
nation	isizwe	eeseezwe'
nationality	isizalo	eeseezaalo'
native – of ---	owokuzalwa e---	o'wo'koozaalwaa e'---
nephew	umshana	oomshaanaa
niece	umshanakazi	oomshaanaakaazee
noble	asemakhosini ohlanga	aase'maako'seenee o'hlaangaa
nobleman	owasemakhosini ezwe	o'waase'maako'seenee e'zwe'
noblesse	amakhosi ohlanga	aamaako'see o'hlaangaa
parent	umzali	oomzaalee
parents	abazali	aabaazaalee
prince	inkosana yohlanga	eenko'saana yo'hlaangaa
princess	inkosazana yenkosi	eenko'saazaana ye'nko'see
queen	inkosikazi / ukhwini	eenko'seekaazee / ookweenee
royal	nobukhosi	no'booko'see
royalty	abomuzi wenkosi	aabo'moozee we'nko'see
sister	udade / usisi	oodaade'/ ooseesee
sister-in-law	umlamu / usibali	oomlaamoo / ooseebaalee
sisters	osisi / abasesi	o'seesee / aabaase'see
son	indodana / umfana	eendo'daanaa / oomfaanaa
sons	amadodana / abafana	aamaado'daanaa / aabaafaanaa
son-in-law	umkhwenyana	oomkwe'nyaanaa
spinster	umjendevu	ooje'nde'voo
tribe	uhlobo / isizwana	oohlo'bo' / eeseezwaanaa
tribesman	owesizwana	o'we'seezwaanaa
uncle	umalume	oomaaloome'
widow	umfelokazi	oomfe'lo'kaazee
widower	umfelwa	oomfe'lwaa
wife	umfazi / umakoti / inkosikazi	oomfaazee / oomaako'tee / eenko'seekaazee
young lady	inkosazana	eenko'saazaanaa
young man	insizwa	eenseezwaa
young woman / girl	intombazana	eento'mbaazaanaa

81.

GREETINGS	IZILOKOTHO	EEZEELO´KO´TO´
Happy birthday.	Usuku lokuzalwa oluhle.	Oosooko lo´koozaalwaa o´loohle´.
Happy anniversary.	Umkhosi omuhle	Oomko´see o´moohle´.
Merry christmas.	Ukhisimuzi omuhle.	Ookeeseemoozee o´moohle´.
Merry christmas and a	Ukhisimuzi omuhle	Ookeeseemoozee o´moohle´
happy new year.	nonyaka omusha omuhle.	no´nyaakaa o´mooshaa o´moohle´.
Thank you	Ngiyabonga	Ngeeyaabo´ngaa
Congratulations!	Halala!	Haalaalaa!
I congratulate you.	Ngiyakubongela. /	Ngeeyaakoobo´nge´laa. /
	Ngiyakuhalalisela.	Ngeeyaakoohaalaaleese´laa.
We congratulate you.	Siyakubongela. /	Seeyaakoobo´nge´laa. /
	Siyakuhalalisela.	Seeyaakoohaalaaleese´laa.
Get well soon. /	Sengathi ungasinda	Se´ngaatee oongaaseendaa
	masinyane / ngokushesha. /	maaseenyaane´ / ngo´kooshe´shaa. /
Get well soon.	Sengathi ungalulama	Se´ngaatee oongaaloolaamaa
	ngokushesha.	ngo´kooshe´shaa.
I love you.	Ngiyakuthanda.	Ngeeyaakootaandaa.
Thinking of you.	Ngicabanga ngawe.	Ngeecaabaangaa ngaawe´.
Good luck. /	Ngikufisela inhlanhla. /	Ngeekoofeese´laa eenhlaanhlaa. /
Good luck. /	Sengathi ungaba	Se´ngaatee oongaabaa
	nenhlanhla. /	ne´nhlaanhlaa. /
Good luck.	Ube nenhlanhla.	Oobe´ ne´nhlaanhlaa.
Happy mother's day.	Usuku oluhle lomama.	Oosookoo o´loohle´ lo´maamaa.
Happiest mother's day.	Usuku lomama olunenjabulo	Oosookoo lo´maamaa o´loone´njaaboolo´
	enkulu kaakooloo.	e´nkooloo kakhulu.
Happy father's day.	Osuku oluhle lobaba.	O´sookoo o´loohle´ lo´baabaa.
Happiest father's day.	Usuku lobaba olunenjabulo	Oosookoo lo´baabaa o´loone´njaaboolo´
	enkulu kakhulu.	e´nkooloo kaakooloo.
Happy valentine's day.	Usuku oluhle	Oosookoo o´loohle´
	lwezithandani.	lwe´zeentaandaanee.
Happiest valentine's day.	Usuku lwezithandani	Oosookoo lwe´zeetaandaanee
	olunenjabulo enkulu kakhulu.	o´loone´njaaboole´ e´nkooloo kaakooloo.
Be my valentine.	Yiba ngothandiweyo wami.	Yeebaa ngo´taandeewe´yo´ waamee.
Wishing you a ---	Ngikufisela ---	Ngeekoofeese´laa ---
Just to say ---	Ngifuna ukuthi nje ---	Ngeefoonaa ookootee nje´ ---
Just to say I love you.	Ngifuna ukuthi	Ngeefoonaa ookootee
	ngiyakuthanda.	ngeeyaakootaandaa.
Good luck on your	Ngikufisela inhlanhla	Ngeekoofeese´laa eenhlaanhlaa
wedding day. /	ngosuku lwakho lomshado. /	ngo´sookoo lwaako´ lo´mshaado´. /
Good luck on your	Ube nenhlanhla	Oobe´ ne´nhlaanhlaa
wedding day.	ngosuku lwakho lomshado.	ngo´sookoo lwaako´ lo´mshaado´.
Good luck on your	Ngikufisela inhlanhla	Ngeekoofeese´laa eenhlaanhlaa
engagement. /	ekuthenjisweni kwakho. /	e´koote´njeeswe´nee kwaako´. /
Good luck on your	Ube nenhlanhla	Oobe´ ne´nhlaanhlaa
engagement.	ekuthenjisweni kwakho.	e´koote´njeeswe´nee kwaako´.
It's your special day.	Wusuku lwakho lwekhethelo.	Woosookoo lwaako´ lwe´ke´te´lo´.
Enjoy it!	Ube nenjabulo!	Oobe´ ne´njaaboolo´!
Good luck for the exams. /	Ubhale kahle	Oobaale´ kaahle´
	ukuhlolwa kwakho. /	ookoohlo´lwaa kwaako´. /

English	Zulu	Phonetic
Good luck for the exams. /	Ube nenhlanhla ekuhlolweni kwakho. /	Oobe´ ne´nhlaanhlaa e´koohlo´lwe´nee kwaako´. /
Good luck for the exams.	Ngikufisela inhlanhla ekuhlolweni kwakho.	Ngeekoofeese´laa eenhlaanhlaa ekoohlo´lwe´nee kwaako´.
Bon voyage.	Uhambo oluhle.	Oohaambo´ o´loohle´.
Enjoy your holiday. /	Ube neholide elimnandi. /	Oobe´ ne´ho´leede´ e´leemnaandee. /
Enjoy your holiday. /	Ube neholide elihle. /	Oobe´ ne´ho´leede´ e´leehle´. /
Enjoy your holiday. /	Iholide elihle. /	Eeho´leede´ e´leehle´. /
Enjoy your holiday.	Ulijabulele iholide lakho.	Ooleejaaboole´le´ eeho´leede´ laako´.
Congratulations on the birth ---	Ngiyakuhalalisela ekuzalweni ---	Ngeeyaakoohaalaaleese´laa e´koozaalwe´nee ---
of your son /	kwendodana yakho /	kwe´ndo´daanaa yaako´ /
of your daughter /	kwendodakazi yakho /	kwe´ndo´daakaazee yaako´ /
grandchild /	komzukulu /	ko´mzookooloo /
grandson /	komzukulu wesilisa /	ko´mzookooloo we´seeleesaa /
granddaughter.	komzukulu wesifazane.	komzookooloo we´seefaazaane´.
With sympathy.	Ngozwelo.	Ngo´zwe´lo´.
With deepest sympathy on your tragic loss.	Ngozwelo olujulile ekulahlekelweni kwakho okushaqisayo.	Ngo´zwe´lo´ o´loojooleele´ e´koolaahle´ke´lwe´nee kwaako´ o´kooshaaqeesaayo´.
With sympathy on the loss of a loved one.	Ngozwelo ngokulahlekelwa ngothandwayo.	Ngo´zwe´lo´ ngo´koolaahle´ke´lwaa ngo´taandwaayo´.
May God be with you during your time of loss. /	iNkosi ibe nawe kule sikhathi sokulahlekelwa kwakho. /	eeNko´see eebe´ naawe´ koole´ seekaatee so´koolaahle´ke´lwaa kwaako´. /
May God be with you during your time of loss.	unKulunkulu abe nawe kulesi sikhathi sokulahlekelwa kwakho.	oonKooloonkooloo aabe´ naawe´ koole´see seekaatee so´koolaahle´ke´lwaa kwaako´.
Your kindness has made a difference, thank you.	Umusa wakho wenze umehluko, ngiyabonga.	Oomoosaa waako´ we´nze´ oome´hlooko´, ngeeyaabo´ngaa.
Shoot for the moon, even if you miss, you will land among the stars.	Dubula inyanga, noma ugeja, uyohlala phakathi kwezinkanyezi.	Dooboolaa eenyaangaa, no´maa ooge´jaa, ooyo´hlaalaa paakaatee kwe´zeenkaanye´zee.
Life is made up of memories. May today be one of the fondest.	Impilo yakhiwe nezinkumbulo. Sengathi namhlanje kungaba ngeyedlulele.	Eempeelo´ yaakeewe´ ne´zeenkoomboolo´. Se´ngaatee naamhlaanje´ koongaabaa nge´ye´dloole´le´.
I wanted to wish you the best, because you are the best.	Bengifuna ukukufisela okuhle kakhulu, ngoba umuhle kakhulu kunabo bonke.	Be´ngeefoonaa ookookoofeese´laa o´koohle´ kaakooloo, ngo´baa oomoohle´ kaakooloo koonaabo´ bo´nke´.

Happy birthday to you	'Suk' olumnandi kuwe	'Sook' o'loomnaandee koowe'
Happy birthday to you	'Suk' olumnandi kuwe	'Sook' o'loomnaandee koowe'
Happy birthday dear Marc	'Suk' olumnandi kuwe Marc	'Sook' o'loomnaandee koowe'
Happy birthday to you.	'Suk' olumnandi kuwe.	'Sook' o'loomnaandee koowe'.

For they are jolly good fellows and so say all of us.	Bangabahlobo abahle kusho thina sonke.	Baangaabaahlo'bo aabaahle' koosho' teenaa so'nke'.

anniversary	usuku lomnyaka	oosookoo lo'mnyaakaa
birthday	usuku lokuzalwa	oosookoo lo'koozaalwaa
celebration	umkhosi	oomko'see
ceremony	umkhosi	oomko'see
Christmas	uKhisimuzi	ooKeeseemoozee
death	ukushona	ookoosho'naa
easter	ista	eestaa
engagement	ukuthenjiswa umshado	ookoote'njeeswaa oomshaado'
funeral	umngcwabo	oomgcwaabo'
year	umnyaka	oomnyaakaa
new year's day	usuku lomnyaka omusha	oosookoo lo'mnyaakaa o'mooshaa
passover	phasika	paaseekaa
wedding	umshado	oomshaado'
wedding celebration	umgcagco	oomgcaagco'

NOTE :

In Zulu the noun consists of a prefix and a stem – for example Ubaba (father) u -baba (oobaabaa).
Therefore, all nouns are shown in their full form in most cases.

ENGLISH	ZULU	PHONETIC

A

ENGLISH	ZULU	PHONETIC
aardvark	isambane	eesaambaane´
abandon (v)	lahla / yeka / shiya	laahlaa / ye´kaa / sheeyaa
abandoned	lahliwe / shiyiwe	laahleewe´ / sheeyeewe´
abattoir	amadela	aamaade´laa
abbreviate (v)	finyeza / nciphisa	feenye´zaa / nceepeesaa
abbreviation	isifinyezo	eeseefeenye´zo´
abdicate (v)	dela / yeka / duba	de´laa / ye´ kaa / doobaa
abdication /	ukudela /	ookoode´laa /
abdication	ukulahlwa kobukhosi	ookoolaahlwaa ko´booko´see
abdomen	isisu	eeseesoo
abdominal	esisu	e´seesoo
abduct (v)	thumba	toombaa
abduction	ukuthumba	ookootoombaa
abide (v) – home	hlala	hlaalaa
abide (v) – tolerate	nyamezela	nyaame´ze´laa
ability – know how	ilikhono / ukwazi	eeleeko´no´ / ookwaazee
ability – power	amandla	aamaandlaa
able	-kwazi	-kwaazee
ablution	ukugeza / ukuhlanza	ookooge´zaa / ookoohlaanzaa
abnormal	ngavamile / ngafani	ngaavaameele´/ ngaafaanee
abnormality	okungavamile	o´koongaavaameele´
aboard	emkhunjini	e´mkoonjeenee
abode – home / place	ikhaya / indawo / umuzi	eekaayaa / eendaawo´/ oomoozee
abode – my present	indawo engisahlala kuyo	eendaawo´ e´ngeesaahlaalaa kooyo´
abolish (v)	susa / qeda	soosaa / qe´daa
abomination	isinengeko	eeseene´nge´ko´
aboriginal	emvelo	e´mve´lo´
aborigines – Australian	abomdabu base Ostreyliya	aabo´mdaaboo baase´ O´stre´leeyaa
aborigines	abantu bemvelo	aabaantoo be´mve´lo´
abort (v) – animal	phunza	poonzaa
abort (v) – child	khipha isisu	keepaa eeseesoo
abortion – animal	umphunzo / ukuphunza	oompoonzo´/ ookoopoonzaa
abortion – human	ukuphuphuma kwesisu	ookoopoopoomaa kwe´seesoo
about – walk about (v)	hambahamba	haambaahaambaa
about	ngakhona	ngaako´naa
above	phezulu	pe´zooloo
absent (he / she is)	akekho / -kho	aake´ko´ / -ko´
absent-minded	alukile / ndwazile	aalookeele´/ ndwaazeele´
accelerate (v)	sheshisa	she´sheesa
accident	ingozi	eengo´zee
accidentally	ngengozi	nge´ngo´zee
accommodate (v)	nika indawo	neeka eendaawo´
accommodation	indawo yokuhlala nokulala	eendaawo´ yo´koohlaalaa no´koolaalaa
accompany (v)	phelezela	pe´le´ze´laa
account (n)	i - akhawunti	ee -aakaawoontee

English		
accuse (v)	beka icala	be'ka eecaala
ache	ubuhlungu	ooboohloongoo
achieve (v)	feza	fe'zaa
achievement	impumelelo	eempoome'le'lo'
acid / sour	muncu	mooncoo
acknowledge (v)	vuma	voomaa
acquaint (v)	azisa	aazeesaa
acquire (v)	zuza / thola	zooza / to'laa
across (through) / lie across	phambana na	paambaana naa
across (yonder)	phesheya	pe'she'ya
active (energetic)	khuthele	koote'le'
adapt (v)	vumelanisa	voome'laaneesa
add (v)	enezela / engeza	e'ne'ze'la / e'nge'zaa
address (P.O.Box)	ikheli	eeke'lee
adequate	anele	aane'le'
adhere (v)	namathela	naamaate'laa
admire (v)	babaza	baabaaza
admission	ukwamukelwa	ookwaamooke'lwa
admit (v)	mukela	mooke'la
adopt (v) - a child	thola intandane	to'la eentaandaane'
adoption	ukuthola intandane	ookooto'laa eentandaane'
adore - worship	khulekela	koole'ke'laa
adult (a)	osekhulile	o'se'kooleele'
adult (n)	umuntu osekhulile	oomoontoo o'se'kooleele'
advance (n) - move on	ukuqhubeka	ookooqoobe'kaa
advance (v) - move on	qhubeka	qoobe'kaa
advancement	inqubekela phambili	eenqoobe'ke'la paambeeli
advantage - benefit (n)	inzuzo	eenzoozo'
advertise (v)	azisa	aazeesaa
advertisement	isaziso	eesaazeeso'
advice - instruction	iseluleko / isiyalo	eese'loole'ko' / eeseeyaalo'
advise (v)	eluleka / qondisa	e'loole'kaa / qo'ndeesaa
adviser	umeluleki	oome'loole'kee
aeroplane	ibhanoyi / indiza	eebaano'yee / eendeezaa
affair - love	indaba yothando	eendaaba yo'taando'
affair	indaba	eendaabaa
affect (v)	thinta	teentaa
affection	uthando	ootaando'
affidavit	isifungo	eeseefoongo'
afford / supply / give (v)	veza / nika	ve'zaa / neekaa
afraid	novalo / sabayo	no'vaalo' / saabaayo'
after	emuva kwa	e'moovaa kwaa
afternoon	intambama	eentaambaamaa
afterwards	kamuva	kaamoovaa
again	futhi	footee
again - again and again	futhi futhi	footee footee
again - once again	kanye futhi	kaanye' footee
again - never again	neze - neze	ne'ze' ne'ze'
against - lean (v)	ncika	nceekaa
against - run up against	nqwamana na	nqwaamaanaa naa

against - in opposition to	phambene na	paambe'ne' naa
against - warn against	xwayisa	xwaayeesaa
age (n)	ubudala	ooboodaalaa
age (v)	guga	googaa
aged	gugile	googeele'
agile	lula	loolaa
agree (v)	vumelana	voome'laanaa
agreeable (adv)	mnandi	mnaandee
agreement	isivumelwano	eeseevoome'lwaano'
ahead	ngaphambili	ngaapaambeelee
aid (n) – help	usizo	ooseezo'
aid (v)	siza	seezaa
aids – illness	ingculazi	eengcoolaazee
aim (v)	khomba / -hlosa	ko'mba / -hlo'saa
air (n)	umoya	oomo'yaa
air (v)	shayisa umoya	shaayeesaa oomo'yaa
alarm (scare)	ethusa / esabisa	e'toosa / e'saabeesaa
albino /	inkawu /	eenkaawoo /
albino	umuntu oyinkawu	oomoontoo o'yeenkaawoo
alcohol /spirits	ugologo / utshwala	oogo'lo'go' / ootshwaalaa
alcoholic	isidakwa	eeseedaakwaa
alert	xwayile	xwaayeele'
alike	fanayo	faanaayo'
alive - well	phila	peelaa
alive - living	philile	peeleele'
all (beings) / we	sonke / thina	so'nke' / teenaa
all (things)	konke	ko'nke'
allow (v)	vumela	voome'laa
almost	cishe	ceeshe'
alone	o-dwa / e- dwa	o'dwa / e'dwaa
alone - Leave me alone.	Ngiyeke.	Ngeeye'ke'.
aloud	nomsindo	no'mseendo'
also	futhi	footee
alternate	phambanisiweyo	paambaaneeseewe'yo'
alternate (v)	phambana	paambaanaa
although	noma	no'maa
always	njalo	njaalo'
amaze (v)	mangalisa	maangaaleesaa
ambition	ukulangazela	ookoolaangaaze'la
ambulance	i-ambulense	ee-aamboole'nse'
amid	phakathi kwa-	paakaatee kwaa-
ammunition	izindubulo	eezeendooboolo'
amputate (v)	nquma	nqoomaa
amputation	ukunqunywa	ookoonqoonywaa
amuse (v)	thokozisa	to'ko'zeesaa
anaesthetic	ianesithethiki	eeaane'seethe'teekee
anaesthetist	umuntu ofaka	oomoontoo o'faakaa
	umuthi	oomootee
	wokuqeda ukuzwa	wo'kooqe'daa ookoozwaa
anaesthetize (v)	qeda ukuzwa	qe'da ookoozwaa

and / again	na / futhi	naa / footee
anger	ulaka	oolaaka
angry	thukuthele	tookoote´le´
animal	isilwane	eeseelwaane´
announce (v)	memezela	me´me´ze´laa
annoy (v)	casula	caasoolaa
anointed	ogcotshiweyo	o´gco´tsheewe´yo´
answer (v)	phendula	pe´ndoolaa
answer	impendulo	impe´ndoolo´
ant	intuthwane	intootwaane´
antagonism	umbango	oombaango´
anthem	ilihubo / ingoma	eeleehoobo´ / eengo´maa
anxious / scared / wary	xwayile	xwaayeele´
any	noma	no´maa
anybody	noma ubani	no´ma oobaanee
anyhow	noma kunjani	no´ma koonjaanee
anything	noma yini	no´ma yeenee
anywhere	noma kuphi	no´ma koopee
ape	inkawu	eenkaawoo
apologise	xolisa	xo´leesaa
appetite	inkanuko	eenkaanooko´
applaud (v)	halalisa	haalaaleesaa
apple	i-apula	ee-aapoolaa
applicant	ofaka isicelo	o´faakaa eeseece´lo´
apply (v)	faka isicelo	faakaa eeseece´lo´
appoint (v)	qasha / khetha	qaasha / ke´taa
approval	imvume	eemvoome´
approve (v)	vumela	voome´laa
apron	iphinifo	eepeeneefo´
argue (v)	phikisana	peekeesaanaa
arid	omile	o´meele´
arise (v)	vuka	vookaa
arm	ingalo	eengaalo´
army worm	isinambuzane	eeseenaamboozaane´
army	impi	eempee
arouse (v)	vusa	voosaa
arrange (v)	hlela	hle´laa
arrest (v)	bopha / bamba	bo´paa / baambaa
arrest (n)	ukuboshwa	ookoobo´shwaa
arrive(v)	fika	feekaa
article	into	eento´
artificial respiration	ukusizwa	ookooseezwaa
	ukuphefumulisa	ookoope´foomooleesaa
artificial respirator	umshini yokwelekelela	oomsheenee yo´kwe´le´ke´le´laa
	ukuphefumula	ookoope´foomoolaa
as is / as though	sengathi	se´ngaatee
ash	umlotha	oomlo´taa
ashamed	namahloni	naamaahlo´nee
aside	ngasese	ngaase´se´
aside – put aside (v)	beka eceleni	be´kaa e´ce´le´nee

ask (v)	buza	boozaa
asleep	lele	le'le'
assault (v)	hlasela	hlaase'laa
assist (v)	sekela / siza	se'ke'laa / seezaa
assistant	umsizi	oomseezee
asthma	umbefu / isifuba somoya	oombe'foo / eeseefoobaa so'mo'yaa
astronaut	isiphuphutheki	eeseepoopoote'kee
athlete	ihatileti / umdlali	eehaateele'tee / oomdlaalee
athletes	amahatileti / abadlali	aamaahaateele'tee /aabaadlaalee
athletics meeting	imikhuba yamahatileti	eemeekoobaa yaamaahaateele'tee
atmosphere (space)	isibhakabhaka / umkhatini	eeseebaakaabaakaa / oomkaateenee
atmosphere - friendly	isimo sokuzwana	eeseemo' so'koozwaanaa
attach (v)	hlanganisa	hlaangaaneesaa
attempt (n)	umzamo	oomzaamo'
attempt (v)	zama	zaamaa
avalanche	isiwulukuhlu	eeseewoolookoohloo
aviation	ukundiza komuntu emoyeni	ookoondeezaa ko'moontoo e'mo'ye'nee
aviator	ondizayo emoyeni	o'ndeezaayo' e'mo'ye'nee
avocado pear	ukwatapheya	ookwaataape'yaa
avoid (v)	xwaya	xwaayaa
awake (a)	vukile / xwayile	vookeele' / xwaayeele'
awake (v)	vuka	vookaa
axe (n)	imbazo / izembe	eembaazo' / eeze'mbe'

B

baby	umntwana	oomntwaanaa
back (adv)	emuva	e'moovaa
back (n)	umhlane	oomhlaane'
bacon	ubhekeni	oobe'ke'nee
badge	ibheji / indonya	eebe'jee / eendo'nyaa
badly	kabi	kaabee
bag (sack)	isaka	eesaakaa
bake at (temp.)	bhaka ku 180 deg.	baakaa koo 180 deg.
bake till . . .	bhaka kuze ku . . .	baakaa kooze' koo . . .
bake (v)	bhaka	baakaa
baked potato	izambane	eezaambaane'
	elibhakiwe	e'leebaakeewe'
bald person	impandla	eempaandlaa
banana	ubhanana	oobaanaanaa
banner	ibhanela	eeebaane'laa
bark (v- dog)	khonkotha	ko'nko'taa
basin	ubheseni	oobe'se'nee
basket	ubhasikidi	oobaaseekeedee
bath (v)	ukubhava / bhava	ookoobaavaa / baavaa
bath	ubhavu	oobaavoo
bathroom	ibhavulumu	eebaavooloomoo
battle field	inkundla yempi	eenkoondlaa ye'mpee
beat (v - egg)	shaya	shaayaa
beat (v – hit)	shaya	shaayaa
beat till . . .	shaya kuze ku . . .	shaayaa kooze' koo . . .
because	ngesimanga / ngoba	nge'seemaangaa / ngo'baa
bed – make a bed (v)	endlala umbhede	e'ndlaalaa oombe'de'
bed of flowers / flower bed	indinyana	eendeenyaanaa
bed of roses	ukunethezeka	ookoone'te'ze'kaa
bed	umbhede	oombe'de'
bedbug	imbungulu	eemboongooloo
bedclothes	izingubo zokulala	eezeengoobo' zo'koolaalaa
bedroom	ikamelo lokulala	eekaame'lo' lo'koolalaa
bee	inyosi	eenyo'see
beef	inyama yenkomo	eenyaamaa ye'nko'mo'
beer	utshwala	ootshwaalaa
before . . .	phambi kwa- / kuka-. . .	paambee kwaa / kookaa-
beg (v)	cela / nxiba	ce'laa / nxeebaa
beggar	isinqibi / isiceli	eeseenqeebee / eeseece'lee
begin (v)	qala	qaalaa
behind	emuva	e'moovaa
bell	insimbi	eenseembee
belly	isisu	eeseesoo
belong / mine	kwa / kwami	kwaa / kwaamee
belt	ibhande	eebaande'
best department	umnyango ovelele	oomnyaango' o've'le'le'
best leader	umholi ovelele	oomho'lee o've'le'le'
best team	ithimu elivelele	eeteemoo e'leeve'le'le'

better	ngcono	ngco'no'
between	ngaphakathi	ngaapaakaatee
beware	qaphela	qaape'laa
big	khulu	kooloo
birthday	usuku lokuzalwa	oosookoo lo'koozaalwaa
birthmark	umkhangu	oomkaangoo
biscuit	ibhisikidi	eebeeseekeedee
bit by bit	kancane kancane	kaancaane' kaancaane'
bit - piece	isihlephu	eeseehle'poo
bite (v)	luma	loomaa
bitter	muncu	mooncoo
black	mnyama	mnyaamaa
bladder	isinye	eeseenye'
blame (n)	insolo / isijeziso	eenso'lo' / eeseeje'zeeso'
blame (v) – someone else	esulela ngecala / sola	e'soole'laa nge'caalaa / so'laa
blame (v)	sola	so'laa
blanket	ingubo	eengoobo'
bleach (v)	cacisa umbala	caaceesaa oombaalaa
	omhlophe	o'mhlo'pe'
bleed (v)	opha	o'paa
bless (v)	busisa	booseesaa
blind /	ngaboni /	ngaabo'nee /
blind	yimpumputhe	yeempoompoote'
blob (of butter)	isicucwana	eeseecoocwaanaa
block (v)	vimbela	veembe'laa
block	isigaxa	eeseegaaxaa
blood	igazi	eegaazee
blouse	ibhulawuzi	eeboolaawoozee
blow (v)	phephetha	pe'pe'taa
blunt	buthuntu	bootoontoo
board	ibhodi	eebo'dee
body	umzimba	oomzeembaa
boil (v)	bilisa	beeleesaa
boiled (egg / water)	elibilisiwe	e'leebeeleeseewe'
boiling water	amanzi abilayo	aamaanzee aabeelaayo'
bone	ithambo	eetaambo'
book	incwadi / ibhuku	eencwaadee / eebookoo
boot (car)	ibhuthi	eebootee
both	bobabili	bo'baabeelee
bottle	ibhodlela	eebo'dle'laa
bottom - under	ngaphansi	ngaapaansee
bow down – respect (v)	thoba	to'baa
bowl	isitsha	eeseetshaa
box	ibhokisi	eebo'keesee
boy	umfana	oomfaanaa
brass - metal / money	ithusi	eetoosee
bread board	uqwembe lokusikela	ooqwe'mbe' lo'kooseeke'laa
	isinkwa	eeseenkwaa
bread crumbs	imvuthu yesinkwa	eemvootoo ye'seenkwaa
bread slicer	ummese wesinkwa	oome'se' we'seenkwaa

English	Zulu	Pronunciation
bread	isinkwa	eeseenkwaa
break – a leg (v)	aphuka umlenze	aapookaa oomle′nze′
break – to pieces (v)	hlakaza	hlaakaazaa
break (n) gap	isikhala	eeseekaalaa
break (n) pause	isikhawu	eeseekaawoo
break (v)	ephuka / bulala	e′pookaa / boolaalaa
breakfast	ibhulakufesi	eeboolaakoofe′see
breath	umphefumulo	oompe′foomoolo′
breathe (v)	phefumula	pe′foomoolaa
breeze	umoya omnandi	oomo′yaa o′mnaandee
bridal party	umthimba	oomteembaa
bride	umakoti	oomaako′tee
bridegroom	umyeni / umkhwenyana	oomye′nee / oomkwe′nyaanaa
bridesmaid	impelesi	eempe′le′see
bring (v)	letha	le′taa
broken	file / phukile	feele′ / pookeele′
broken limb	isinqekle	eeseenqe′kle′
broom	umshanelo	oomshaane′lo′
brother	umfowethu	oomfo′we′too
brother-in-law	umlamu	oomlaamoo
brown sugar	ushukela onsundu	ooshooke′laa o′nsoondoo
brown	nsundu	nsoondoo
bruise	isisihla	eeseeseehlaa
brush	ibhulashi	eeboolaashee
bubbles (boil)	amagwebu	aamaagwe′boo
bucket	ibhakede	eebaake′de′
build (v)	akha	aakaa
burglar	umgqekezi	oomgqe′ke′zee
burn - must not	kungashi	koongaashee
burn (v)	shisa	sheesaa
burn (n)	isibashu	eeseebaashoo
burn down (v)	lotha	lo′taa
burning	-shayo	-shaayo′
burst (v)	qhuma	qoomaa
bury (v)	ngcwaba	ngcwaabaa
bus	ibhasi	eebaasee
bush	ihlathi	eehlaatee
bustle around (v)	gqigqizela	gqeegqeeze′laa
but	kodwa	ko′dwaa
butcher	ubhusha	oobooshaa
butchery	ibhusha / isilaha	eebooshaa / eeseelaaghaa
butter	ibhotela	eebo′te′laa
buttered (greased)	eligcotshiwe	e′leegco′tsheewe′
butterfly	uvemvane	oove′mvaane′
butternut	ibhathanathi	eebaataanaatee
buy (v)	thenga	te′ngaa

C

English		
cabbage	ikhabishi / iklabishi	eekaabeeshee / eeklaabeeshee
cafe	ikhefi	eeke´fee
cake	ikhekhe	eeke´ke´
calculate	bala / balisisa	baalaa / baaleeseesaa
calender	ikhalenda	eekaale´ndaa
call (v)	biza	beezaa
called – who / which is---	esibizwa ngokuthi	e´seebeezwaa ngo´ kootee
caller - a visitor	isivakashi	eeseevaakaashee
calm	thulile	tooleele´
camera	ikhamera	eekaame´raa
cancer	umdlavuza	oomdlaavoozaa
candle	ikhandlela	eekaandle´laa
cane rat	imbuzimeshe	eemboozeeme´she´
canvas (n) / sail	useyili	oose´yeelee
canvas (tent)	useyili	oose´yeelee
cap / hat	ikepisi	eeke´peesee
cap / lid	isivalo	eeseevaalo´
car	imoto	eemo´to´
care - take care (v)	qaphela	qaape´laa
care (v)	ukunakelela	ookoonaake´le´laa
careful	nakekela	naake´ke´laa
careless	nganaki	ngaanaakee
caretaker	umbheki	oombe´kee
carrot	ukherothi	ooke´ro´tee
carry - on back (v)	beletha	be´le´taa
carry (v)	thwala	twaalaa
cart (n)	ikalishi	eekaaleeshee
casserole dish	indishi yokupheka	eendeeshee yo´koope´kaa
catch (v)	bamba	baambaa
caterpillar	icimbi / bupha	eeceembee / boopaa
cattle	izinkomo	eezeenko´mo´
cauliflower	ukholiflawa	ooko´leeflaawaa
cause (n)	imbangela	eembaange´laa
cause (v)	banga / enza	baangaa / e´nzaa
cease (v)	khawula	kaawoolaa
ceiling	isilingi	eeseeleengee
celery	useleri	oose´le´ree
cent	isenti	eese´ntee
chainsaw	ibhalantoni / ihonela	eebaalaanto´nee / eeho´ne´laa
chair	isihlalo	eeseehlaalo´
chance / opportunity	ithuba	eetoobaa
change (v)	shintsha	sheentshaa
change (v) – change subject	guqula indaba	gooqoolaa eendaabaa
charm (n)	ubuhle	ooboohle´
chat (v)	xoxa	xo´xaa
cheap	shibhile	sheebeele´
check (v)	hlolisisa	hlo´leeseesaa
cheek — insolence	uluphondo	ooloopo´ndo´

93.

cheek - face	isihlathi	esseehlaatee
cheeky	yimpompo / delelayo	yeempo´mpo´/ de´le´laayo´
cheer (v)	halalisa	haalaaleesaa
cheerful	thokozile	to´ko´zeele´
cheese	ushizi	oosheezee
chicken - white	umkhwepha	oomkwe´paa
chicken pieces	amaphisizi enkukhu	aamaapeeseezee e´nkookoo
chicken	inkukhu	eenkookoo
child	umntwana	oomntwaanaa
childishness	ubuntwana	ooboontwaanaa
chilli	upelepele	oope´le´pe´le´
chimney	ushimula	oosheemoolaa
chin	isilevu	eeseele´voo
chip (piece)	ucezu	ooce´zoo
chips (fish &)	amashipsi	aamaasheepsee
chocolate	ushokolethi	oosho´ko´le´tee
choice	ukukhetha	ookooke´taa
cholera	ikholera	eeko´le´raa
choose (v)	khetha	ke´taa
chop (v - tree)	gawula	gaawoolaa
chop (v -meat & vegies)	qoba	qo´baa
chop (n- meat)	ishopsi	eesho´psee
chopped	qotshiwe / nqumile	qo´tsheewe´ / nqoomeele´
Christmas	uKhisimusi	ooKeeseemoosee
church	isonto	eeso´nto´
chutney	ushatini	ooshaateenee
cigarette / tobacco	usikilidi / ugwayi	ooseekeeleedee /oogwaayee
cinder - coal	ilahle	eelaahle´
cinema	ibhayisikobho	eebaayeeseeko´bo´
circle	isiyingi	eeseeyeengee
circumcise (v)	soka	so´kaa
circumcision	ukusoka	ookooso´kaa
cistern	ithangi	eetaangee
citizen	umphakathi	oompaakaatee
citizenship	ubuphakathi / ubuzwe	ooboopaakaatee / ooboozwe´
city	idolobha	eedo´lo´baa
civilisation	impucuko	eempoocooko´
civilize (v)	phucula	poocoolaa
claim (v) demand	banga / biza	baangaa / beezaa
claim (v) against	mangalela	maangaale´laa
claim (v)	ukubanga / ukubiza	ookoobaangaa / ookoobeezaa
clairvoyant	isangoma	eesaango´maa
clan	isizalo / isizwe	eeseezaalo´/ eeseezwe´
clap (v) – on the back	ukumbambatha emhlane	ookoombaambaataa e´mhlaane´
clap (v) hands	shaya izandla	shaayaa eezaandlaa
clash (n)	ukuxabana	ookooxaabaanaa
clash (v)	xabana / phambana	xaabaanaa / paambaanaa
class – first class	okwedlula okunye	o´kwe´dloolaa o´koonye´
class – top of the class	inhloko yekilasi	eenhlo´ko´ ye´keelaasee

94.

class – upper class	abakhulu	aabaakooloo
class – poorer class	okhwahla	o´ kwaahlaa
classify	ahlukanisa	aahlookaaneesaa
claw	uzipho	oozeepo´
clay pot	ibumba / ukhamba	eeboombaa / ookaambaa
clay	udongwe	oodo´ngwe´
clean (v- floor / food)	geza / washa	ge´zaa / waashaa
clean (v)	hlanza	hlaanzaa
clean	hlanzekile	hlaanze´keele´
cleanliness	ubunono	ooboono´no´
clear – a clear head	ingqondo	eenqo´ngo´
	ehlakahlekile	e´hlaakaahle´keele´
clear – become clear (v)	hlambuluka	hlaamboolookaa
clear – clear sky	izulu elicwebile	eezooloo e´leecwe´beele´
clear – of the mind	-hlakahlekile	-hlaakaahle´keele´
clear – to the eye	bonakele	bo´naake´le´
clear – water	amanzi acwebile	aamaanzee aacwe´beele´
climb (v)	khwela	kwe´laa
cling (v)	nombela	no´mbe´laa
clinic	ikliniki	eekleeneekee
clock	iwashi elikhulu	eewaashee e´leekooloo
close (a) - near	eduze	e´dooze´
close (v)	vala	vaalaa
clot – blood / lump	isigaxa	eeseegaaxaa
cloth	indwangu	eendwaangoo
clothe (v)	embesa	e´mbe´saa
clothes	izingubo	eezeengoobo´
clothes horse	umgibe	oomgeebe´
cloud	ifu	eefoo
cloudy (it is cloudy)	liguqubele	leegooqoobe´le´
club (tennis)	ikilabhu	eekeelaaboo
clumsy	ndaxandaxa	ndaaxaandaaxaa
coal	amalahle	aamaalaahle´
coast (beach)	ugu	oogoo
coat (n)	ibhantshi	eebaantshee
cobweb	ubulembu	ooboole´mboo
cock	iqhude	eeqoode´
cockroach	iphela	eepe´laa
cocoa	ukhokho	ooko´ko´
coconut	ukhukhunathi	ookookoonaatee
coffee	ikhofi	eeko´fee
coffin	ibhokisi lomngcwabo	eebo´keesee lo´mngcwaabo´
coin	uhlamvu lwemali	oohlaamvoo lwe´maalee
cold – calm, cool	pholile	po´leele´
cold – illness	umkhuhlane	oomkoohlaane´
cold – shiver	godola	go´do´laa
cold	makhaza	maakaazaa
colic	isilumo	eeseeloomo´
collar	isiphika	eeseepeekaa
collect (v)	qoqa / butha	qo´qaa / bootaa

college	ikholiji	eeko´leejee
collide (v)	shayana / shayisana	shaayaanaa / shaayeesaanaa
collision	ukushayana / ukushayisana	ookooshaayaanaa / ookooshaayeesaanaa
colour	umbala	oombaalaa
comb (v)	kama	kaamaa
comb	ikama / ikamu	eekaamaa / eekaamoo
combine (v)	hlanganisa	hlaangaaneesaa
come out (oven) (v)	kuphuma kuhavini	koopoomaa koohaaveenee
come (v)	-za / woza	-zaa / wo´zaa
comfort (v)	duduza	doodoozaa
comfort (n)	induduzo	eendoodoozo´
community service	abasebenzela umphakathi	aabaase´be´nze´laa oompaakaatee
companion	umhlanganyeli	oomhlaangaanye´lee
companionship	ubungane	ooboongaane´
compensate (v)	linganisa / buyisela	leengaaneesaa / booyeese´laa
compensate for (v)	hlawula	hlaawoolaa
compensation	inhlawulo / imbuyiselo	eenhlaawoolo´ / eembooyeese´lo´
compete (v)	phikisana	peekeesaanaa
competence	ukwazi	ookwaazee
competition /	umncintisano /	oomnceenteesaano´ /
competition	umqhudelwano	oomqoode´lwaano´
competitive	-ncintisanayo	-nceenteesaanaayo´
complain (v)	khala	kaalaa
complaint	isikhalo	eeseekaalo´
complete (a)	pheleleyo	pe´le´le´yo´
complete (v)	qedela	qe´de´laa
compose (v)	qamba	qaambaa
compost	umquba	oomqoobaa
conceal (v - hide)	fihla	feehlaa
conceited	ziqhayisa	zeeqaayeesaa
conceive (baby) (v)	mitha / khulelwa	meetaa / koole´lwaa
concrete	ukhonkolo	ooko´nko´lo´
condition	ubunjani / isimo	ooboonjaanee / eeseemo´
condom	ijazi lomkhwenyane	eejaazee lo´mkwe´nyaane´
conduct (v)	ziphatha kahle	zeepaataa kaahle´
conference	umhlangano	oomhlaangaano´
confess (v)	vuma	voomaa
confession	ukuvuma	ookoovoomaa
confide (v)	hlebela	hle´be´laa
confidential	yisifuba	yeeseefoobaa
conflict (v)	phambana	paambaanaa
confuse (v)	dida	deedaa
congeal (v)	shuba	shoobaa
congratulate (v)	halalisela	haalaaleese´laa
connect (v)	hlanganisa	hlaangaaneesaa
consent	ukuvuma	ookoovoomaa
consent (v)	vuma	voomaa
console (v)	duduza	doodoozaa

console (v)	khuza	koozaa
constipation	ukuqumba	ookooqoombaa
consult (v)	xoxa / bonana	xo´xaa / bo´naanaa
consult (v)	xoxisana	xo´xeesaanaa
consultation	ukubonisana	ookoobo´neesaanaa
consume (v)	idla / qeda	eedlaa / qe´daa
consumption (water etc)	umthamo	oomtaamo´
consumption - food etc.	okudliwayo	o´koodleewaayo´
contact (v)	thintana	teentaanaa
contact lens	ingilazi yezibuko	eengeelaazee ye´zeebooko´
contagious	thathelana	taate´laanaa
contain (v)	phatha	paataa
container / drum	idlelo / umgqomo	eedle´lo´ / oomgqo´mo´
content (happy)	enamile	e´naameele´
contents	okuqukethwe	o´kooqooke´twe´
continue (v - to go on)	qhubeka	qoobe´kaa
continue (v - with this)	qhubeka nalokhu	qoobe´kaa naalo´koo
continue (v - persevere)	qhubisa	qoobeesaa
contraception	ukuzivala /	ookoozeevaalaa /
	ukuvikela	ookooveeke´laa
contract	isivumelwano	eesseevoome´lwaano´
contraction	ukufinyeza	ookoofeenye´zaa
contradict (v)	phikisa	peekeesaa
control (v)	phatha	paataa
controversial	impikiswano	eempeekeeswaano´
controversy	ukuphikisana	ookoopeekeesaanaa
convalesce (v)	lulama	loolaamaa
convenient	vumekayo	voome´kaayo´
conversation	inkulumo	eenkooloomo´
conversion	impenduko	eempe´ndooko´
convert (v)	phendula / guqula	pe´ndoolaa / gooqoolaa
convict (n)	isiboshwa	eeseebo´shwaa
convince (v)	gculisa	gcooleesaa
convulsion	ukudikiza	ookoodeekeezaa
cook (n)	umpheki	oompe´kee
cook (v)	pheka	pe´kaa
cooked (when cooked)	sekuvuthiwe	se´koovooteewe´
cool (v)	phola	po´laa
cool off (v - temp.)	yehlisa ukushisa	ye´hleesaa ookoosheesaa
cool - temperature	pholile	po´leele´
co-operate (v)	sizana	seezaanaa
co-operation	ukusizana	ookooseezaanaa
cord	umchilo	oomcheelo´
cork	ikhokho	eeko´ko´
corner	ikhona	eeko´naa
corpse	isidumbu	eeseedoomboo
correct (v)	lungisa	loongeesaa
correct - ok	lungile	loongeele´
costly	dulile / - biza	dooleele´ / - beezaa
cottage	indlwana	indlwaanaa

cotton	ukotini	ooko'teenee
cottonwool	uvolo	oovo'lo'
cough	ukukhwehlela	ookookwe'hle'laa
count (v)	bala	baalaa
country folk	abantu basemakhaya	aabaantoo baase'maakaayaa
cover (n)	isivalo	eeseevaalo'
cover (v- close)	vala / yemboza	vaalaa / ye'mbo'zaa
cover with -lid (v)	yemboza	ye'mbo'zaa
cow (female)	inkomazi	eenko'maazee
cow	inkomo	eenko'mo'
coward	igwala	eegwaalaa
crab	inkalankala	eenkaalaankaalaa
crack (n) feet / fissure	umnkenke / umdabuko	oomnke'nke' / oomdaabooko'
crack (v)	qhekeka / dabuka / ifa	qe'ke'kaa / daabookaa / eefaa
cramp (n)	inkwantshu	eenkwaantshoo
crawl (v)	khasa	kaasaa
cream	ulaza / ukhilimu	oolaazaa / ookeeleemoo
crease (n)	ikhrisi	eekreesee
crease (v)	shwabanisa	shwaabaaneesaa
creature	isidalwa	eeseedaalwaa
credit (a/c)	ukukweletisa	ookookwe'le'teesaa
creeper	intandela	eentaande'laa
cricket – insect	inyendle	eenye'ndle'
cricket - sport	ikhilikithi	eekeeleekeetee
crime	ubugebengu	ooboogeꞌbe'ngoo
criminal	isigebengu	eeseegeꞌbe'ngoo
cripple (n)	isishosha / unyonga	eeseeshoꞌshaa / oonyo'ngaa
cripple (v)	goga	goꞌgaa
criticise (v)	hlaba / gxeka	hlaabaa / gxeꞌkaa
crockery	izitsha	eezeetshaa
crocodile	ingwenya	eengwe'nyaa
crooked	okugwegwile	oꞌkoogweꞌgweele'
crop – bumper	inala	eenaalaa
crop – poor crop	inkwico	eenkweeco'
crop (n – farming)	okuvunwayo / isilimo	oꞌkoovoonwaayoꞌ/ eeseeleemo'
cross (temper)	thukuthela	tookooteꞌlaa
cross (v) – cross over	dabula / wela / eqa	daaboolaa / weꞌlaa / eꞌqaa
crowd	isixuku	eeseexookoo
cruel	nonya	noꞌnyaa
crumb	imvuthu	eemvootoo
crumble (v)	bhuduza	boodoozaa
crust	uqweqwe	ooqweꞌqwe'
cry	khala	kaalaa
cub	iwundlu lesilo	eewoondloo leꞌseelo'
cubes - cut into	sika ibe amakhyubhu	seekaa eebeꞌ aamaakeeyooboo
cube	ikhyubhu	eekeeyooboo
cucumber	ikhukhamba	eekookaambaa
culprit	umoni	oomoꞌnee
cultivate (v)	lima	leemaa
culture – upbringing	isimo sempucuko	eeseemoꞌ seꞌmpoocooko'

culture	isiko	eeseeko´
cunning	nobuqili	no´booqeelee
cup	inkomishi	eenko´meeshee
cupboard	ikhabethe	eekaabe´te´
curdle (v)	jiya	jeeyaa
cure (n)	ukuphilisa	ookoopeeleesaa
cure (v)	philisa	peeleesaa
curry	ukhali	ookaalee
curse (v)	thuka / qalekisa	tookaa / qaale´keesaa
curse	isiqalekiso	eeseeqaale´keeso´
curtain	ikhethini	eeke´teenee
cushion	umqamelo / ikhushini	oomqaame´lo´ / eekoosheenee
cut (n)	umsiko	oomseeko´
cut (v)	sika	seekaa
cute	nobuqili / bukekayo	no´booqeelee / booke´kaayo´
cutlery	izinto okudliwa	eezeento´ o´koodleewaa
	ngazo	ngaazo´

D

daily	nsuku zonke	nsookoo zo´nke´
dam	idamu	eedaamoo
damage (v)	limaza	leemaazaa
damage (n)	ukulimaza	ookooleemaazaa
damp (dampness)	umswakama	oomswaakaamaa
damp (a)	manzana	maanzaanaa
damp (n)	ubumanzi	ooboomaanzee
dampen (v)	manzisa	maanzeesaa
dance (v)	gida / dansa	geedaa / daansaa
danger	ingozi	eengo´zee
dangerous	nengozi	ne´ngo´zee
dare (v)	lokotha	lo´ko´taa
dark	-mnyama	-mnyaamaa
darkness	ubumnyama	ooboomnyaamaa
darn (v)	dana	daanaa
date (v - to go out)	khipha / thathela	keepaa / tate´laa
date	usuku / idethi	oosookoo / eede´tee
daughter in law	umakoti	oomaako´tee
daughter	indodakazi	eendo´daakaazee
dawn	ukusa	ookoosaa
day	usuku	oosookoo
daze (n)	ukuphuphutheka	ookoopoopoote´kaa
daze (v)	phuphuthekisa	poopoote´keesaa
dead	file / shonile	feele´ / sho´neele´
deaf	ngenakuzwa / ngezwa	nge´naakoozwaa / nge´zwaa
death	ukufa	ookoofaa
debt	isikweletu	eeseekwe´le´too
decay (v)	bola	bo´laa
deceased	shonileyo	sho´neele´yo´
deceit	inkohliso	eenko´hleeso´
deceive (v)	khohlisa	ko´hleesaa
decide (v)	nquma	nqoomaa
decision	isinqumo	eeseenqoomo´
decorate (v)	hlobisa	hlo´beesaa
decrease (v)	ncipha / nciphisa	nceepaa / nceepeesaa
deep	shonile / julile	sho´neele´ / jooleele´
defend (v)	vikela	veeke´laa
delay (v)	bambezela	baambe´ze´laa
deliberately – do---	enza ngabomu	e´nzaa ngaabo´moo
delicious	mnandi	mnaandee
delight (n)	injabulo	eenjaaboolaa
delight (v)	jabulisa	jaabooleesaa
deliver (v)	nikeza	neeke´zaa
demand (v)	biza / funa	beezaa / foonaa
demolish (v)	diliza	deeleezaa
demon	idimoni	eedeemo´nee
demonstrate (v) in street	bhikisha / bhokela	beekeeshaa / bo´ke´laa
demonstrate (v) show	bonisa	bo´neesaa

demonstration - protest	ukubhikisha	ookoobeeheeshaa
demonstartion (n) - show	isibonakaliso	eeseebo´naakaaleeso´
dentist	udokotela	oodo´ko´te´laa
	wamazinyo	waamaazeenyo´
deny (v)	phika	peekaa
deodorant	isiqedaphunga	eeseeqe´daapoongaa
depart (v)	emuka / hlukana	e´mookaa / hlookaanaa
deposit (v)	faka / beka / bekelela	faakaa / be´kaa / be´ke´le´laa
deposit	isibeko	eeseebe´ko´
descend (v)	ehla	e´hlaa
deserve (v)	fanela	faane´laa
desire (v)	khanuka	kaanookaa
desk	ideski	eede´skee
detective	ufokisi	oofo´keesee
detest (v)	enyanya	e´nyaanyaa
detour	umshekelelo	oomshe´ke´le´lo´
devil	usathane	oosaataane´
diarrhoea	uhudo	oohoodo´
die (v)	- fa / i+fa / shona	- faa / eefaa / sho´naa
differ (v)	ahlukana	aahlookaanaa
differ from (v)	ehluka	e´hlookaa
difference – quarrel	ukuxabana	ookooxaabaanaa
difference –make no---	-ngabi – lutho /	-ngaabee looto´/
	akwenzi mahluko	aakwe´nzee maahlooko´
difference - make a ---	enza ubungcono	e´nzaa ooboongco´no´
difference- unlikeness	ukwahlukana /	ookwaahlookaanaa /
	umahluko	oomaahlooko´
different (unalike)	ahlukile / ngafani	aahlaakeele´ / ngaafaanee
differently	ngenye indlela	nge´nye´ eendle´laa
difficult	nzima / kulukhuni	nzeemaa / koolookoonee
difficulty-with---	kanzima	kaanzeemaa
dig (v)	-mba / imba / lima	-mbaa / eembaa / leemaa
dilute (v)	hlambulula	hlaambooloolaa
dim (stupid)	fiphele	feepe´le´
dine (v)	-dla / idla	- dlaa / eedlaa
dining room	ikamelo lokudlela	eekaame´lo´ lo´koodle´laa
dinner	idina	eedeenaa
dip (into) (v)	cwilisa	cweeleesaa
dip (v) dip a dog	dipha	deepaa
dipping tank	idiphu	eedeepoo
dips – the road dips	umgwaqo uyashona	oomgwaaqo´ ooyaasho´naa
direct (straight)	qondile	qo´ndeele´
direct (v)	khombisa	ko´mbeesaa
direction (n)- way	inkomba	eenko´mbaa
dirty	ngcolile	ngco´leele´
disabled	khubazekile	koobaaze´keele´
disagree (v)	phambana / ngavumelani	paambaanaa / ngaavoome´lanee
disagreement /	ukuphambana /	ookoopaambaanaa /
disagreement	ukungavumelani	ookoongaavoome´laanee
disappear (v)	nyamalala	nyaamaalaalaa

101.

disagreement /	ukuphambana /	ookoopaambaanaa /
disagreement	ukungavumelani	ookoongaavoome'laanee
disappear (v)	nyamalala	nyaamaalaalaa
disappoint (v)	dumaza	doomaazaa
disappointment	indumalo / injabhiso	eendoomaalo' / eenjaabeeso'
disaster /	ingozi enkulu /	eengo'zee e'nkooloo /
disaster	isidumo	eeseedoomo'
discipline	umthetho	oomte'to'
disconnect (v)	ahlukanisa	aahlookaaneesaa
discourage (v)	khubeza / aphula	koobe'zaa / aapoolaa
discover (v)	fumanisa / tholwa	foomaaneesaa / to'lwaa
discriminate (v)	bandlulula	baandlooloolaa
discrimination	ubandlululo	oobaandlooloolo'
discuss (v) with	xoxisana nga	xo'xeesaanaa ngaa
discussion	ingxoxo	eengxo'xo'
disease	isifo	eeseefo'
disgrace	ihlazo	eehlaazo'
disgust (n)	isicasulo	eeseecaasoolo'
dish (n) / in a dish	isitsha / esitsheni	eeseetshaa / e'seetshe'nee
dish up (v)	phaka / phakela	paakaa / paake'laa
dish	indishi / isitsha	eendeeshee / eeseetshaa
dishonest /	khohlisayo /	ko'hleesaayo' /
dishonest	ngathembekile	ngaate'mbe'keele'
dishonesty /	inkohliso /	eenko'hleeso' /
dishonesty	ukungathembeki	ookoongaate'mbe'kee
disinfect / kill germs (v)	bulala amagciwane	boolaalaa aamaagceewaane'
disinfectant /	isihlanzisisi /	eeseehlaanzeesee /
disinfectant	isibulalamagciwane	eeseeboolaalaamaagceewaane'
disloyalty	ukuhlubuka	ookoohloobookaa
dismiss (v) - remove	xosha	xo'shaa
dismiss (v) - let go	mukisa	mookeesaa
dismissal	ukuxoshwa	ookooxo'shwaa
disobedience	ukungalaleli	ookoongaalaale'lee
disobey (v)	ngalaleli	ngaalaale'lee
dispute (v)	banga / phikisa	baangaa / peekeesaa
disregard (v)	delela	de'le'laa
dissatisfaction	ukungeneliseki	ookoonge'ne'leese'kee
dissolve (melt) (v)	ncibilikisa	nceebeeleekeesaa
district	isigodi	eeseego'dee
distrust (n)	ukungathembi	ookoongaate'mbee
distrust (v)	ngathembi	ngaate'mbee
disturb (v)	phazamisa	paazaameesaa
ditch	umsele	oomse'le'
dive (v) - in water	cwila	cweelaa
diver	umcwili	oomcweelee
divorce /	idivosi /	eedeevo'see /
divorce	isehlukaniso	eese'hlookaaneeso'
divorce (v)	divosa / hlukanisa	deevo'saa / hlookaaneesaa
dizziness	inzululwane	eenzooloolwaane'
do (v)	enza	e'nzaa

doctor	udokotela	oodo'ko'te'laa
document	umbhalo / umqulo	oombaalo' / oomqoolo'
dog	inja	eenjaa
doll	udoli	oodo'lee
domestic (a)	asendlini	aase'ndleenee
donate (v)	nikela	neeke'laa
donation	umnikelo	oomneeke'lo'
done	enziwe	e'nzeewe'
donkey	imbongolo	eembo'ngo'lo'
door	umnyango	oomnyaango'
dose (n)	ithamo	eetaamo'
dose (v) – spray / muti	thela umuthi / phuzisa umuthi	te'laa oomootee / poozeesaa oomootee
double (a)	phindiwe	peendeewe'
double (n)	okuphindiweyo	o'koopeendeewe'yo'
doubt (v)	sola / ngabaza	so'laa / ngaabaazaa
doubt (n)	ukungabaza / ukusola	ookoongaabaazaa / ookooso'laa
dough	inhlama	eenhlaamaa
down	phansi	paansee
doze (v)	hlwathiza	hlwaateezaa
dozen	idazini	eedaazeenee
drag (v)	hudula	hoodoolaa
drain (liquid) (v)	cwenga amanzi	cwe'ngaa aamaanzee
drain (v) – drain away	khameka	kaame'kaa
drain (n)– for water	umsele / idileni	oomse'lee / eedeele'nee
drained	ahluziwe	aahloozeewe'
drainpipe	ipayipi	eepaayeepee
draw (pull) (v)	donsa	do'nsaa
draw (v) - picture	dweba	dwe'baa
dread	uvalo	oovaalo'
dream (v)	phupha	poopaa
dream (n)	iphupho	eepoopo'
dress (v)	gqokisa	gqo'keesaa
dress	ilokwe / ingubo	eelo'kwe' / eengoobo'
drink (v)	phuza	poozaa
drink (n)	isiphuzo	eeseepoozo'
drip (v)	consa	co'nsaa
drip (n)	iconsi	eeco'nsee
drive (v)	shayela	shaaye'laa
driver	umshayeli	oomshaaye'lee
driveway	umgwaqo oya-endlini	oomgwaaqo' o'ya e'ndleenee
drizzle (v)	khiza	keezaa
drizzle	umkhizo	oomkeezo'
droop (v)	yenda	ye'ndaa
drop (v)	wisa	weesaa
drought	ukomisa kwezulu / isomiso	ooko'meesaa kwe'zooloo / eeso'meeso'
drown (v)	emuka namanzi	e'mookaa naamaanzee
drown (v)	minza / cwila / muka	meenzaa / cweelaa / mookaa

103.

drowse (v)	ozela	o'ze'laa
drug addict	isigqila sezidakamizwa	eeseegqeelaa se'zeedaakaameezwaa
drug	isidakamizwa	eeseedaakaa-meezwaa
drum (container)	umphongolo	oompo'ngo'lo'
drum	isigubhu	eeseegooboo
drummer	umshayi wesigubhu	oomshaayee we'seegooboo
drunk	dakiwe	daakeewe'
drunkard	isidakwa	eeseedaakwaa
dry (v)	omisa	o'meesaa
dry	omile	o'meele'
dryclean (v)	drayiklina	draayeekleenaa
drycleaner	ilondolo /	eelo'ndo'lo' /
	umdrayiklina	oomdraayeekleenaa
duck	idada	eedaadaa
duiker	impunzi	eempoonzee
dumb	yisimungulu	yeeseemoongooloo
dust (v)	sula uthuli	soolaa ootoolee
dust (n)	uthuli	ootoolee
duster (n)	isesulo sothuli /	eese'soolo' so'toolee /
	idasta	eedaastaa
duty	imfanelo / umsebenzi	eemfaane'lo' / oomse'be'nzee
dwarf	isichwe	eeseechwe'
dwelling	ikhaya	eekaayaa

E

each	yilowo	yeelo'wo'
eager	nkamunkamu	nkaamoonkaamoo
eagle	ukhozi	ooko'zee
ear	indlebe	eendle'be'
earache	ubuhlungu bendlebe	ooboohloongoo be'ndle'be'
early	masisha	maaseeshaa
earn (v- money)	holwa / hola	ho'lwaa / ho'laa
earn (v- praise)	zuza	zoozaa
earnings	imali eholwayo	eemaalee e'ho'lwaayo'
earring	icici	eeceecee
earth	umhlaba	oomhlaabaa
earthquake /	indudumela yomhlaba /	eendoodoome'laa yo'mhlaabaa /
earthquake	indudumela	eendoodoome'laa
earthworm	umsundu	oomsoondoo
east- in the east	empumalanga	e'mpoomaalaangaa
east - direction	impumalanga	eempoomaalaangaa
easy to cook	okulula ukuphekwa	o'kooloolaa ookoope'kwaa
easy	lula	loolaa
eat (v)	idla / yidla	eedlaa / yeedlaa
edge / on the edge	icala / eceleni	eecaalaa / e'ce'le'nee
edible	dlekayo	dle'kaayo'
educate (v)	fundisa	foondeesaa
education	imfundo	eemfoondo'
eel	umbokwane	oombo'kwaane'
effect (n)	imiphumela	eemeepoome'laa
effort	umzamo	oomzaamo'
effortless	kalula	kaaloolaa
egg - hard	iqanda eliqinile	eeqaandaa e'leeqeeneele'
egg - soft	iqanda elithambile	eeqaandaa e'leetaambeele'
egg	iqanda	eeqaandaa
eggbeater	isiphehli samaqanda	eeseepe'hlee saamaaqaandaa
eggshell	igobolondo leqanda	eego'bo'lo'ndo' le'qaandaa
either - or	noma muphi	no'maa moopee
eland	impofu	eempo'foo
elastic	injoloba	eenjo'lo'baa
elbow	indololwane	eendo'lo'lwaane'
eldest	dala kakhulu	daalaa kaakooloo
	kunabobonke	koonaabo'bo'nke'
elect / elected	khetha / khethiwe	ke'taa / ke'teewe'
election	ukhetho	ooke'to'
electric mixer	umshini wokuxuba	oomsheenee wo'kooxoobaa
electric	kagesi	kaage'see
electricity	ugesi / i-elektriki	ooge'see / ee-e'le'ktreekee
elephant	indlovu	eendlo'voo
eliminate (v)	susa	soosaa
elongate (v)	elula	e'loolaa
elope (v)	eqa / baleka	e'qaa / baale'kaa
elsewhere	kwenye indawo	kwe'nye' eendaawo'

emaciated	nciphile	nceepeele'
embarrass - they are ---	banamahloni	baanaamaahlo'nee
embarrass (v)	phoxa	po'xaa
embrace (n)	ukugona / ukwanga	ookoogo'naa / ookwaangaa
embrace (v)	gona	go'naa
emerge (v)	phuma	poomaa
emergency -accident	ingozi	eengo'zee
emergency - at work	phutumayo	pootoomaayo'
emigrate (v)	thuthela kwelinye izwe	toote'laa kwe'leenye' eezwe'
employ (v)	qasha	qaashaa
employee	isisebenzi	eeseese'be'nzee
employer	umqashi	oomqaashee
employment	umsebenzi	oomse'be'nzee
empty (a)	ngenalutho	nge'naalooto'
empty (v)	chitha / thulula	ceetaa / tooloolaa
enclose (v)	zungezeleka / faka	zoonge'ze'le'kaa / faakaa
encourage (v)	khuthaza	kootaazaa
end (n)	ukugcina	ookoogceenaa
end (v)	gcina	gceenaa
endanger (v)	faka engozini	faakaa e'ngo'zeenee
endear (v)	thandekisa	taande'keesaa
enema	uchatho	oocaato'
enemy	isitha	eeseetaa
energetic	khuthele	koote'le'
energy	umfutho	oomfooto'
engaged (busy)	bambekile	baambe'keele'
engine	injini	eenjeenee
English	isiNgisi	eeseeNgeesee
enjoy (v)	jabulela	jaaboole'laa
enlarge (v)	andisa / khulisa	aandeesaa / kooleesaa
enormous	khulukazi	koolookaazee
enough	anele	aane'le'
enrol (v)	joyina	jo'yeenaa
ensure (v)	qiniseka	qeeneese'kaa
enter (v)	ngena	nge'naa
entire	pheleleyo	pe'le'le'yo'
entrails	amathumbu	aamaatoomboo
entry	ukungena	ookoonge'naa
envelope	imvilophu	eemveelo'poo
envy (n)	umhawu / inkanuko	oomhaawoo / eenkaanooko'
envy (v)	hawukela	haawooke'laa
epilepsy	isifo / isiguli	eeseefo' /eeseegoolee
	sesithuthwane	se'seetootwaane'
epileptic fit	isithuthwane	eeseetootwaane'
equal (v)	lingana na	leengaana naa
equal	lingene	leenge'ne'
erase (v)	esula / sula	e'soolaa / soolaa
eraser	isesulo	eese'soolo'
erect (v) build	akha	aakaa
error	isiphosiso	eeseepo'seeso'

erupt (v)	qhuma	qoomaa
escape (v)	baleka / eqa	baale'kaa / e'qaa
escort (v)	phelezela	pe'le'ze'laa
escort	umphelezeli	oompe'le'ze'lee
eskimo	umEskimo	oomE'skeemo'
essential	funekayo	foone'kaayo'
ethnic	kohlobo lobuzwe	ko'hlo'bo' lo'boozwe'
even (a)	lingene	leenge'ne'
even amount	lingene	leenge'ne'
even so	noma kunjalo	no'maa koonjaalo'
evening	ukuhlwa / kusihlwa	ookoohlwaa / kooseehlwaa
event	isehlakalo	eese'hlaakaalo'
every	o- nke	o'-nke'
every - now & then	futhifuthi / phindaphinda	footeefootee / peendaapeenda
evict (v)	xosha	xo'shaa
evidence	ubufakazi	ooboofaakaazee
evil	i- bi	ee-bee
exact	qinisile	qeeneeseele'
exaggerate (v)	bhumbela / yenza ihaba	boombe'laa / ye'nzaa eehaabaa
example (make eg.) (v)	enza isibonelo	e'nzaa eeseebo'ne'lo'
example (n)	isibonelo	eeseebo'ne'lo'
except (for)	ngaphandle kwa	ngaapaandle' kwaa
excercise (v) - work	sebenza	se'be'nzaa
excercise (n) - work	umsebenzi	oomse'be'nzee
exercise (v) – training / gym	ukwelula umzimba	ookwe'loolaa oomzeembaa
excuse (v)	xolela	xo'le'laa
excuse	izaba	eezaabaa
exemption	igunya	eegoonyaa
exhale (v)	khipha umoya	keepaa oomo'yaa
exit (v)	phuma	poomaa
expect (v)	ethemba / lindela	e'te'mbaa / leende'laa
expenses	izindleko	eezeendle'ko'
expensive / it is --	dulile / kuyabiza	dooleele' / kooyaabeezaa
experience (n)	ulwazi	oolwaazee
experiment (n)	ukulinga	ookooleengaa
experiment (v)	linga	leengaa
expert	isazi	eesaazee
explain – at length	chaza kabanzi	caazaa kaabaanzee
explain (v)	chaza	caazaa
explore (v)	hlola	hlo'laa
explosion	ukuqhuma	ookooqoomaa
extinguish (v)	cima	ceemaa
extra	ngaphezulu	ngaape'zooloo
eye	iso	eeso'
eyebrow	ishiya	eesheeyaa
eyelash	ukhophe	ooko'pe'
eyelid	ijwabu lehlo	eejwaaboo le'hlo'
eyewitness	isibukeli	eeseebooke'lee

F

face	ubuso	oobooso´
fact	iqiniso	eeqeeneeso´
factory	ifekthri	eefe´ktree
fade (v)	fiphala	feepaalaa
faeces	amasimba / uthuvi	aamaaseembaa / ootoovee
fail (v)	hluleka	hloole´kaa
failure	ukwahluleka	ookwaahloole´kaa
faint (v)	quleka	qoole´kaa
fainting fit	isinxi	eeseenxee
faith	ithemba	eete´mbaa
faithful	thembekile	te´mbe´keele´
fake (v)	khohlisa	ko´hleesaa
fall (v)	i- wa	ee- waa
falter / make mistake (v)	phazama	paazaamaa
fame	udumo	oodoomo´
family	uzalo / umndeni	oozaalo´ / oomnde´nee
famine	indlala	eendlaalaa
famous	dumile	doomeele´
fan (n) - air	isiphephezelo	eeseepe´pe´ze´lo´
fan (v)	bhebhezela	be´be´ze´laa
far	kude	koode´
farm (v)	lima	leemaa
farm	ipulazi	eepoolaazee
farmer	umlimi	oomleemee
fashion	imfeshini	eemfe´sheenee
fast	masinyane	maaseenyaane´
fasten	bopha	bo´paa
fat (n)	amafutha	aamaafootaa
fat - obese	khuluphele	kooloope´le´
father	ubaba	oobaabaa
father-in-law	ubabezala	oobaabe´zaalaa
fatigue	ukukhathala	ookookaataalaa
fault	isiphosiso	eeseepo´seeso´
favour (v)	khetha	ke´taa
favour	umusa	oomoosaa
favourite	khethekayo	ke´te´kaayo´
fear (v)	esaba	e´saabaa
fear	ukwesaba	ookwe´saabaa
feast (v)	dikiza	deekeezaa
feast	idili	eedeelee
feather	uphaphe	oopaape´
feed (v)	phakela	paake´laa
feel (v)	i - zwa	ee-zwaa
female	isifazane	eeseefaazaane´
fence (n)	ucingo / ifensi	ooceengo´ / eefe´nsee
fence (wire)	ucingo	ooceengo´
fence (v)	biyela	beeye´laa
fester (v)	vunda	voondaa

108.

fetch (v)	landa	laandaa
fever	imfiva	eemfeevaa
few	ncane / mbalwa	ncaane´ / mbaalwaa
field	indawo yasendle / insimu	eendaawo´ yaase´ndle´ / eenseemoo
fierce	nolaka	no´laakaa
fight (v)	ilwa	eelwaa
fight	ukulwa	ookoolwaa
fill (v)	gcwalisa	gcwaaleesaa
filling	okugcwalisayo	o´koogcwaaleesaayo´
filth	udoti	oodo´tee
final	isigcino / isiphetho	eeseegceeno´ / eeseepe´to´
find (v)	thola	to´laa
finger	umunwe	oomoonwe´
fingernail	uzipho	oozeepo´
fingerprints	iminwe	eemeenwe´
finish (n)	ukuphela	ookoope´laa
finish (v)	phelisa / qeda	pe´leesaa / qe´daa
finish completely (v)	shaya ubhuqe	shaayaa oobooqe´
fire	umlilo	oomleelo´
fireplace	iziko	eezeeko´
firewood	izinkuni	eezeenkoonee
firm (hard)	qinile	qeeneele´
first aid	usizo lokuqala	ooseezo´ lo´kooqaalaa
first	ukuqala	ookooqaalaa
firstborn	izibulo	eezeeboolo´
fish (v)	doba	do´baa
fish	inhlanzi	eenhlaanzee
fishing rod	udobo / uthi lokudoba	oodo´bo´ / ootee lo´koodo´baa
fishmoth	umvunya	oomvoonyaa
fist	inqindi	eenqeendee
fit (n)-epileptic	ukuquleka	ookooqoole´kaa
fit (v)	lingana	leengaanaa
fix (v)	lungisa	loongeesaa
flash (torch)	umbani / ukukhanya	oombaanee / ookookaanyaa
flashlight	ithoshi	eeto´shee
flavour (v)	nandisa	naandeesaa
flavour	isinandisi	eeseenaandeesee
flea	izeze	eeze´ze´
flesh	inyama	eenyaamaa
floor (n)	phansi	paansee
flour - baking	ufulawa	oofoolaawaa
flower - garden	imbali	eembaalee
fluid	ngamanzi	ngaamaanzee
fluoride	iflorayidi	eeflo´raayeedee
fly (n)	impukane	eempookaane´
fly (v)	ndiza	ndeezaa
foe	isitha	eeseetaa
fog	inkungu	eenkoongoo
fold (n) - in clothes	umpheco	oompe´co´

fold (v) - paper / clothes	songa / pheca / goqa	so'ngaa / pe'caa / go'qaa
follow (v)	landela	laande'laa
food	ukudla	ookoodlaa
fool	isilima	eeseeleemaa
foot	unyawo	oonyaawo'
footsteps	izigi	eezeegee
forever	naphakade	naapaakaade'
forbid (v)	ala	aalaa
force (n)	amandla	aamaandlaa
force (v) (press)	cindezela	ceende'ze'laa
foreskin	ijwabu	eejwaaboo
forest	ihlathi	eehlaatee
forget (v)	khohlwa	ko'hlwaa
forgive (v)	thethelela / xolela	te'te'le'laa / xo'le'laa
fork	imfologo	eemfo'lo'go'
fortunately	ngenhlanhla	nge'nhlaanhlaa
forward	ngaphambili	ngaapaambeelee
fowl	inkukhu	eenkookoo
free (v)	khulula	kooloolaa
free - for free	mahala	maahaalaa
freedom	inkululeko	eenkooloole'ko'
freeze (v)	qandisa	qaandeesaa
freezer	isiqandisi	eeseeqaandeesee
fresh	i- sha	ee-shaa
fridge - inside	efrijini	e'freejeenee
fridge	ifriji	eefreejee
friend	umngane	oomngaane'
friendship	ubungane	ooboongaane'
frighten (v)	ethusa	e'toosaa
frog	isele	eese'le'
from	kusuka ku	koosookaa koo
front	phambili	paambeelee
frost - garden	isithwathwa	eeseetwaatwaa
frown (v)	hwaqabala / hwaqa	hwaaqaabaalaa / hwaaqaa
fruit	isithelo	eeseete'lo'
fry (v)	thosa	to'saa
frying pan	ipani lokuthosa	eepaanee lo'kooto'saa
fuel (for a fire)	okokubasela umlilo	o'ko'koobaase'laa oomleelo'
full	gcwele	gcwe'le'
fun	ukudlala	ookoodlaalaa
funeral	umngcwabo	oomngcwaabo'
funnel	isetho / ifonela	eese'to' / eefo'ne'laa
funny	hlekisayo	hle'keesaayo'
fur	uboya	oobo'yaa
furniture	ifenisha	eefe'neeshaa
further along / on top of	phambili / ngaphezu	paambeelee / ngaape'zoo

G

gain (v)	zuza	zoozaa
gain	inzuzo	eenzoozo´
game (play)	umdlalo	oomdlaalo´
gang	igenge	eege´nge´
garage	igalaji	eegaalaajee
garden	ingadi	eengaadee
gargle (v)	hahaza	haahaazaa
garlic	ugaliki	oogaaleekee
gas (n)	igesi	eege´see
gasp (v)	befuzela	be´fooze´laa
gastric	okusesiswini	o´koose´seesweenee
gate	isango	eesaango´
gecko	intulo	eentoolo´
geese	amahansi	aamaahaansee
gentle	mnene	mne´ne´
gently	ngobunono	ngo´boono´no´
germ	igciwane	eegceewaane´
get (v)	thola	to´laa
ghost	isipoki	eeseepo´kee
giddy	nesizunguzane	ne´seezoongoozaane´
gift / talent	isiphiwo	eeseepeewo´
gill (fish)	isiphefumulo	eeseepe´foomoolo´
girl	intombazane	eento´mbaazaane´
girlfriend	intombi	eento´mbee
give (v)	i- pha / nika	ee-paa / neekaa
glad	jabulile	jaabooleele´
gland	indlala	eendlaalaa
glass	ingilazi	eengeelaazee
glasses - for eyesight	izibuko zamehlo	eezeebooko´ zaame´hlo´
glove	igilavu	eegeelaavoo
glow (v)	nkemuzela	nke´mooze´laa
glue (n)	isinamathelisi / iglu	eeseenaamaate´leesee / eegloo
glue (v)	namathelisa	naamaate´leesaa
go (v) - go / go to	hamba / -ya	haambaa / -yaa
God	uNkulunkulu	ooNkooloonkooloo
going	ukuhamba	ookoohaambaa
gold	igolide	eego´leede´
gone	hambile	haambeele´
good - she is pretty / it is ---	mu-hle / ku-hle	moohle´ / koohle´
goodness	ubuhle	ooboohle´
goods	izimpahla	eezeempaahlaa
gossip (n)	amahemuhemu	aamaahe´moohe´moo
gossip (v)	hemuza / hleba	he´moozaa / hle´baa
government	uhulumeni	oohooloome´nee
grain	uhlamvu	oohlaamvoo
grandchild	umzukulu	oomzookooloo
grandfather	ubabamkhulu / umkhulu	oobaabaamkooloo / oomkooloo

grandmother	ugogo	oogo´go´
grandson	umzukulu wesilisa	oomzookooloo we´seeleesa
grant (v)	thola	to´laa
grapes	amagrebhisi /	aamaagre´beesee /
	amagilebhisi	aamaageele´beesee
grasp (v)	bamba	baambaa
grass	utshani	ootshaanee
grate (v)	khuhluza / greytha	koohlooza / gre´ytaa
grated (cheese)	ushizi ogreythiwe	oosheezee o´gre´yteewe´
grateful	-bongayo	-bo´ngaayo´
grater	igreytha	eegre´ytaa / eegre´taa
grave (n)	ithuna	eetoonaa
grave (sad)	nzima	nzeemaa
gravel - road / stoney gravel	uhlalwane /	oohlaalwaane´/
	amatshana	aamaatshaanaa
gravy	umhluzi / isobho	oomhloozee / eeso´bo´
grease (v -pan)	gcoba	gco´baa
grease	igrisi	eegreesee
greasy / oily	m a t i f i t i f i /	maateefeeteefee /
	namafutha	naamaafootaa
green - colour / unripe	luhlaza	loohlaazaa
greenpepper	upelepele oluhlaza	oope´le´pe´le´ o´loohlaazaa
greet (v)	bingelela	beenge´le´laa
grill (v)	osa	o´saa
grill	insimbi yokosa	eenseembee yo´ko´saa
grilled (v)	egriliwe	e´greeleewe´
grin	sineka	seene´kaa
grind (v – mealies)	gaya	gaayaa
groan (v)	bubula	booboolaa
groceries	igilosa	eegeelo´saa
ground (sand)	umhlabathi	oomhlaabaatee
grow (v) - crops	mila	meelaa
grow (v) – height	khula	koolaa
growl (dog)	hhahhama	hhaahhaamaa
grumble (v)	khononda	ko´no´ndaa
guarantee (n)	isiqinisekiso	eeseeqeeneese´keeso´
guarantee (v)	qinisekisa	qeeneese´keesaa
guard (n)	ugadi	oogaadee
guard (v)	gada	gaadaa
guilt	icala	eecaalaa
guilty	necala	ne´caalaa
guineafowl	impangele	eempaange´le´
gum (teeth)	insini	eenseenee
gun	isibhamu	eeseebaamoo
gutter	igatha / ugedasi	eegaataa / ooge´daasee

H

habit	injwayelo	eenjwaaye'lo'
hack-saw	isaha lokusika insimbi	eesaaghaa lo'kooseekaa eenseembee
haemorrhage (v) - bleed	opha	o' paa
haemorrhage (v) - nose bleed	umongozima	oomo'ngo'zeemaa
haemorrhage (n) - nose bleed	umongula	oomo'ngoolaa
haemorrhoids	imizoko	eemeezo'ko'
hair	izinwele	eezeenwe'le'
haircut	ukugunda izinwele	ookoogoondaa eezeenwe' le'
hairdresser	umcwali wezinwele	oomcwaalee we'zeenwe'le'
hairy	noboya	no'bo'yaa
half	uhhafu / ingxenye	oohaafoo / eengxe'nye'
hall	ihholo	eehallo' / eeho'lo'
halt (v)	i-ma / u-ma	eema / ooma
halve (v)	caza kabili	caaza kaabeelee
ham	ihemu	eehe'moo
hamburger	ihembhega	eehe'mbe'gaa
hammer	isando	eesaando'
hand	isandla	eesaandlaa
handkerchief	iduku	eedookoo
handle (n)	isibambo	eeseebaambo'
hang (washing) (v)	lengisa / neka	le'ngeesaa / ne'kaa
hang (v) - body	phanyeka	paanye'kaa
hang (v) – pictures	lengisa izithombe	le'ngeesaa eezeeto'mbe'
hang – hang one's head	ngxolombisa	ngxo'lo'mbeesaa
happen (v)	enzeka	e'nze'kaa
happiness	injabulo	eenjaaboolo'
happy	jabula	jaaboolaa
hard (a)	lukhuni	lookoonee
hard (difficult)	nzima	nzeemaa
harm (v)	limala	leemaalaa
harm	ukulimala	ookooleemaalaa
harmful	nengozi	ne'ngo'zee
harmless	ngenangozi	nge'naango'zee
harvest (v)	vuna	voonaa
haste	ukusheshisa	ookooshe'sheesaa
hasty	sheshisa	she'sheesaa
hat	isigqoko	eeseegqo'ko'
hate (v)	zonda	zo'ndaa
hate each other	zondana	zo'ndaanaa
have (v) - they have	-na / bane	-naa / baane'
hawk	uklebe	ookle' be'
he	yena	ye'naa
head	ikhanda	eekaandaa
headache	ukuphathwa ikhanda	ookoopaatwaa eekaandaa
heal (v)	elapha	e'laapaa
health	impilo	eempeelo'
healthy	philile	peeleele'
heap (n) - of rubbish	inqwaba	eenqwaabaa

113.

heap (v) – heap up rubbish	futhuza	footoozaa
heap (v)	nqwabela	nqwaabe´laa
hear (v)	i-zwa	eezwaa
heart	inhliziyo	eenhleezeeyo´
heartburn	isilungulela	eeseeloongoole´laa
hearth	iziko	eezeeko´
heat (n)	ukushisa	ookoosheesaa
heat up (v -food)	fudumeza	foodoome´zaa
heaven	izulu	eezooloo
heavy	sinda	seendaa
hedge (n)	uthango	ootaango´
heifer	isithole	eeseeto´le´
height - tall / altitude	ubude	ooboode´
height - elevation	ukuphakama	ookoopaakaamaa
hello - to a male friend	sawubona mfo	saawoobo´naa mfo´
hello - to female friend	sawubona sisi	saawoobo´naa seesee
hello - to a granny	sawubona gogo	saawoobo´naa go´go´
hello	sawubona	saawoobo´naa
help (n)	usizo	ooseezo´
help (v)	siza	seezaa
helpful	sizayo	seezaayo´
helpless person - scared	thithibele	teeteebe´le´
helpless person - not hear	ngenasizo	nge´naaseezo´
hem (n)	umthungo / umphetho	oomtoongo´ / oompe´to´
hen	inkukhu	eenkookoo
her	yena	ye´naa
herbs - edible	imfino	eemfeeno´
herbs - medicinal	ikhambi	eekaambee
herd (n)	umhlambi	oomhlaambee
herd (v)	lusa	loosaa
herdman / driver	umelusi / umqhubi	oome´loosee / oomqoobee
here	lapha / khona lapha	laapaa / ko´naa laapaa
hero / heroes	iqhawe / amaqhawe	eeqaawe´ / aamaaqaawe´
hers	okwakhe	o´kwaake´
hiccough	intwabi	eentwaabee
hidden	fihliwe	feehleewe´
hide (v)	fihla	feehlaa
high pressure	umfutho onamandla	oomfooto´ o´naamaandlaa
high	phakeme / kude	paake´me´ / koode´
hijack (v)	ukubamba inkunzi	ookoobaambaa eenkoonzee
him	yena	ye´naa
hinge	ihinji	eeheenjee
hip	inqulu	eenqooloo
hippopotamus	imvubu	eemvooboo
hire (v)	qasha	qaashaa
his	okwakhe	o´kwaake´
hit (v)	shaya	shaayaa
hobby	umsebenzana	oomse´be´nzaanaa
hockey	ihokhi	eeho´kee
hockey stick	induku yehokhi	eendookoo ye´ho´kee

hoe (v)	hlakula	hlaakoolaa
hoe (n)	ikhuba / igeja	eekooba / eege´jaa
hold (v)	bamba	baambaa
hold	ukubamba	ookoobaambaa
hole (n) in ground / clothes	umgodi / imbobo	oomgo´dee / eembo´bo´
holes - make holes	vula imbobo / bhoboza	voola eembo´bo´ / bo´ bo´zaa
holiday	iholide	eeho´leede´
holy	ngcwele	ngcwe´le´
home	ikhaya	eekaayaa
homework	umsebenzi wasekhaya	oomse´be´nzee waase´kaaya
homosexual	isitabane	eeseetaabaane´
honest	qotho / thembekile	qo´to´ / te´mbe´keele´
honesty	ubuqotho / ukuthembeka	oobooqo´to´ / ookoote´mbe´kaa
honey	uju	oojoo
honeymoon	ihanimuni	eehaaneemoonee
honour (v)	hlonipha	hlo´neepaa
hoof	isondo	eeso´ndo´
hook (v)	hhuka	hhookaa
hook	ihhuku	eehookoo
hoot (v)	papaza / shaya ihutha	paapaazaa / shaayaa eehootaa
hop (v)	kheleza	ke´le´zaa
hope	ithemba	eete´mbaa
horn (cow)	uphondo	oopo´ndo´
horror	okwesabekayo	ookwe´saabe´kaayo´
horse	ihhashi	eehaashee
hose	ithumbu	eetoomboo
hospital	isibhedlela	eeseebe´dle´laa
hot - as in curry	obabayo	o´baabaayo´
hot - as in weather	fudumele	foodoome´le´
hotel	ihhotela	eeho´te´laa
hour	i- awa / ihora	ee-aawa / eeho´raa
house (v)	hlalisa	hlaaleesaa
house	indlu	eendloo
how	kanjani	kaanjaanee
humanity	ubuntu	ooboontoo
humble (v) – to be humble	thoba	to´baa
humid	manzana	maanzaanaa
humour	inhliziyo	eenhleezeeyo´
hundred	ikhulu	eekooloo
hunger	ukulamba	ookoolaambaa
hungry	lambile	laambeele´
hunt (v)	zingela	zeenge´laa
hunter	umzingeli	oomzeenge´lee
hurry	phangisa / shesha	paangeesaa / she´shaa
hurt (v)	limaza	leemaazaa
hurt, get hurt (v)	limala	leemaalaa
husband	umyeni / indoda	oomye´nee / eendo´daa
hut — a thatch hut	iqhugwane / indlu yotshani	eeqoogwaane´ / eendloo yo´tshaani
hypnotise (v)	lutha	lootaa
hypnotist	umluthi	oomlootee

I

I	ngi	ngee
ibis	inkankane	eenkaankaane'
ice	iqhwa	eeqwaa
icecream	ayisikhilimu	aayeeseekeeleemoo
icing	ayisingi	aayeeseengee
idea	umcabango	oomcaabaango'
identical	fana	faanaa
identify (v)	khomba	ko'mbaa
identity	uqobo lwa --	ooqo'bo' lwaa –
identity number	inombolo kamazisi	eeno'mbo'lo' kaamaazeesee
idiot	isilima	eeseeleemaa
idle	ngenzi lutho / vilaphayo	nge'nzee looto' / veelaapaayo'
if	uma	oomaa
if you like	uma uthanda	oomaa ootaandaa
ignorance	ukungazi	ookoongaazee
ignore (v)	nganaki	ngaanaakee
iguana	uxamu	ooxaamoo
ill	gula	goolaa
ill treat	phatha kabi	paataa kaabee
illegal	ngavumelani nomthetho	ngaavoome'laanee no'mte'to'
ill – mannered	ngahloniphi	ngaahlo'neepee
illiterate	ngafundile	ngaafoondeele'
illness / disease	ukugula / isifo	ookoogoolaa / eeseefo'
ill-tempered	nolaka	no'laakaa
illustrate	bonisa / hlobisa	bo'neesaa / hlo'beesaa
illustration	isiboniso	eeseebo'neeso'
ill-will	inzondo	eenzo'ndo'
image	isithombe	eeseeto'mbe'
imagination	umcabango	oomcaabaango'
imagine (v)	cabanga	caabaangaa
imbecile	isithutha	eeseetootaa
imitate (v)	lingisa / fanisa	leengeesaa / faaneesaa
imitation	ukulinganisela	ookooleengaaneese'laa
immaculate	-ngengasisihla	-nge'naaseeseehlaa
immature	-ngakakhuli	-ngaakaakoolee
immediate	manje	maanje'
immediately	masinyane	maaseenyaane'
immediately - just now	khona manje	ko'naa maanje'
immense	khulukazi	koolookaazee
immerse (v)	cwilisa	cweeleesaa
immigrant	isifiki	eeseefeekee
immigrate (v)	fika ezweni	feekaa e'zwe'nee
immigration	ukuthuthela kwelinye izwe	ookootoote'laa kwe'leenye' eezwe'
immobile	ngasahambi	ngaasaahaambee
immobilize (v)	misa	meesaa
immoral	nobubi / ngalungile	no'boobee / ngaaloongeele'
immoral person	isifebe	eeseefe'be'
immovable	ngenakususwa	nge'naakoosooswaa

immune	gomekile	go´me´keele´
immunization	ukugonywa	ookoogo´nywaa
immunity	ukugomeka	ookoogo´me´kaa
immunize (v)	goma	go´maa
impartial	ngakhethi	ngaake´tee
impatience	ukungabekezeli	ookoongaabe´ke´ze´lee
impatient	ngabekezeli	ngaabe´ke´ze´lee
imperfect	ngaphelele	ngaape´le´le´
impetuous	namawala	naamaawaalaa
impinge (v)	gudlana na	goodlaanaa naa
implant (v)	ngenisa	nge´neesaa
implicate (v)	ngenisa / xabhelela	nge´neesaa / xaabe´le´laa
imply (v)	qonda / gudlisa	qo´ndaa / goodleesaa
impolite	ngahloniphi	ngaahlo´neepee
import (v)	ngenisa impahla	nge´neesaa eempaahlaa
	ezweni	e´zwe´nee
importance	ubukhulu	oobookooloo
important	qavile / balulekile	qaaveele´ / baaloole´keele´
important - it is ----	isemqoka	eese´mqo´ kaa
impose (v)	thwalisa / khohlisa	twaaleesaa / ko´hleesaa
imposition / burden	ukweleka / umthwalo	ookwe´le´kaa / oomtwaalo´
impossible	ngenakwenzeka	nge´naakwe´nze´kaa
impostor	umkhohlisi	oomko´hleesee
impound (v)	bamba impahla	baambaa eempaahlaa
impoverish (v)	phofisa / khohlisa	po´feesaa / ko´hleesaa
impregnate (v)	mithisa / zalisa	meeteesaa / zaaleesaa
impress (v) - affect	zwisisa	zweeseesaa
impress (v) -enforce	phoqa	po´qaa
impressive	nesithunzi	ne´seetoonzee
imprison (v)	bopha	bo´paa
improper	ngafanele	ngaafaane´le´
improve (v)	thuthukisa	tootookeesaa
improvement	intuthuko	eentootooko´
improvise (v)	ciciyela	ceeceeye´laa
impudence	ukweyisa	ookwe´yeesaa
in (inside)	phakathi kwa	paakaatee kwaa
inaccurate	ngalungile	ngaaloongeele´
inactive	ngasebenzi	ngaase´be´nzee
inadequate	nganele	ngaane´le´
inaudible	ngezwakali	nge´zwaakaalee
inbred	segazini	se´gaazeenee
incapable –too weak	ngenamandla	nge´naamaandle´
incapable – not know	ngenakwazi	nge´naakwaazee
incentive	isivuso / umvuso	eeseevooso´ / oomvooso´
inception	isiqalo	eeseeqaalo´
inch	iyintshi	eeyeentshee
incidence	ukuvama	ookoovaamaa
incident	isigameko	eeseegaame´ko´
incinerate (v)	shisa	sheesaa
incision	umsiko / ukusika	oomseeko´/ ookooseekaa

include (v)	faka / ngenisa	faakaa / nge'neesaa
inclusion	ukungeniswa	ookoonge'neeswaa
income	iholo	eeho'lo'
incompatible	ngafanelene	ngaafaane'le'ne'
incomplete	ngaphelele	ngaape'le'le'
inconceivable	ngenakukholwa	nge'naakooko'lwaa
inconclusive	ngadelisanga	ngaade'leesaangaa
inconsiderate	ngenaluzwela	nge'naaloozwe'laa
inconvenience	ukukhathazeka	ookookaataaze'kaa
incorrect	ngalungile	ngaaloongeele'
increase (v) grow / add	ukukhula / andisa	ookookoolaa / aandeesaa
increase (v)	ukwenyusa / anda	ookwe'nyoosaa / aandaa
indecision	ukuzindla	ookoozeendlaa
indeed	impela	eempe'laa
indemnity	imbuyiselo	eembooyeese'lo'
independence	ukuzimela	ookoozeeme'laa
independent	zimeleyo	zeeme'le'yo'
index	inkomba	eenko'mbaa
Indian	iNdiya	eeNdeeyaa
indicate (v)	khombisa	ko'mbeesaa
indication	inkomba	eenko'mbaa
indicator	isikhombiso	eeseeko'mbeeso'
indifference	ukunganaki	ookoongaanaakee
indigenous	kwemvelo	kwe'mve'lo'
indigenous tree	umuthi womdabu	oomootee wo'mdaaboo
individual	umuntu munye	oomoontoo moonye'
indoors	phakathi endlini	paakaatee e'ndleenee
inequality	ukungalingani	ookoongaaleengaanee
inexcusable	ngenakuxolelwa	nge'naakooxo'le'lwaa
inexpensive	shibhile	sheebeele'
infant	usana / ingane	oosaana / eengaane'
infect (v)	esulela / thelela	e'soole'laa / te'le'laa
infectious	thathelanayo	taate'laanaayo'
inflate (v) (air)	futha	footaa
influence (n)	imfundiso	eemfoondeeso'
influence (v)	fundisa / thonya	foondeesaa / to'nyaa
influential	nesithunzi	ne'seetoonzee
inform (v)	bonisa / azisa / ceba	bo'neesaa / aazeesaa / ce'baa
information	umbiko / ulwazi	oombeeko' / oolwaazee
informer	umcebi / impimpi	oomce'bee / oompeempee
ingratitude	ukungabongi	ookoongaabo'ngee
ingredients	izithako	eezeetaako'
inhabit (v)	hlala / akha	hlaalaa / aakaa
inhabitant	ohlalayo	o'hlaalaayo'
inherit (v)	thola ngefa	to'laa nge'faa
inhuman	nonya	no'nyaa
initiate (v)	qalisa / fundisa	qaaleesaa / foondeesaa
initiative	ukuzisusela / okuqaliwe	ookoozeesoose'laa / o'kooqaaleewe'
inject (v)	jova	jo'vaa

injection	umjovo	oomjo'vo'
injure (v)	limaza	leemaazaa
injury	ingozi	eengo'zee
ink	uyinki	ooyeenkee
innings - cricket	isikhathi sokudlala	eeseekaatee so'koodlaalaa
innocent – not guilty	ngenacala	nge'naacaalaa
innocent – not know	msulwa	msoolwaa
inoculate (v)	jova	jo'vaa
inquire (v)	buza	boozaa
inquiry	umbuzo	oomboozo'
insane	hlanyayo	hlaanyaayo'
insanitary	ngcolile	ngco'leele'
insanity	ukuhlanya	ookoohlaanyaa
insect	isinambuzane	eeseenaamboozaane'
insert (v)	ngenisa / faka	nge'neesaa / faakaa
inside	phakathi	paakaatee
insincere	ngenaqiniso	nge'naaqeeneeso'
insinuate	bhekisa	be'keesaa
insist (v)	qinisa	qeeneesaa
insolent	delelayo	de'le'laayo'
insolvency	ukushona emalini	ookoosho'naa e'maaleenee
insomnia	ukungalali	ookoongaalaalee
inspect (v)	hlola	hlo'laa
inspection	ukuhlola	ookoohlo'laa
inspiration	ukukhuthaza	ookookootaazaa
inspire (v)	khuthaza	kootaazaa
instability	ukuxega	ookooxe'gaa
install (v)	faka / beka	faakaa / be'kaa
instalment - of an account	inthela / isigamu	eente'la / eeseegaamoo
instantly	khona manje	ko'na maanje'
instead	endaweni yokuba	e'ndaawe'nee yo'koobaa
instigate (v)	qala	qaalaa
instruct (v)	fundisa	foondeesaa
instruction	imfundiso	eemfoondeeso'
instructor	umfundisi	oomfoondeesee
insufficient	ngalingene / nganele	ngaaleenge'ne'/ ngaane'le'
insult (n)	isithuko	eeseetooko'
insult (v)	thuka	tookaa
insurance	umshuwarensi	oomshoowaare'nsee
insure (v)	faka emshuwarensi	faakaa e'mshoowaare'nsee
integrate (v)	hlanganisa	hlaangaaneesaa
	ngokuphelelisa	ngo'koope'le'leesaa
integrity	ubuqotho	oobooqo'to'
intellect	ingqondo	eengqo'ndo'
intelligence	ukuhlakanipha	ookoohlaakaaneepaa
intention	umqondo / isifiso	oomqo'ndo'/ eeseefeeso'
interact (v)	bonisana	bo'neesaanaa
interbreed (v)	zalana	zaalaanaa
intercept (v)	vimbela	veembe'laa
intercourse	ukulalana	ookoolaalaanaa

interest (n) - in a person	uthando	ootaando´
interfere (v)	xhaka / qekelela	xaakaa / qe´ke´le´laa
intermingle (v)	hlangana	hlaangaanaa
internal	ngaphakathi	ngaapaakaatee
interpret (v)	humusha	hoomooshaa
interpretation	ukuhumusha	ookoohoomooshaa
interrogate (v)	buzisisa	boozeeseesaa
interrogation	ukubuzisiswa	ookooboozeeseeswaa
interrupt (v)	phazamisa	paazaameesaa
interruption	isiphazamiso	eeseepaazaameeso´
intervene (v)	lamula	laamoolaa
interview (v)	xoxa	xo´xaa
interview	ingxoxo	eengxo´xo´
intestines	amathumbu	aamaatoomboo
intimidate (v)	esabisa	e´saabeesaa
into	phakathi	paakaatee
introduce (v)	ethula / azisa	e´toolaa / aazeesaa
intrude (v)	xhaka / xhakela	xaakaa / xaake´laa
intruder	iselelesi	eese´le´le´see
invade (v)	hlasela	hlaase´laa
invalid – sick person	isiguli	eeseegoolee
invalid	ngenasiqiniseko	nge´naaseeqeeneese´ko´
invasion	ukuhlaselwa kwezwe	ookoohlaase´lwaa kwe´zwe´
invent (v)	qamba	qaambaa
inventor	umqambi	oomqaambee
invest (v)	faka imali ukuze izale	faakaa eemaalee ookooze´ eezaale´
investigate (v)	hlola / phenya	hlo´laa / pe´nyaa
investigation	ukuhlola	ookoohlo´laa
investment	ukufakwa imali ukuze izale	ookoofaakwaa eemaalee ookooze´ eezaale´
invitation	isimemo	eeseeme´mo´
invite (v)	mema	me´maa
iron (n) - washing	insimbi yoku-ayina	eenseembee yo´koo - aayeena
iron (v)	ayina	aayeenaa
irreparable	ngasenakulungiswa	ngaase´naakooloongeeswaa
irrespective	ngaphandle kwa	ngaapaandle´ kwaa
irresponsible	ngenacala	nge´naacaalaa
irrigate (v)	nisela ngamanzi	neese´laa ngaamaanzee
irrigation	ukunisela	ookooneese´laa
irritate (v)	cunula / casula	coonoolaa / caasoolaa
island	isiqhingi	eeseeqeengee
isolate (v)	ahlukanisa kubekodwa	aahlookaaneesaa koobe´ko´dwaa
it	lokhu	lo´koo
itch	utwayi	ootwaayee
itch (v)	luma	loomaa

J

jack - for punctures	ujeke	ooje'ke'
jackal	impungushe	eempoongooshe'
jacket	ibhantshi	eebaantshee
jail	ijele	eeje'le'
jam	ujamu	oojaamoo
jar	imbizana / isitsha	eembeezaanaa / eeseetshaa
jaw	umhlathi	oomhlaatee
jelly	ujeli	oojelly /ooje'lee
jealous	nomona	no'mo'naa
jealousy	umona	oomo'naa
jersey	ijezi	eeje'zee
Jesus	uJesu	ooJe'soo
jetty	ijethi	eeje'tee
Jew	iJuda	eeJoodaa
jewel	itshana eliyigugu	eetshaanaa e'leeyeegoogoo
jewelry	iqoqo legugu	eeqo'qo' le'googoo
job	umsebenzi	oomse'be'nzee
jockey	ujoki	oojo'kee
jog (v)	dledlezela	dle'dle'ze'laa
join (v)	hlanganisa	hlaangaaneesaa
joke	ihlaya	eehlaayaa
joker	isinteli	eeseente'lee
jolly	hlekayo	hle'kaayo'
journey	uhambo	oohaambo'
joy	injabulo	eenjaaboolo'
judge (n)	ijaji / umgwebi	eejaajee / oomgwe'bee
judge (v)	gweba	gwe'baa
judgement	isahlulelo	eesaahloole'lo'
jug	ujeke	ooje'ke'
juggle	gila	geelaa
juggler	isigilamkhuba	eeseegeelaamkoobaa
juice	ijusi	eejoosee
jump (v)	gxuma	gxoomaa
jungle	ihlathi / igxa	eehlaatee / eegxaa
jury	ijuri	eejooree
justify	vumela	voome'laa
juvenile	ingane encane	eengaane' e'ncaane'

K

keen	shisekela	sheese´ke´laa
keep (v) - not reveal	gcina	gceenaa
keep (v) - hold	thatha / khweza	taataa / kwe´zaa
keepsake	isikhumbuzo	eeseekoomboozo´
kennel	indlu yenja	eendloo ye´njaa
kettle	igedlela / iketelo	eege´dle´laa / eeke´te´lo´
key	ukhiye	ookeeyaa
khaki weed	unsangwana	oonsaangwaana
kick (v)	khahlela	kaahle´laa
kidnap	thumba	toombaa
kidney	inso	eenso´
kill (v)	bulala	boolaalaa
kill (v) - slaughter	hlaba	hlaabaa
kind - nature	nomusa	no´moosaa
kind (n) - sort	uhlobo	oohlo´bo´
kindly	ngomusa	ngo´moosaa
kindness	umusa	oomoosaa
king	inkosi	eenko´see
kingdom /	ubukhosi / yezwe /	oobooko´see / ye´zwe´ /
kingdom	umbuso	oombooso´
kiss (n)	ukuqabula	ookooqaaboolaa
kiss (v)	qabula	qaaboolaa
kitchen	ikhishi	eekeeshee
knead (v)	xova	xo´vaa
knee	idolo	eedo´lo´
kneecap	ivi	eevee
kneel (v)	guqa ngamadolo	gooqaa ngaamaado´lo´
knew	azile	aazeele´
knife	ummese	oome´se´
knit(v)	nitha	neetaa
knit (v) - bone broken	hlumelela	hloome´le´laa
knitting	ukunitha	ookooneetaa
knock (v)	ngqongqoza	ngqo´ngqo´zaa
knock knock	ngqo ngqo	ngqo´ ngqo´
knot (n)	ifindo	eefeendo´
knot (v)	bopha ifindo	bo´paa eefeendo´
know	azi	aazee
knowledge	ulwazi	ˮoolwaazee
kraal	umuzi / isibaya	oomoozee / eeseebaayaa

L

label (n)	ilebula	eele'boolaa
labour (n)	umsebenzi	oomse'be'nzee
labour (v)	sebenza	se'be'nzaa
lack (v)	ntula	ntoolaa
ladder	isikhwelo / iladi	eeseekwe'lo' / eelaadee
ladle (n)	indebe	eende'be'
lady - married	inkosikazi	eenko'seekaazee
lamp	isibani / ilambu	eeseebaanee / eelaamboo
land	umhlaba	oomhlaabaa
language /	inkulumo /	eenkooloomo' /
language	ulimi	ooleemee
language - bantu language	isintu	eeseentoo
large	-khulu	-kooloo
last – at the end	-gcinayo	-gceenaayo'
late (evening)	-shonile	-sho'neele'
late (arriving	phuzile ukufika	poozeele' ookoofeekaa
laugh (v)	hleka	hle'kaa
laughter	uluhleko	ooloohle'koo
laundry	ilondolo	eelo'ndo'lo'
law	umthetho	oomte'to'
lawn	utshani	ootshaanee
lawyer	ummeli	oome'lee
lay (v) - table	deka itafula	de'kaa eetaafoolaa
lay (v) - an egg	zala	zaalaa
layered	okwenziwe ngezilayi	o'kwe'nzeewe' nge'zeelaayee
lazy (person)	livila / ivila	leeveelaa / eeveelaa
lead (v)	hamba phambili	haambaa paambeelee
leaf	ikhasi / ihlamvu	eekaasee / eehlaamvoo
leak (v)	vuza	voozaa
learn (v)	funda	foondaa
leave (n) - holiday	ilivi / ilivu	eeleevee / eeleevoo
leave (v) - behind	shiya	sheeyaa
lefthanded person	inxele	eenxe'le'
leftover	insalela / sala	eensaale'laa / saalaa
leg	umlenze	oomle'nze'
lemon	ulamula	oolaamoolaa
lend (v)	bolekisa	bo'le'keesaa
less	ngaphansi	ngaapaansee
lessen (v)	nciphisa	nceepeesaa
lesson	isifundo	eeseefoondo'
letter	incwadi	eencwaadee
lettuce	uletisi	oole'teeseee
level (n)	ileveli	eele've'lee
level (v) make even	linganisa	leengaaneesaa
liar	umqambi manga	oomqaambee maangaa
library	ilayibhrari	eelaayeebraaree
licence	ilayisense	eelaayeese'nse'
lick (v)	khotha	ko'taa

lid	isivalo	eeseevaalo´
lie (sleep - v)	lala	laalaa
lie (liar - n)	amanga	aamaangaa
lie (v) – be dishonest	qamba amanga	qaambaa aamaangaa
life	impilo	eempeelo´
lift (elevator)	ilifti	eeleeftee
lift (raise- v)	phakamisa	paakaameesaa
light (n)	ukukhanya	ookookaanyaa
light (v)	khanyisa	kaanyeesaa
light (v- set alight)	thungela	toonge´laa
lightening	umbani	oombaanee
lightening - there is---	liyabaneka	leeyaabaane´kaa
like (love-v)	thanda	taandaa
like (same)	njenga	nje´ngaa
like that	kanjalo	kaanjaalo´
line- cord / row	intambo / umugqa	eentaambo´ / oomoogqaa
line – washline	umgibe	oomgeebe´
line – fishing line	udobo	oodo´bo´
linen	ilineni	eeleene´nee
lion /	ibhubesi /	eeboobe´see /
lion	ingonyama	eengo´nyaamaa
lion's share	inxenye enkulu	eenxe´nye´ e´nkooloo
lip	udebe	oode´be´
liquid	-manzi	-maanzee
liquidiser	isenzaluketshezi	eese´nzaalooke´tshe´zee
liquor	ugologo / utshwala	oogo´lo´go´/ ootshwaalaa
listen (v)	lalela	laale´laa
little	ncane / kancane	ncaanee / kaancaane´
live (v)	phila	peelaa
live (v) - I live at home	hlala	hlaalaa
liver	isibindi	eeseebeendee
load (v)	layisha	laayeeshaa
load	umthwalo	oomtwaalo´
loaf - bread	isinkwa	eeseenkwaa
loan /	isikweledu /	eeseekwe´le´doo /
loan	isikweletu	eeseekwe´le´too
loathe (v)	enyanya	e´nyaanynaa
lock (n)	isikhiye	eeseekeeye´
lock (v)	khiya	keeyaa
log / wood	isigodo	eeseego´do´
log	ugodo	oogo´do´
long (for -v)	langazela	laangaaze´laa
long - length	ku -de	koo -de´
look (v)	bheka	be´kaa
look carefully (v)	bheka kahle	be´kaa kaahle´
look	ukubheka	ookoobe´kaa
loose - not tight	xegezela / xegayo	xe´ge´ze´laa / xe´gaayo´
loquat	ulokwata	oolokwaata
lorry	iloli	eelo´lee
lose (v)	lahlekelwa	laahle´ke´lwaa

loss	ukulahlekelwa	ookoolaahle´ke´lwaa
lost	-lahlekelwe	-laahle´ke´lwe´
loud	nomsindo	no´mseendo´
lounge	ilawunji	eelaawoonjee
love	uthando	ootaando´
love (v)	thanda	taandaa
low heat	emlilweni ophansi	e´mleelwe´nee o´paansee
low pressure	umfutho omncane	oomfooto´ o´mncaane´
low	-ehlile	-e´hleele´
lower (under)	ngaphansana	ngaapaansaanaa
lower heat (v)	yehlisa umlilo	ye´hleesaa oomleelo´
loyal	-thembekile	-te´mbe´keele´
luck	inhlanhla	eenhlaanhlaa
luggage /	izimpahla yendlela /	eezeempaahlaa ye´ndle´laa /
luggage	izimpahla	eezeempaahlaa
luke warm	-mthuku	-mtookoo
lump	isigaxa	eeseegaaxaa
lunch	idina	eedeenaa
lung	iphaphu	eepaapoo
lure (v)	yenga	ye´ngaa

M

maccaroni	imakharoni	eemaakaaro´nee
machine	umshini	oomsheenee
mad – drive mad (v)	hlanyisa	hlaanyeesaa
mad - insane	luhlanya / uhlanya	loohlaanyaa / oohlaanyaa
madam /	nkosikazi /	nko´seekaazee /
madam	nkosazana	nko´saazaanaa
maggot	isibungu	eeseeboongoo
mail (n)	iposi	eepo´ssee
mail (v)	posa	po´saa
maim (v)	limaza	leemaazaa
maintain (v –family)	ondla	o´ndlaa
maintenance	isondlo	eeso´ndlo´
maize	ummbila	oombeelaa
make (n) - type	uhlobo	oohlo´bo´
make (v)	enza	e´nzaa
man - fellow	umfo	oomfo´
man – hello / greeting	sawubona mfo	saawoobo´naa mfo´
man	indoda	eendo´daa
manage - able to	. . .ukwazi uku	. . . ookwaazee ookoo
manage (v)	phatha	paataa
manager	umphathi	oompaatee
mannered - well mannered	-nesimo esihle	-ne´seemo´ e´seehle´
mannered - bad mannered	-nesimo esibi	-ne´seemo´ e´seebee
manners - good manners	inhlonipho	eenhlo´neepo´
manners - bad manners	ukungahloniphi	ookoongaahlo´neepee
manure	umquba	oomqoobaa
many	-ningi	-neengee
march (v)	masha	maashaa
mark (v)	maka	maakaa
mark (n) - sign / stain	isici / ibala	eeseecee / eebaalaa
market	imakethe	eemaake´te´
market place	indawo yemakethe	eendaawo´ ye´maake´te´
market (v)	thengisa	te´ngeesaa
marriage	umshado	oomshaado´
marry (v)	shada	shaadaa
mash (potato)	imeshi	eeme´shee
massage (v)	voca voca / dovadova	vo´caa vo´caa / do´vaa do´vaa
mat - mat / grass mat	umata / icansi	oomaataa / eecaansee
match – game	umbango / umdlalo	oombaango´/ oomdlaalo´
match – to light fire with	umentshisi	oome´ntsheesee
match (v) look alike eg.	fanisa / fanela	faaneesaa / faane´laa
material	indwangu	eendwaangoo
matter - does not	akunalutho	aakoonaalooto´
matter - What is the matter?	Yini ndaba?	Yeenee ndaabaa?
mattress	umatilasi	oomaateelaasee
mature (a)	khulile	kooleele´
maul (v)	shikashika	sheekaasheekaa
may (v)	-nga	ngaa

maybe	mhlawumbe	mhlaawoombe´
me	mina	meenaa
meal	isidlo	eeseedlo´
mean (v)	qonda	qo´ndaa
measure (v)	linganisa	leengaaneesaa
measure (v-weigh)	kala	kaalaa
measuring jug	ujeke wokukala	ooje´ke´ wo´kookaalaa
meat	inyama	eenyaamaa
medal	imendlela	eeme´ndle´laa
medallion	imendlela enkulu	eeme´ndle´laa e´nkooloo
mediate (v)	lamula / xazulula	laamoolaa / xaazooloolaa
mediation	ukulamula	ookoolaamoolaa
mediator	umlamuli	oomlaamoolee
medicine	umuthi	oomootee
medicine - preventative ---	ukuvimbele	ookooveembe´le´
meet (v)	hlangana na	hlaangaanaa naa
meeting (n)	umhlangano	oomhlaangaano´
melon - watermelon	ikhabe	eekaabe´
melt (v)	ncibilika	nceebeeleekaa
member	ilunga / abantu	eeloongaa / aabaantoo
memory	inkumbulo	eenkoomboolo´
men	amadoda	aamaado´daa
mend	lungisa	loongeesaa
mercy	umusa	oomoosaa
mess (n)	isibhixi	eeseebeexee
mess (v)	bhixiza	beexeezaa
message	umbiko	oombeeko´
messy	nesibhixi	ne´seebeexee
method	indlela yokwenza	eendle´laa yo´kwe´nzaa
microwave	imayikhroweyivi	eemaayeekro´we´yeevee
midday	imini	eemeenee
midwife	umbelethisi	oombe´le´teesee
mild - taste	pholile	po´leele´
mildew	isikhunta	eeseekoontaa
milk (v) - a cow	senga	se´ngaa
milk	ubisi	oobeesee
mince (v)	-kugaya / gaya	-koogaayaa / gaayaa
mince meat	inyama egayiweyo	eenyaamaa e´gaayeewe´yo´
mincer	isigayo senyama	eeseegaayo´ se´nyaamaa
mind (n)	umqondo	oomqo´ndo´
mine	ami / lami / sami	aamee / laamee / saamee
minister - church	umfundisi	oomfoondeesee
minute (time)	iminithi / umzuzu	eemeeneetee / oomzoozoo
mirror	isibuko	eeseebooko´
misfortune	ilishwa	eeleeshwaa
Miss - Miss Illman	iNkosazana	eeNko´saazaanaa
mist	inkungu	eenkoongoo
mistake	isiphosiso	eeseepo´seeso´
Mister - Mr. Greene	uMnumzane	ooMnoomzaane´
misunderstand (v)	ngezwa / ngizwanga kahle	nge´zwaa / ngeezwaangaa kaahle´

mix (v) /	xubanisa / xuba	xoobaaneesaa / xoobaa
mix (v)	hlanganisa	hlaangaaneesaa
mix all together	hlanganisa konke	hlaangaaneesaa ko´nke´
mixed together	okuhlanganisiwe	o´koohlaangaaneeseewe´
mixed	xubile	xoobeele´
mixture	ixube / ingxube	eexoobe´/ eengxoobe´
moan (v)	thetha	te´taa
moist	manzana	maanzaanaa
moisten (v)	manzisa	maanzeesaa
moisture	ubumanzi	ooboomaanzee
mole - on body	umkhanga	oomkaangaa
mole - in ground	imvukazane	eemvookaazaane´
money	imali	eemaalee
monkey	inkawu	eenkaawoo
month	inyanga	eenyaangaa
moon	inyanga	eenyaangaa
moon - new	inyanga elucezu	eenyaangaa e´looce´zoo
moon - full moon	inyanga ehlangene	eenyaangaa e´hlaange´ne´
more	ningi	neengee
morning	ekuseni	e´koose´nee
mosquito	umiyane	oomeeyaane´
mother	umama	oomaamaa
motorcar	imoto	eemo´to´
mount (v)	khwela	kwe´laa
mountain	intaba	eentaabaa
mourn (v)	lilela / zila	leele´laa / zeelaa
mouse	igundane	eegoondaane´
moustache	amadevu	aamaade´voo
mouth	umlomo	oomlo´mo´
move (v) (trek)	emuka	e´mookaa
move (v) move about	nyakaza / hlela	nyaakaazaa / hle´laa
move (v) take away	susa	soosaa
Mr. (Mr. Greene)	uMnumzane	ooMnoomzaane´
Mrs. (Mrs. Greene)	uNkosikazi	ooNko´seekaazee
mud	udaka	oodaakaa
muddy	nodaka	no´daakaa
muffin tins	izitsha zokubhaka	eezeetshaa zo´koobaakaa
mug (n)	imagi	eemaagee
murder (v)	bulala	boolaalaa
murder (n)	ukubulala	ookooboolaalaa
murderer	umbulali	oomboolaalee
muscle	umsipha	oomseepaa
mushroom	ikhowe	eeko´we´
music	umculo / umnyuziki	oomcoolo´ / oomnyoozeekee
mussel	imbaza	eembaazaa
must	kufanele	koofaane´le´
mustard	umasitadi	oomaaseetaadee
mutton	inyama yemvu	eenyaamaa ye´mvoo
my	mi / yami / ami / sami	mee / yaamee / aamee / saamee

N

nail (tack)	isipikili	eeseepeekeelee
nail (finger)	uzipho	oozeepo´
naked	-nqunu	-nqoonoo
name (v)	biza	beezaa
name	igama	eegaamaa
name - make name for oneself	zenzela udumo	ze´nze´laa oodoomo´
name - good name	umkhokha	oomko´kaa
name - bad name	isihlamba	eeseehlaambaa
name - name after	biza ngegama la---	beezaa nge´gaamaa laa---
namely	ngokuthi	ngo´kootee
namesake	ubizo / ugama	oobeezo´ / oogaamaa
nappy	inephi / inabukeni	eene´pee / eenaabooke´nee
narrow (v)	nciphisa	nceepeesaa
narrow	-ncane	-ncaane´
narrow minded	-nengqondo emfishane	-ne´ngqo´ndo´ e´mfeeshaane´
nasty	-bi / mubi / -casulayo	-bee / moobee / -caasoolaayo´
nation / race / tribe	isizwe	eeseezwe´
national	-esizwe	-e´seezwe´
national anthem	iculo lesizwe	eecoolo´ le´seezwe´
nationality	isizwe / isizalo	eeseezwe´ / eeseezaalo´
natural	yimvelo	yeemve´lo´
naturally	nempela	ne´mpe´laa
nature reserve	isiqiwi	eeseeqeewee
nature	imvelo	eemve´lo´
naughty	delela / ngezwa	de´le´laa / nge´zwaa
nausea	isicanucanu	eeseecaanoocaanoo
nauseate (v)	canula	caanoolaa
navel	inkaba	eenkaabaa
near	eduze	e´dooze´
nearly	cishe	ceeshe´
neat	-nobunono	-no´boono´no´
neatness	ubonono	oobo´no´no´
neatly	ngobunono	ngo´boono´no´
necessary	dingekile	deenge´keele´
neck	intamo	eentaamo´
necklace	umgexo	oomge´xo´
need (n) (poorness)	isidingo	eeseedeengo´
need (need something -v)	dinga / swela	deengaa / swe´laa
need (v)	swela	swe´laa
needle	inaliti	eenaaleetee
negotiate (v)	xoxisana	xo´xeesaanaa
neighbour	umakhelwane	oomaake´lwaane´
neighbourhood	komakhelwane	ko´maake´lwaane´
neighbourhood watch	umbheki abomuzi	oombe´kee aabo´moozee
nephew	umshana	oomshaanaa
nerve - courage	isibindi	eeseebeendee
nervous	namatata / novalo	naamaataataa / no´vaalo´

nest - bird	isidleke	eeseedle´ke´
net (n)	inetha	eene´taa
never	ngeke	nge´ke´
new moon	ethwasa kwenyanga	e´twaasaa kwe´nyaangaa
new year	ethwasa konyaka	e´twaasaa ko´nyaakaa
new	-sha / yintsha	-shaa / yeentshaa
news	izindaba	eezeendaabaa
newspaper	iphephandaba	eepe´paandaabaa
next to	-seceleni kwa	-se´ce´le´nee kwaa
next	-landelayo	-laande´laayo´
nice (taste)	mnandi	mnaandee
nice - looking	-bukekayo	-booke´kaayo´
nickname	isifenqo	eeseefe´nqo´
niece /	umshana /	oomshaanaa /
niece	umshanakazi	oomshaanaakaazee
night	ubusuku	ooboosookoo
nightmare	iphupho elisabisayo	eepoopo´ e´leesaabeesaayo´
night watchman	umantshingelana	oomaantsheenge´laanaa
nipple – animal	umbele	oombe´le´
nipple – human	isibele	eeseebe´le´
no	cha / qha	caa / qaa
no matter what happens	nakanjani	naakaanjaanee
nobody	akukho - muntu	aakooko´- moontoo
noise	umsindo	oomseendo´
none – there is none	akukho	aakooko´
noodles	izibhunge	eezeeboonge´
nor	noma	no´maa
normal	-lunge	-loonge´
nose	ikhala	eekaalaa
not - not so	qhabo	qaabo´
nothing – for nothing	mahala	maahaalaa
nothing / it is nothing	ize / akulutho	eeze´ / aakoolooto´
nothing at all	ngisho ini	ngeesho´ eenee
notice (n) -attention	umnako	oomnaako´
notice (n) - note	isimemezelo	eeseeme´me´ze´lo´
notice - message	imbiko	eembeeko´
notice - at short notice	masishane	maaseeshaane´
notice - until further notice	kuze kwaziswe	kooze´ kwaazeeswe´
notice (v)	naka / bona	naakaa / bo´naa
notify (v)	azisa	aazeesaa
now	manje	maanje´
nuisance	inkathazo	eenkaataazo´
number	inombolo	eeno´mbo´lo´
nun	isistela	eeseeste´laa
nurse (v)	nesa	ne´saa
nurse (n)	unesi	oone´see
nursery - children	ikamelo lezingane	eekaame´lo´ le´zeengaane´
nut (kernel)	inhlamvu	eenhlaamvoo
nut (peanut -n)	intongomane	eento´ngo´maane´
nuts (peanuts)	amantongomane	aamaanto´ngo´maane´

O

obedient	ukulalela	ookoolaale'laa
obey (v)	lalela	laale'laa
object (n)	into	eento'
object (v)	yala	yaalaa
observe (v)	qaphela	qaape'laa
obstacle /	isivimbelo /	eeseeveembe'lo' /
obstacle	isiphazamiso	eeseepaazaameeso'
obstinate	nenkani	ne'nkaanee
obstruct (v)	vimbela / phazamisa	veembe'laa / paazaameesaa
obtain (v)	zuza / thola	zoozaa / to'laa
occasion	umkhosi	oomko'see
occur (v)	vela	ve'laa
ocean	ulwandle	oolwaandle'
offend (v)	cunula / casula	coonoolaa / caasoolaa
offer (n)	isithembiso	eeseete'mbeeso'
offer (v)	thembisa	te'mbeesaa
office	ihhovisi	eeho'veesee
often	kaningi / njalo	kaaneengee / njaalo'
oil	i-oyili	ee- o'yeelee
old	dala	daalaa
omelette	-omilethe	-o'meele'te'
omit (v) / leave	shiya / yega	sheeyaa / ye'gaa
on (the side)	eceleni	e'ce'le'nee
on - on top	phezulu kwa	pe'zooloo kwaa
once	kanye	kaanye'
one	kunye	koonye'
onion - cut up	u-anyanisi oqotshiwe	oo-aanyaaneesee o'qo'tsheewe'
onion	u-anyanisi	oo-aanyaaneesee
only (a)	-dwa / o+dwa	-dwa / o'dwaa
only (adv)	kuphela	koope'laa
onward	phambili	paambeelee
open (v)	vula	voolaa
open	vuliwe	vooleewe'
operate (v -surgery)	hlinza	hleenzaa
operation	ukuhlinza	ookoohleenzaa
opportunity	ithuba	eetoobaa
or	noma	no'maa
orange - fruit	iwolintshi	eewo'leentshee
order (v) clothes etc.	oda izimpahla	o'daa eezeempaahlaa
order (v) instruct	layeza / tshela	laaye'zaa / tshe'laa
ordinary	vamile	vaameele'
organisation	inhlangano	eenhlaangaano'
organize (v)	hlela	hle'laa
ornament	umhlobiso	oomhlo'beeso'
ostrich	intshe	eentshe'
other / others	- nye / enye / abanye	- nye' / e'nye'/ aabaanye'
other - somewhere or other	nakuphi	naakoopee

otherwise (adv) / otherwise	kungenjalo / ngokunye	koonge'njaalo' / ngo'koonye'
our	-ethu	e'too
ours	abethu	aabe'too
ourselves	thina	teenaa
out	phandle	paandle'
outside	ngaphandle	ngaapaandle'
oven	uhhavini	oohaaveenee
over - on other side	phesheya	pe'she'yaa
over (v) - talk over	xoxisana	x'oxeesaanaa
over (v) - fall over	-iwa	-eewaa
over (v) - roll over	gingqa	geengqaa
over (v) - turn over	phenduka	pe'ndookaa
over (v) - take over	welisa	we'leesaa
over (v) - bring over	letha	le'taa
over (v) - jump over	eqa	e'qaa
over (v) - knock / run over	wisa / nyathela	weesaa / nyaate'laa
over (v) - think over	cabanga	caabaangaa
over - over there	laphaya	laapaayaa
over - left over food	sele	se'le'
overall	i-ovaloli	ee-o'vaalo'lee
overflow (v)	chichima	cheecheemaa
overgrown	-enile	e'neele'
overseas	phesheya	pe'she'yaa
overtake (v)	edlula	e'dloolaa
owe (v)	-kweleta	-kwe'le'taa
owl	isikhova	eeseeko'vaa
own - my own / mine	wami / yami / kwami	waamee / yaamee / kwaamee
own - their own	zabo / yabo / wabo	zaabo' / yaabo' / waabo'
own - possess - mine	anayo / ami	aanaayo' / aamee
own - own up to (v)	vuma	voomaa
owner	umnikazi	oomneekaazee

P

pack (v) suitcase	pakisha	paakeeshaa
pack (v) put together	hlanganisa	hlaangaaneesaa
paddock	inkambu	eenkaamboo
padlock	ingidi / iqhaga	eengeedee / eeqaagaa
page	ikhasi	eekaasee
pail (bucket)	ithunga	eetoongaa
pain	ubuhlungu	ooboohloongoo
paint (v)	penda	pe'ndaa
paint	upende	oope'nde'
pale	-mhloshana /	-mhlo'shaanaa /
	phaphathekile	paapaate'keele'
pan	ipani	eepaanee
pancake	panikuku	paaneekookoo
pane (window)	iwindi /	eeweendee /
	ingilazi yefasitela	eengeelaazee ye'faaseete'laa
panic (v)	tatazela	taataaze'laa
pant (v)	hefuzela	he'fooze'laa
pantry	iphandolo	eepaando'lo'
paper towel	ithawula lephepha	eetaawoolaa le'pe'paa
paper	iphepha	eepe'paa
paraffin	uphalafini	oopaalaafeenee
paralyse (v)	thwebula	twe'boolaa
parcel	iphakethe	eepaake'te'
pardon (v)	xolela	xo'le'laa
parent	umzali	oomzaalee
park (n)	ipaki	eepaakee
park (v)	paka	paakaa
parsley	ipasili	eepaaseelee
party	inhlangano	eenhlaangaano'
pass (v)	dlula	dloolaa
passenger	umgibeli	oomgeebe'lee
past (n) - time	isikhathi esidlulileyo	eeseekaatee e'seedlooleele'yo'
past - ago	dlulile	dlooleele'
paste (v) /	namathelisa /	naamaate'leesaa /
paste (v)	namathisela	naamaateese'laa
pastry	uqweqwe lukaphayi	ooqwe'qwe' lookapaayee
pasture /	edlelweni /	e'dle'lwe'nee /
pasture	idlelo	eedle'lo'
pat down (v)	cindezela	ceende'ze'laa
path	indlela	eendle'laa
patience	ukubekezela	ookoobe'ke'ze'laa
patient (a -to be)	bekezela	be'ke'ze'laa
patient (n)	isiguli	eeseegoolee
pawpaw	upopo	oopawpaw / oopo'po'
pay (n)	inkokhelo	eenko'ke'lo'
pay (v)	khokha	ko'kaa
payer	umkhokhi	oomko'kee
payment	inkokhelo	eenko'ke'lo'

pea	uphizi	oopeezee
peace	ukuthula	ookootoolaa
peach	ipetshisi / ipentshisi	eepe'tsheesee / eepe'ntsheesee
peacock	ipigogo	eepeego'go'
peanuts	amantongomane	aamaanto'ngo'maane'
pear	ipheya	eepe'yaa
peel (n)	ikhasi	eekaasee
peel (v)	hluba	hloobaa
peep (v)	lunguza	loongoozaa
peg (n) - wooden nail / plug	isikhonkwane	eeseeko'nkwaane'
peg (v) - fasten	bethela	be'te'laa
peg - clothes peg	iphekisi	eepe'keesee
pen	ipeni	eepe'nee
pencil	ipensela	eepe'nse'laa
penetrate (v)	ngena	nge'naa
penis	umthondo / umphambili	oomto'ndo'/ oompaambeelee
pension	impesheni	eempe'she'nee
people	abantu	aabaantoo
peoples' person	umuntu wabantu	oomoontoo waabaantoo
pepper	upelepele / uphepha	oope'le'pe'le' / oope'paa
perform (v)	enza	e'nzaa
perfume	usende	oose'nde'
perish (v)	bhubha / ifa	boobaa / eefaa
permanent	hlalayo	hlaalaayo'
permission	imvume	eemvoome'
permit (n)	iphomede	eepo'me'de'
permit (v)	vumela	voome'laa
persevere (v)	bekezela	be'ke'ze'laa
person	umuntu	oomoontoo
perspiration	umjuluko	oomjoolooko'
perspire (v)	juluka	joolookaa
persuade (v)	bonisa	bo'neesaa
perturb (v)	ethusa	e'toosaa
pest – a problem	inkathazo	eenkaataazo'
pest - killer	isifo esibulalayo	eeseefo' e'seeboolaalaayo'
pest - thing / person	inkathazo	eenkaataazo'
pester (v)	khathaza	kaataazaa
pet (n)	isilwane sasendlini	eeseelwaane' saase'ndleenee
petrol	uphethroli	oope'tro'lee
petticoat	ipitikoti	eepeeteeko'tee
pharmacist	usokhemisi	ooso'ke'meesee
photograph	isithombe	eeseeto'mbe'
pick (v) - choose	khetha	ke'taa
pick (n) - tool	ipiki	eepeekee
pick (v) - fruit	ikha	eekaa
picnic	ipikiniki	eepeekeeneekee
picture - photo	isithombe	eeseeto'mbe'
picture (n)	umfanekiso	oomfaane'keeso'
pie	uphaya / uphayi	oopaayaa / oopaayee
piece	isiqephu / ucezu	eeseeqe'poo / ooce'zoo

pierce (v)	bhoboza	bo'bo'zaa
pig	ingulube	eengooloobe'
pile (n)	isitaki	eeseetaakee
pile (v)	taka	taakaa
pill	iphilisi	eepeeleesee
pillow	umcamelo	oomcaame'lo'
pin (v) (tie)	bopha ngesipeleti	bo'paa nge'seepe'le'tee
pin - safety pin	isipeleti	eeseepe'le'tee
pinch (v) / steel / nip	ncweba / ncinza	ncwe'baa / nceenzaa
pineapple	uphayinaphu	oopaayeenaapoo
pip	inhlamvu	eenhlaamvoo
pipe - smoking	ipipi	eepeepee
pipe - tube / water	ipayipi	eepaayeepee
pit	umgodi	oomgo'dee
place – of assembly	umkhandlu	oomkaandloo
place – of refuge	inqaba	eenqaabaa
place (n)	indawo	eendaawo'
place (v)	beka / faka / hlalisa	be'kaa / faakaa / hlaaleesaa
place-into (v)	faka	faakaa
place-onto (v)	beka	be'kaa
plan (n)	isu / icebo / iplani	eesoo/ eece'bo' / eeplaanee
plan (v)	klama / songoza	klaamaa / so'ngo'zaa
planet	iplanethi	eeplaane'tee
plank	ipulangwe	eepoolaangwe'
plant (n)	isithombo	eeseeto'mbo'
plant (v)	tshala	tshaalaa
plaster of paris	ukhonkolo	ooko'nko'lo'
plastic	iplastiki	eeplaasteekee
plate	isitsha	eeseetshaa
play (v)	dlala	dlaalaa
plead – a cause (v)	khulumela inhloso	kooloome'laa eenhlo'so'
plead – guilty (v)	vuma icala	voomaa eecaalaa
plead – not guilty (v)	-ngavumi icala	-ngaavoomee eecaalaa
plead (v)	phendula ecaleni	pe'ndoolaa e'caale'nee
pleasant	mnandi / mtoti	mnaandee / mto'tee
please – please may I--	ngicela --	ngeece'laa---
please – wish / choose	thanda / bona	taandaa / bo'naa
please – Yes please!	Yeboke!	Ye'bo'ke'!
please (v)	jabulisa	jaabooleesaa
please don't	musa bo uku ----	moosaa bo' ookoo ----
pleasure	injabulo	eenjaaboolo'
plenty	ningi	neengee
pliers	udlawu / impintshisi	oodlaawoo / eempeentsheesee
plough (v)	lima	leemaa
plough (n)	igeja	eege'jaa
plug (n) (basin)	isivimbo	eeseeveembo'
plug (v)	vimba	veembaa
plum	iplamu	eeplaamoo
plumber	upulamba	oopoolaambaa
poached (egg)	eliphoshiwe	e'leepo'sheewe'

pocket	isikhwama	eeseekwaamaa
point (v) - out	khomba	ko´mbaa
point - tip	isihloko	eeseehlo´ko´
point - of view	umqondo / umbono	oomqo´ndo´/ oombo´no´
poison (snake)	ubuthi	oobootee
poison (v)	bulala ngobuthi	boolaalaa ngo´bootee
poison (v) - infect	faka isihlungu	faakaa eeseehloongoo
poison (n)	isihlungu / ushevu	eeseehloongoo / ooshe´voo
poisonous snake	inyoka enesihlungu	eenyo´kaa e´ne´seehloongoo
poisonous	nobuthi	no´bootee
pole	isigxobo	eeseegxo´bo´
police	iphoyisa	eepo´yeesa
polish (v)	pholisha	po´leeshaa
polish	upholishi	oopo´leeshee
polite	thobekile	to´be´keele´
pool – swimmimg pool	ichibi lokubhukuda	eecheebee lo´koobookoodaa
poor	-mpofu	-mpo´foo
popular	aziwayo	aazeewaayo´
pork	inyama yengulube	eenyaamaa ye´ngooloobe´
porridge	iphalishi	eepaaleeshee
portion	inxenye	eenxe´nye´
position	isimo / isikhundla	eeseemo´ / eeseekoondlaa
post (n)	iposi	eepo´see
post (v)	posa	po´saa
postage stamp	isitembu	eeseete´mboo
postal order	iposoda	eepo´so´daa
postcard	iposikhadi	eepo´seekaadee
postman	umuntu weposi	oomoontoo we´po´see
postoffice	iposi / iposihovisi	eepo´see / eepo´seeho´veesee
pot	ibhodwe	eebo´dwe´
potato	izambane	eezaambaane´
pound (v)	gxoba	gxo´baa
pour (v)	thela	te´laa
power	amandla	aamaandlaa
practical	nokwenzeka	no´kwe´nze´kaa
practise (v)	zijwayeza	zeejwaaye´zaa
praise (v)	bonga	bo´ngaa
praise	ukubonga	ookoobo´ngaa
prawn /	ishebenisi /	eeshe´be´neesee /
prawn	umdambi	oomdaambee
pray (v)	khuleka / thandaza	koole´kaa / taandaazaa
preach (v)	shumayela	shoomaaye´laa
precious	thandekayo	taande´kaayo´
prefer (v)	enyula / khetha	e´nyoolaa / ke´taa
pregnant	khulelwe / nesisu	koole´lwe´ / ne´seesoo
prepare that way (v)	lungisa kanjalo	loongeesaa kaanjaalo´
prepare	lungisa	loongeesaa
present (v)	-pha / ipha	paa / eepaa
present / gift	isiphiwo / isipho	eeseepeewo´ / eeseepo´
preserve (v)	londoloza	lo´ndo´lo´zaa

president	umongameli	oomo'ngaame'lee
press (v)	cindezela	ceende'ze'laa
pressure (water)	umfutho	oomfooto'
pretend	zenzisa	ze'nzeesaa
pretty	-hle / muhle	-hle' / moohle'
prevent (v)	vimbela	veembe'laa
price	intengo	eente'ngo'
prick (v)	bhoboza	bo'bo'zaa
pride	ukuzidla /	ookoozeedlaa /
	ukuziqhenya	ookoozeeqe'nyaa
pride - take pride in	-ziqhenya nga --	-zeeqe'nyaa ngaa---
pride - of lions	iviyo lamabhubesi	eeveeyo' laamaaboobe'see
priest	umphristi / umfundisi	oompreestee/ oomfoondeesee
prime minister	undunankulu	oondoonaankooloo
primitive	asendulo	aase'ndoolo'
prince	inkosana	eenko'saanaa
princess	inkosazana	eenko'saazaana
principal -headmaster /	uthishomkhulu /	ooteesho'mkooloo /
principal - headmaster	uthishanhloko	ooteeshaanhlo'ko'
principle	umthetho	oomte'to'
print (v)	bhala	baalaa
prison	ijele	eeje'le'
prisoner	isiboshwa	eeseebo'shwaa
private (on own) - personal	akhe yedwa	aake' ye'dwaa
private - life	impilo esithekile	eempeelo' e'seete'keele'
private -affairs / secret	-asesifubeni	-aase'seefoobe'nee
private - in private	ngasese	ngaase'se'
private property	akungenwa lapha	aakoonge'nwaa laapaa
prize	klomela	klo'me'laa
problem	inkinga	eenkeengaa
procedure	inqubo	eenqoobo'
proceed (v)	qhubeka	qoobe'kaa
produce (v- eg. fruit)	thela	te'laa
produce (v)	khiqhiza	keeqeezaa
product (eg. fruit)	isithelo	eeseete'lo'
product (n)	umkhiqizo	oomkeeqeezo'
progress (n)	inqubeko	eenqoobe'ko'
progress (v)	qhubeka	qoobe'kaa
promise (v)	thembisa	te'mbeesaa
promise	isithembiso	eeseete'mbeeso'
pronounce (v)	phumisela	poomeese'laa
proof	ubufakazi	ooboofaakaazee
properly	kahle	kaahle'
property (belongings)	impahla	eempaahlaa
propose (v)	songoza	so'ngo'zaa
prosecute (v)	mangalela	maangaale'laa
prosper (v)	chuma	choomaa
protect (v)	vikela	veeke'laa
protest (v)	nqaba	nqaabaa
proud	-zidlayo	-zeedlaayo'

137.

proud of --	-zigqaja nga ---	-zeegqaajaa ngaa---
proudly	ngokuzazi	ngo'koozaazee
prove (v)	bonisa	bo'neesaa
provide (v)	nika	neekaa
prune (v)	nquma	nqoomaa
public (people)	imiphakathi	eemeepaakaatee
public	umphakathi	oompaakaatee
publish	shicilela	sheeceele'laa
pudding bowl	isitsha sikaphudingi	eeseetshaa seekaapoodeengee
pudding	uphudingi	oopoodeengee
pull (v)	donsa	do'nsaa
pump (n)	iphampu	eepaampoo
pump (v)	futha	footaa
pumpkin	ithanga	eetaangaa
punch (v)	shaya isibhakela	shaayaa eeseebaake'laa
puncture (n) - hole	imbobo	eembo'bo'
puncture (v) - make hole	bhobhoza	bo'bo'zaa
puncture (n) - tyre	impontsholo / iliphantsha	eempo'ntsho'lo' / eeleepaantshaa
punish (v)	jezisa	je'zeesaa
punishment	isijeziso	eeseeje'zeeso'
pupil (n- school)	umfundi	oomfoondee
purse	isikhwama semali	eeseekwaamaa se'maalee
pus	ubovu	oobo'voo
push / push aside (v)	sunduza	soondoozaa
put (v)	beka / faka	be'kaa / faakaa
puzzle (n) / secret	indida / imfihlo	eendeedaa / eemfeehlo'
puzzle (toy)	indida	eendeedaa
puzzle (v)	dida	deedaa
puzzle over (v)	dideka	deede'kaa
pyjamas	amaphijama	aamaapeejaamaa
python	inhlwathi	eenhlwaatee

Q

quack - sound	uthi gwee	ootee gwee
quagmire	ubishi	oobeeshee
quake (v)	thuthumela	tootoome'laa
qualification	ilungelo / ukufanela	eeloonge'lo' / ookoofaane'laa
qualified - able to	-nelungelo / -lingene	-ne'loonge'lo' / -leenge'ne'
qualify (v)- what you say	fanelisa	faane'leesaa
qualify (v) - pass	phasela	paase'laa
quality - type	ubunjani	ooboonjaanee
quality - excellence	ubuhle	ooboohle'
quality - how good it is	ikhwalithi	eekwaaleetee
quantity - how much / lots	ubungako / ubuningi	ooboongaako' /oobooneengee
quantity - small amount	ingcosana	eengco'saanaa
quantity - lots of	ubuningi	oobooneengee
quarantine	ukuvalelwa ngenxa yesifo	ookoovaale'lwaa nge'nxaa ye'seefo'
quarrel	ukuxabana	ookooxaabaanaa
quarrel (v)	xabana	xaabaanaa
quarry	inkwali	eenkwaalee
quarter - section	ilikwata	eeleekwaataa
quarter – 1st q. of moon	isilucezu	eeseelooce'zoo
quarter – last q. of moon	isihlephukile	eeseehle'pookeele'
quarter – from every q.	emagumeni onke	e'maagoome'nee o'nke'
quarters – lodgings	indawo yokuhlala	eendaawo' yo'koohlaalaa
quarters – at close q.	eduze impela / ngezifuba	e'dooze' eempe'laa / nge'zeefoobaa
queen	indlovukazi / ukhwini	eendlo'vookaazi / ookweenee
queen ant	uqumbu	ooqoomboo
queer - odd	mangalisayo	maangaaleesaayo'
quench (v- finish thirst)	qeda ukoma	qe'da ooko'maa
query (v)	buza	boozaa
query	umbuzo	oomboozo'
question – It is beyond q.	Kuyiqiniso impela.	Kooyeeqeeneeso' eempe'laa.
question – It is out of the q.	Akunakwenzeka.	Aakoonaakwe'nze'kaa.
question (v)	buza	boozaa
question	umbuzo	oomboozo'
question - it is a q. of---	yindaba ya---	yeendaabaa yaa---
queue	ihele / umugqa	eehe'le' / oomoogqaa
queue up (v)	hlaba ihele	hlaabaa eehe'le'
quick (hurry up)	shesha / sheshisa	she'shaa / she'sheesaa
quick - dishes	ukudla okusheshayo	ookoodlaa o'kooshe'shaayo'
quick - speedy	sheshayo	she'shaayo'
quick - temper	ulaka	oolaakaa
quick - tempered	inhliziyo encane	eenhleezeeyo' e'ncaane'
quick - time, hurry	sheshisa / ngokuphazima	she'sheesaa / ngo'koopaazeemaa
quick - walk	ukunyathela ngokushesha	ookoonyaate'laa ngo'kooshe'shaa
quicken (v)	sheshisa	she'sheesaa
quickly /	ngokushesha /	ngo'kooshe'shaa /

quickly	sheshisa / masinya	she'sheesaa / maaseenyaa
quickness	ukushesha	ookooshe'shaa
quicksand	ulubishi	ooloobeeshee
quiet (n)	ukuthula	ookootoolaa
quiet (v)	thulisa / thula	tooleesaa / toolaa
quiet life	impilo ezothile	eempeelo' e'zo'teele'
quiet	thulile	tooleele'
quiet (v) - keep quiet	thula	toolaa
quieten (v)	thulisa	tooleesaa
quietly	ngokuthula	ngo'kootoolaa
quilt	ikhwilithi	eekweeleetee
quill	usiba	ooseebaa
quill – porcupine q.	inungu	eenoongoo
quit (v)-leave	yeka / shiya	ye'kaa / sheeyaa
quit – work	lahla umsebenzi	laahlaa oomse'be'nzee
quit – go away	muka / yeka	mookaa / ye'kaa
quite – completely	impela	eempe'laa
quiz (v)	buzisisa	boozeeseesaa
quiz	imibuzo	eemeeboozo'
quorom	ikworamu / ikhoramu	ekwo'raamoo / eeko'raamoo
quota	isabelo	eesaabe'lo'
quotation	impinda /	eempeenda /
	okucashuniwe	o'koocaashooneewe'
quotation marks	iziphawulo zemphinda	eezeepaawoolaa ze'mpeendaa
quote (n)	isiphawulo sempinda	eeseepaawoolo' se'mpeendaa
quote (v)	phinda amazwi	peendaa aamaazwee

140.

R

rabbit	unogwaja	oono'gwaajaa
rabid	yisifo sobuhlanya	yeeseefo' so'boohlaanyaa
rabies	isifo esihlanyisa	eeseefo' e'seehlaanyeesaa
race (n-run)	umjaho	oomjaagho'
race (v)	jaha	jaaghaa
racial	ngokwezinhlanga zobuzwe	ngo'kwe'zeenhlaangaa zo'boozwe'
racialism	ubandlululo lobuzwe	oobaandlooloolo' lo'boozwe'
radio	irediyo / umsakazo	eere'deeyo' / oomsaakaazo'
radish	uredishi	oore'deeshee
rag	isidwedwe	eeseedwe'dwe'
rage (n)	ulaka	oolaakaa
rage (v)	dlanga	dlaangaa
ragged – tatters	manikiniki	maaneekeeneekee
raid (v)	hlasela	hlaase'laa
raid (n)	ukuhlasela	ookoohlaase'laa
rail – metal rail	umshayo wensimbi	oomshaayo' we'nseembee
rail – travel by	hamba ngesitimela	haambaa nge'seeteeme'laa
rail (v)	thumela ngesitimela	toome'laa nge'seeteeme'laa
rails – go off r.	phambuka endleleni	paambookaa e'ndle'le'nee
rail (curtain)	umshayo wensimbi	oomshaayo' we'nseembee
railway	umgwaqo wesitimela	oomgwaaqo' we'seeteeme'laa
railway line	ujantshi	oojaantshee
railway station	isiteshi	eeseete'shee
railway works	uloliwe	oolo'leewe'
rain (v) - it is raining	-na / liyana	-naa / leeyaanaa
rain	imvula	eemvoolaa
rainbow	uthingo lwenkosazane	ooteengo' lwe'nko'saazaane'
raincoat	ijazi lemvula	eejaazee le'mvoolaa
raise (v) – lift	phakamisa	paakaameesaa
raise (v) – objection	phikisa	peekeesaa
raise (v) – one's hat	ethula isigqoko	e'toolaa eeseegqo'ko'
raise (v) – increase	khulisa	kooleesaa
raise (v) – voice	phakamisa izwi	paakaameesaa eezwee
raise (v) – wages	khulisa umholo	kooleesaa oomho'lo'
raise (v) – hopes	ethembisa	e'te'mbeesaa
raise (v) – erect	misa	meesaa
raised – upwards	phezulu / phakeme	pe'zooloo / paake'me'
raisin	ireyizini	eere'yeezeenee
rake (v)	hhala	haalaa
ransom	inhlengo	eenhle'ngo'
ransom (v) – pay r.	hlenga	hle'ngaa
rape (v)	dlwengula	dlwe'ngoolaa
rapid	ngejubane	nge'joobaane'
rapidly	ngokushesha	ngo'kooshe'shaa
rare	ngavamile	ngaavaameele'
rarely	ngokuconsa / kancane / ngavamile	ngo'kooco'nsaa / kaancaane' / ngaavaameele'
rash (n)	umqubuko	oomqoobooko'

rat	igundane	eegoondaane'
rat trap	unoxhaka	oono'xaakaa
	wamagundane	waamaagoondaane'
ration	ilesheni	eele'she'nee
rattle (n)	igenqeza	eege'nqe'za
ravage (v)	phanga	paangaa
rave (v)	bheva	be'vaa
raw – food	luhlaza	loohlaazaa
razor	ireza / impuco /	eere'zaa / eempooco'/
	insingo	eenseengo'
reach (v) – arrive at	fika	feekaa
reach (v) – touch	thinta	teentaa
reach top (v)	dundubala	doondoobaalaa
react (v)	buyisa	booyeesaa
reaction	ukuphatheka	ookoopaate'kaa
read (v)	funda	foondaa
ready	lungile	loongeele'
real	liqiniso	leeqeeneeso'
really	ngempela	nge'mpe'laa
reap (v)	vuna	voonaa
rear (a) -behind	ngemuva	nge'moovaa
rear (v) - breed	khulisa / fuya	kooleesaa / fooyaa
reason (n)	isizathu	eeseezaatoo
reason (v)	cabanga	caabaangaa
reasonable	faneleyo	faane'le'yo'
rebel (n)	imbuka	eembookaa
receipt	irisidi	eereeseedee
receive (v)	amukela / thola	aamooke'laa / to'laa
recipe	isu lokupheka	eesoo lo'koope'kaa
recognize (v)	bona	bo'naa
recommend (v)	ncoma / phakamisa	nco'maa / paakaameesaa
record (v)	qopha	qo'paa
record	irekhodi	eere'ko'dee
recover (v)	sinda	seendaa
recovery	ukusinda	ookooseendaa
rectum	umdidi	oomdeedee
red	bomvu	bo'mvoo
reduce (v)	nciphisa	nceepeesaa
reduction	ukuncipha	ookoonceepaa
refer (v)	dlulisela	dlooleese'laa
referee	unompempe	oono'mpe'mpe'
reference	ireferense	eere'fe're'nse'
refrigerator	ifriji	eefreejee
refund (v)	buyisela	booyeese'laa
refuse (n- dirt)	izibi	eezeebee
refuse / rubbish	imfuhlumfuhlu	eemfoohloomfoohloo
refuse (v)	ala	aalaa
regard (v) – view	buka / bheka	bookaa / be'kaa
regard (v) – the law	gcina umthetho	gceenaa oomte'to'
regard (v) – with respect	hlonipha	hlo'neepaa

regard – as r. to	ngalokhu	ngaalo´koo
register (n)	irejista	eere´jeestaa
register (v)	bhalisa	baaleesaa
regret (v)	dabukela / -zisola	daabooke´laa / -zeeso´laa
regulation / regulations	umthetho / imithetho	oomte´to´ / eemeete´to´
rein (n)	itomu	eeto´moo
rein (v) – catch / tighten	bamba / qinisa	baambaa / qeeneesaa
reincarnate	zala futhi	zaalaa footee
rejoice (v)	jabulisa	jaabooleesaa
relation (family)	isihlobo	eeseehlo´bo´
relationship	ubuhlobo	ooboohlo´bo´
relax (v)	phumula	poomoolaa
relaxation	ukuziphumuza	ookoozeepoomoozaa
release (v)	khulula	kooloolaa
release	inkululeko	eenkooloole´ko´
reliable	thembekile	te´mbe´keele´
relief (n) / help	usizo / ukusiza	ooseezo´ / ookooseezaa
relieve (v)	siza	seezaa
religion	inkolo	eenko´lo´
religious	kholiwe	ko´leewe´
rely (v)	themba	te´mbaa
remain (v) / remain behind	hlala / sala	hlaalaa / saalaa
remainder	insalela	eensaale´laa
remains (n) – pl.	izinsalela	eezeensaale´laa
remember (v)	khumbula	koomboolaa
remembrance	isikhumbuzo	eeseekoomboozo´
remind (v)	khumbuza	koomboozaa
remnants	izinsalela	eezeensaale´laa
removal (v) (move)	ukuthutha	ookootootaa
removal (n)	ukususa	ookoosoosaa
remove (v)	susa	soosaa
rent (n)	intela	eente´laa
rent (v) - hire	qasha	qaashaa
repeat (v)	phinda	peendaa
reply (v)	phendula	pe´ndoolaa
report (n)	umbiko	oombeeko´
report (v)	bika	beekaa
reporter	umbiki	oombeekee
represent (v)	mela	me´laa
repulsive	enyanyekayo	e´nyaanye´kaayo´
request (n)	isicelo	eeseece´lo´
request (v)	cela	ce´laa
rescue (n)	ukusindisa	ookooseendeesaa
rescue (v)	sindisa	seendeesaa
research (n)	ukucwaninga	ookoocwaaneengaa
research (v)	cwaninga	cwaaneengaa
resemble (v)	fana na --	faanaa naa ---
reserve (v)	bamba / bekela	baambaa / be´ke´laa
residence	umuzi	oomoozee
resident	ohlezi owakhile	o´hle´zee o´waakeele´

resign (v)	shiya / duba	sheeyaa / doobaa
resign (v) - from work	yekela umsebenzi	ye´ke´laa oomse´be´nzee
resist (v)	zabalaza	zaabaalaazaa
respect (n)	ukuhlonipha	ookoohlo´neepaa
respect (v)	hlonipha	hlo´neepaa
respectable	nesithunzi	ne´seetoonzee
respond (v)	phendula	pe´ndoolaa
responsible	nesibopho	ne´seebo´po´
responsible person	umuntu onegunya	oomoontoo o´ne´goonyaa
responsibility	isibopho / igunya	eeseebo´po´ / eegoonyaa
rest (n)	ukuphumula	ookoopoomoolaa
rest (v)	phumula	poomoolaa
restaurant	indlu yokudlela	eendloo yo´koodle´laa
restless	-yaluzayo / ngenasinqe	-yaaloozaayo´ / nge´naaseenqe´
restrain (v)	khuza / vimbela	koozaa / veembe´laa
restrict	nqanda / vimbela	nqaandaa / veembe´laa
result (v) - follow / from	landela / phuma	laande´laa / poomaa
result (n)	umphumela	oompoome´laa
retire (v) – from work	hoba	ho´baa
return (v) - home	goduka	go´dookaa
return (v) - it to me	buyisela	booyeese´laa
return (v)	phindela	peende´laa
reveal (v) - secret / in open	ambula / beka obala	aamboolaa / be´kaa o´baalaa
revise (v)	bukeza	booke´zaa
reward (v)	klomela	klo´me´laa
reward	umklomelo	oomklo´me´lo´
rheumatism	ikhunkulo	eekoonkoolo´
rhinoceros	ubhejane	oobe´jaanee
rib	ubambo	oobaambo´
ribbon	iribhini	eereebeenee
rice	irayisi	eeraayeesee
rich	nothile / cebile	no´teele´ / ce´beele´
ride (v)	gibela	geebe´laa
ride	ukugibela	ookoogeebe´laa
rifle	isibhamu	eeseebaamoo
right - straight	qondile	qo´ndeele´
right – it is correct (n)	ukulunga / lungile	ookooloongaa / loongeele´
right (n) / right side	ubunene	ooboone´ne´
right - put right	lungisa	loongeesaa
right - quite right	yiqiniso	yeeqeeneeso´
right - that's right	kulungile	kooloongeele´
right - you are right	uqinisile	ooqeeneeseele´
ring (n) / engagement	iringi / indandatho	eereengee / eendaandaato´
ring (v)	khala / shaya / khalisa	kaalaa / shaayaa / kaaleesaa
ring (n) – noise	ukukhala	ookookaalaa
ring (v) – a bell	shaya insimbi	shaayaa eenseembee
ring (v) – phone	shayela ucingo	shaaye´laa ooceengo´
rinse (v) - clothes out	yakaza	yaakaazaa
rinse (v) - out mouth	hlambulula	hlaambooloolaa
riot (n)	isidumo	eeseedoomo´

144.

riot (v)	susa isidumo	soosaa eeseedoomo´
ripe	vuthiwe	vooteewe´
rise - as in dough	ukukhukhumala	ookookookoomaalaa
rise (n) - to get up	ukukhuphuka	ookookoopookaa
rise (v)	khuphuka / khukhumala	koopookaa / kookoomaalaa
risk (n)	ingozi	eengo´zee
river	umfula	oomfoolaa
road	umgwaqo	oomgwaaqo´
roast	osa / thosa	o´saa / to´saa
rob	phanga	paangaa
rock	itshe	eetshe´
rock rabbit	imbila	eembeelaa
rocket /	isiphuphutheki /	eeseepoopoote´kee /
rocket	umkhumbimkhathi	oomkoombeemkaatee
roll (v) - to rotate	gingqika	geengqeekaa
roll (v) – dough	ginqika / bhomboda	geenqeekaa / bo´mbo´daa
roll (v) – about in pain	bhonqa / gungquza	bo´nqaa / goongqoozaa
roll (v) – along / revolve	gingqa	geenqaa
roll (v) – away / down	gelekeqa	ge´le´ke´qaa
roll – on voter's roll	ohlwini lwabavoti	o´hlweenee lwaabaavo´tee
roll up (v) – paper	goqeka / goqa	goqe´kaa / go´qaa
rolling pin	iphini lokugaya	eepeenee lo´koogaayaa
	inhlama / ufulawa	eenhlaamaa / oofoolaawaa
roof	uphahla	oopaahlaa
room	ikamelo	eekaame´lo´
root	impande	eempaande´
rope	indophi / intambo	eendo´pee / eentaambo´
rot (v)	bola	bo´laa
rotten	bolile	bo´leele´
round	yindilinga	yeendeeleengaa
row (v- boat)	gwedla	gwe´dlaa
row (n) - line	uhlu	oohloo
rub (v)	hlikihla	hleekeehlaa
rubber (eraser)	irabha	eeraabaa
rubbish bin	umgqomo wezibi	oomgqo´mo´ we´zeebee
rubbish	izibi	eezeebee
rude - impolite / unrefined	ngahloniphi / luhlaza	ngaahlo´neepee / loohlaazaa
rule (n)	umthetho	oomte´too
rule (v)	busa	boosaa
ruler (king)	umbusi	oomboosee
ruler – draw line with	irula	eeroolaa
rumours	amahemuhemu	aamaahe´moohe´moo
run (v)	gijima	geejeemaa
rural development	ukuthuthukiswa	ookootootookeeswaa
	kwezindawo	kwe´zeendaawo´
	ezisemaphandleni	e´zeese´maapaandle´nee
rural	asemaphandleni	aase´maapaandle´nee
rush out - in anger	dumela	doome´laa
rush (v)	sheshisa	she´sheesaa

S

sack (n)	isaka	eesaakaa
sack (v)	xosha	xo'shaa
sad	dabukile	daabookeele'
sadden (v)	dabukisa	daabookeesaa
saddle	isihlalo sehhashi	eeseehlaalo'se'haashee
sadness	ukudabuka	ookoodaabookaa
safe (a)	londekile / phephile	lo'nde'keele' / pe'peele'
safe (n) - for money	isisefo	eeseese'fo'
safety pin	isipeletu	eeseepe'le'too
safety	ukulondeka	ookoolo'nde'kaa
sail (v)	-ntweza	ntwe'zaa
sail	useyili	oose'yeelee
salad bowl	isitsha sesaladi	eeseetshaa se'saalaadee
salad dressing	umhluzi wesaladi / okokunongisa isaladi	oomhloozee we'saalaadee / o'ko'koono'ngeesaa eesaalaadee
salad	isaladi	eesaalaadee
salary	iholo	eeho'lo'
sale	indali	eendaalee
saliva	amathe	amaate'
salt cellar /	isitsha setswayi /	eeseetshaa se'tswaayee /
salt cellar	isitsha sikasawoti	eeseetshaa seekaasaawo'tee
salt	itswayi / usawoti	eetswaayee / oosaawo'tee
salvation	insindiso	eenseendeeso'
same	fanayo	faanaayo'
samp	isitambu	eeseetaamboo
sample	isampula	eesaampoolaa
sand	isihlabathi	eeseehlaabaatee
sandal /	ingxabulela /	eengxaaboole'la /
sandal -sandal / zulu sandal	isandali / imbadada	eesaandaalee /eembaadaadaa
sandwich	isemishi	eese'meeshee
sane	-sile	-seele'
sarcasm	ukubhuqa / umbhuqo	ookoobooqaa / oombooqo'
sarcastic	bhuqayo	booqaayo'
satchel	ujosaka	oojo'saakaa
satisfy (v)	anelisa	aane'leesaa
Saturday	uMgqibelo	ooMqeebe'lo'
sauce	usoso / umhluzi	ooso'so' / oomhloozee
saucepan	isosipani	eeso'seepaanee
sausage	isositshi	eeso'seetshee
save (v- my soul)	sindisa	seendeesaa
save (v) - rescue / time	sindisa / onga	seendeesaa / o'ngaa
save (v) - money	londoloza	lo'ndo'lo'zaa
savings	imali elondoloziwe	eemaalee e'londo'lo'zeewe'
savour	zwa / i+ zwa	zwaa / eezwaa
savoury	mnandi	mnaandee
saw (n) - for sawing wood	isaha	eesaaghaa
saw (v) - saw wood	saha	saaghaa
saw (v) - see	bonile	bo'neele'

say (v)	-sho / i+sho / - thi / i+thi	-sho´ / eesho ´/-tee / eetee
say (n)	ukusho	ookoosho´
scab	uqweqwe / utwayi	ooqwe´qwe´ / ootwaayee
scale (n) - weight	isikali	eeseekaalee
scar	isibanda	eeseebaandaa
scare (v)	ethusa / esabisa	e´toosaa / e´saabeesaa
scarecrow	umzamaziso / isithuso	oomzaamaazeeso´ / eeseetooso´
scared / wary	ukuxwaya	ookooxwaayaa
scarf	isikhafu	eeseekaafoo
scatter (v)	sakaza	saakaazaa
scene	indawo	eendaawo´
school	isikole	eeseeko´le´
scissors	isikelo	eeseeke´lo´
scold (v)	thethisa	te´teesaa
scoop (v)	-kha / i+kha	-kaa / eekaa
scorch (v)	shisa	sheesaa
scour (v)	khuhla	koohlaa
scrambled egg	iqanda eliphehliwe	eeqaanda e´leepe´hleewe´
scrape (v)	phala	paalaa
scratch (v)	klwebha	klwe´baa
scream (v)	klabalasa	klaabaalaasaa
scream	ukuklabalasa	ookooklaabaalaasa
screw (n)	isikulufo	eeseekooloofo´
scrub (v)	khuhla	koohlaa
scrunchie (hair tie)	igonondo	eego´no´ndo´
sea	ulwandle	oolwaandle´
seal (n) - lid	isivalo	eeseevaalo´
seal (v)	vala	vaalaa
search (v)	ukucinga	ookooceengaa
season (v-food)	nandisa	naandeesaa
seat	isihlalo	eeseehlaalo´
see (v)	bona	bo´naa
seed	imbewu	eembe´woo
seldom	kancane	kaancaane´
self	ubumina	ooboomeenaa
self esteem	ukuzazi	ookoozaazee
self respect	ukuzihlonipha	ookoozeehlo´neepaa
selfishness	ubugovu	ooboogo´voo
selfish	nomhawu	no´mhaawoo
sell (v)	thengisa	te´ngeesaa
send (v)	thuma	toomaa
separate (a)	ahlukene	aahlooke´ne´
serious accident	yingozi	yeengo´zee
serious- genuine / important	qinsile / -nzima	qeenseele´ / -nzeemaa
servant	isisebenzi	eeseese´be´nzee
serve (v) - as in servant	sebenzela	se´be´nze´laa
serve (v) – attend to	nikeza	neeke´zaa
serve (v) – up food	phakela	paake´laa
serve (v) – one's country	sebenzela izwe	se´be´nze´laa eezwe´
serve (v) – be of use	siza	seezaa

147.

service - give service to	ukusebenzela	ookoose´be´nze´laa
service – religious s.	indumiso / ilisonto	eendoomeeso´ / eeleeso´nto´
service – burial s.	inkonzo yokuncwaba	eenko´nzo´ yo´kooncwaabaa
serviette	iseviyethe	eese´veeye´te´
set (v- table)	deka	de´kaa
set	isethi	eese´tee
sew (v)	thunga	toongaa
sewerage pipe	ipayipi lendle	eepaayeepee le´ndle´
sewing machine	umshini wokuthunga	oomsheenee wo´kootoonga
shake (v)	nyakazisa	nyaakaazeesaa
shame (n)	amahloni	aamaahlo´nee
shape (n)	isimo	eeseemo´
shape (v)	fanisa	faaneesaa
share (v) - with each other	cazelana	caaze´laanaa
share - portion	isabelo	eesaabe´lo´
share (v) – out	abela	aabe´laa
share (v) – with	nqamulela	nqaamoole´laa
shark	imfingo / ushaka	eemfeengo´ / ooshaakaa
sharp	bukhali / sikayo	bookaalee / seekaayo´
sharpen (v) – pencil	lola	lo´laa
shave (v)	shefa	she´faa
she / he	yena	ye´naa
sheep	imvu	eemvoo
sheet	ishidi	eesheedee
shelf	ishalofu	eeshaalo´foo
shell (sea)	igobolondo	eego´bo´lo´ndo´
shelter (v) – hide / shelter	bhacisa / fukamela	baaceesaa / fookaame´laa
shelter (n) – protection	isibhaciso / umbhaciso	eeseebaaceeso´/ oombaaceeso´
shield - small / large	isihlangu / ihawu	eeseehlaangoo / eehaawoo
shield (v) – protect	vikela	veeke´laa
shift (v) – move	gudluka	goodlookaa
shift (n) – work	ishifu	eesheefoo
shin - bone	umbala	oombaalaa
shine (v)	khanya / cwebezela	kaanyaa / cwe´be´ze´laa
ship	umkhumbi	oomkoombee
shirt	ihembe / iyembe	eehe´mbe´ / eeye´mbe´
shock (v)	thuka	tookaa
shock (v) – scare	ethusa	e´toosaa
shoe	isicathulo	eeseecaatoolo´
shoelace	intambo yezicathulo	eentaambo´ ye´zeecaatoolo´
shoot (v)	dubula	dooboolaa
shooting	ukudubula	ookoodooboolaa
shop (n)	isitolo	eeseeto´lo´
shop (v)	thenga	te´ngaa
shop keeper	umninisitolo	oomneeneeseeto´lo´
shopper	umthengeli	oomte´nge´lee
shopping	ukuthenga	ookoote´ngaa
shore – coast	ilicala - se ugu	eeleecaalaa - se´ oogoo
shore – on s.	ogwini	o´gweenee
short (height)	fushane	fooshaane´

shorten (v)	fushanisa	fooshaaneesaa
shorts	isikhindi	eeseekeendee
shotgun	ingebe	eenge´be´
shout (v) – call / shout	memeza / bangalasa	me´me´zaa / baangaalaasaa
shove (v)	sunduza	soondoozaa
shovel	ifosholo	eefo´sho´lo´
show (n) - exhibition	umbukiso	oombookeeso´
show (v)	khombisa / bonisa	ko´mbeesaa / bo´neesaa
show (v) – delight	enanela	e´naane´laa
show (v) – enthusiasm	nconcoza	nco´nco´zaa
show (v) – dislike	ngqongqa	ngqo´ngqaa
show up (v)	qhamuka / vela	qaamookaa / ve´laa
shower (v)	shawa	shaawaa
shower	ishawa	eeshaawaa
shred (v)	sika	seekaa
shrink (v)	shwabana	shwaabaanaa
shrivel (v) – up	shwabana	shwaabaanaa
shrub	isihlahlana	eeseehlaanaa
shut eyes (v)	cimeza	ceeme´zaa
shut mouth (v)	vala umlomo	vaalaa oomlo´mo´
shut (v)	vala	vaalaa
shut	valiweyo	vaaleewe´yo´
shy	-namahloni	-naamaahlo´nee
sick	-gulayo	-goolaayo´
sickness	ukugula	ookoogoolaa
side - by the side of --	ecaleni kwa ---	e´caale´nee kwaa ---
side - on this side	nganeno	ngaane´no´
side - on all sides	nxazonke	nxaazo´nke´
side (n) - edge	icala	eecaalaa
side -on the side	eceleni	e´ce´le´nee
sieve	isisefo	eeseese´fo´
sift (v)	sefa	se´faa
sifted	osefiwe	o´se´feewe´
sight (n)	ukubuka	ookoobookaa
sight / view	umbukiso	oombookeeso´
sight-seeing	ukubona izindawo	ookoobo´naa eezeendaawo´
sight-seer	umbukazwe	oombookaazwe´
sign (v)	sayina / bhala	saayeenaa / baalaa
sign -an agreement	sayina	saayeenaa
	isivumelwano	eeseevoome´lwaano´
signature	ukusayina	ookoosaayeenaa
signboard	ipulangwe lezaziso	eepoolaangwe´ le´zaazeeso´
sign-off	phuma ngokukiloga /	poomaa ngo´kookeelo´gaa /
sign off - time to go home!!	shayisa emsebenzini	shaayeesaa e´mse´be´nzeenee
sign-on / join	joyinisa	jo´yeeneesaa
sign - ones name	sayina igama	saayeenaa eegaamaa
silence (v)	thulisa	tooleesaa
silence	ukuthula	ookootoolaa
silent	thulile	tooleele´
silently	ngokuthulile	ngo´kootooleele´

149.

silly person	isiphukuphuku	eeseepookoopookoo
silly – he is a s. person	yisithutha	yeeseetootaa
simple	sobala / lula	so'baala / loolaa
sin (n)	isono	eeso'no'
sin (v)	ona	o'naa
sing (v)	cula / hlabelela	coolaa / hlaabe'le'laa
singer	isiculi / umhlabeleli	eeseecoolee / oomhlaabe'le'lee
sing sweetly	cula kamtoti	coolaa kaamto'tee
single – alone	-dwa	-dwaa
single handed	eyedwa	e'ye'dwaa
single – unit	into eyodwa	eento' e'yo'dwaa
sink (n)	usinki	ooseenkee
sink (v)	shona / cwila	sho'naa / cweelaa
sip (n)	umhabulo	oomhaaboolo'
sip (v)	habula	haaboolaa
sister	udade / usisi	oodaade' / ooseesee
sit (v)	hlala	hlaalaa
sit down	hlala phansi	hlaalaa paansee
sit – leaning back	qhiyama	qeeyaamaa
situation – locality	indawo	eendaawo'
size	ubukhulu	oobookooloo
skeleton	ugebhezi lwamathambo	ooge'be'zee lwaamaataambo'
skill	ubukhali	oobookaalee
skin (n)	isikhumba	eeseekoombaa
skin-of fruit / bark	igxolo	eegxo'lo'
skin-of milk	ungwengwezi	oongwe'ngwe'zee
skinny	ondile	o'ndeele'
skirt	isiketi	eeseeke'tee
sky	isibhakabhaka / ilizulu	eeseebaakaabaakaa / eeleezooloo
sky rocket	irokhethe	eero'ke'te'
slander (v)	hleba	hle'baa
slap (v) – in face	mukula	mookoolaa
slash (v) – gash	gamula	gaamoolaa
slaughter (v)	hlaba	hlaabaa
slave	isigqila	eeseegqeelaa
sleep	ubuthongo	oobooto'ngo'
sleep (v)	lala	laalaa
sleeping	lele	le'le'
sleepy	nobuthongo	no'booto'ngo'
sleeve	umkhono	oomko'no'
slender	-cuthene	-coote'ne'
slice	ucezu	ooce'zoo
slice (v)	qoba	qo'baa
slide (v)	shelela	she'le'laa
slip (v) – fall	shelela	she'le'laa
slope	ukwehla	ookwe'hlaa
slope (v) – down	ehlela	e'hle'laa
slope (v) – up	khuphukela	koopooke'laa
slow – to be s.	ephuza	e'poozaa

slow - as in coming	ephuzile	e'poozeele'
slowly	kancane	kaancaane'
smack (v) – slap	thwaxula / shaya	twaaxoolaa / shaayaa
small	ncane	ncaane'
smell (v)	nuka	nookaa
smell	iphunga	eepoongaa
smelly	nephunga	ne'poongaa
smile (v)	mamatheka	maamaate'kaa
smoke (v)	bhema	be'maa
smoke (n)	intuthu	eentootoo
smooth	-bushelelezi	-booshe'le'le'zee
snail	umnenke	oomne'nke'
snake	inyoka	eenyo'kaa
sneeze (v)	thimula	teemoolaa
sneeze	ukuthimula	ookooteemoolaa
sniff	hela / hogela	he'laa / ho'ge'laa
snore (v)	hona	ho'naa
snore	ukuhona	ookooho'naa
snow (v)	khithika	keeteekaa
snow	iqhwa	eeqwaa
soak (v)	cwilisa	cweeleesaa
soap	insipho	eenseepo'
sober	ngadakiwe	ngaadaakeewe'
sock	isokisi	eeso'keesee
soft	thambile	taambeele'
soften (v)	thambisa	taambeesaa
softly	kancane	kaancaane'
soil / sand	umhlabathi	oomhlaabaatee
soldier	isosha	eeso'shaa
some	obanye / ezinye	o'baanye' / e'zeenye'
somebody	ubani	oobaanee
someone	omunye	o'moonye'
something	into	eento'
sorry – sad	dabukile	daabookeele'
sorry (v) – be s. for	hawukela	haawooke'laa
sorry – I feel s. for him / her.	Ngiyamhawukela.	Ngeeyaamhaawooke'laa.
sort (n)	uhlobo	oohlo'bo'
sort out (v)	khetha	ke'taa
soul	umoya	oomo'yaa
son	indodana	eendo'daanaa
song	iculo / iliculo	eecoolo' / eeleecoolo'
soon	masinyane	maaseenyaane'
soothe (v) calm	duduza	doodoozaa
soothe with muti (v)	pholisa	po'leesaa
sore (n)	isilonda	eeseelo'ndaa
sore	buhlungu	booghloongoo
sound	umsindo	oomseendo'
soup powder	impuphu yesobho	eempoopoo ye'so'bo'
soup	isobho	eeso'bo'
sour	muncu	mooncoo

151.

sow (v -grow)	tshala	tshaalaa
space ship	umkhumbi	oomkoombee
	wasemkhathini	waase'mkaateenee
space-outer space	emkhathini	e'mkaateenee
spade	ifosholo / isipede	eefo'sho'lo'/ eeseepe'de'
spanner	isipanela	eeseepaane'laa
speak (v)	khuluma	kooloomaa
speak briefly	khuluma kafushane	kooloomaa kaafooshaane'
speak - at length	elula inkhulumo	e'loolaa eenkooloomo'
speaker	okhulumayo	o'kooloomaayo'
special	-esipesheli	-e'seepe'she'lee
special - chosen	khethiwe	ke'teewe'
spectacles	izibuko	eezeebooko'
spectator	obukayo / isibukeli	o'bookaayo'/ eeseebooke'lee
speech	ukukhuluma	ookookooloomaa
speech / language	inkulumo	eenkooloomo'
speed (n)	ijubane	eejoobaane'
speed up (v)	sheshisa	she'sheesaa
spell (v)	pela	pe'laa
spend (v)	chitha / khokha	cheetaa / ko'kaa
spice	isipayisi /	eeseepaayeesee /
	isinandiso	eeseenaandeeso'
spice (v)	nandisa	naandeesaa
spider	ulwembu /	oolwe'mboo /
	isicabucabu	eeseecaaboocaaboo
spider's web	ubulwembu	ooboolwe'mboo
spill (v)	chitha	ceetaa
spin (v)	shwila	shweelaa
spin (v) – a coin	pininiza uhlamvu	peeneeneezaa oohlaamvoo
	lwemali	lwe'maalee
spit (v)	khafula	kaafoolaa
sponge	isipanji	eeseepaanjee
spoon	ukhezo / isipunu	ooke'zo'/ eeseepoonoo
sport	umdlalo	oomdlaalo'
sporting chance	ilithutshana	eeleetootshaanaa
sport - she is a good sport	unhliziyonhle	oonhleezeeyo'nhle'
sportsman	umdlali	oomdlaalee
sportsmanship	ubudlaba	ooboodlaabaa
spot	ibala	eebaalaa
spray (n) liquid	umfafazo	oomfaafaazo'
spray (v)	fafaza	faafaazaa
spread (v) jam	gcoba	gco'baa
spring (v)	-eqa	-e'qaa
sprinkle (v)	fafaza	faafaazaa
sprinkler	isifafazo	eeseefaafaazo'
sprout (v)	hluma	hloomaa
spy (v)	hlola	hlo'laa
squash (n)	isikwashi	eeseekwaashee
squash (v)	pitshiza	peetsheezaa
squat (v)	qoshama	qo'shaamaa

squatter camp	umjondolo	oomjo´ndo´lo´
squeeze (v)	cindezela	ceende´ze´laa
stab (v)	hlaba / gwaza	hlaabaa / gwaazaa
stable (horse)	isitebele	eeseete´be´le´
stain (v)	faka umbala	faakaa oombaalaa
stain (n)	ibala	eebaalaa
stairs	isitezi	eeseete´zee
stale	duvile / dala	dooveele´ / daalaa
stamp (n)	isitembu	eeseete´mboo
stand (v)	-ma / ima	-maa / eemaa
star (sky)	inkanyezi	eenkaanye´zee
starch	isitashi	eeseetaashee
stare (v)	gqolozela	gqo´lo´ze´laa
start (v)	qala	qaalaa
start – at the s.	ekuqaleni	e´kooqaale´nee
starve (v)	lamba	laambaa
station	isiteshi	eeseete´shee
stationery (n)	izincwadi zokubhala	eezeencwaadee zo´koobaalaa
stay (v)	hlala	hlaalaa
stay at home (n)	umhlalakhaya	oomhlaalaakaayaa
stay behind (v)	sala	saalaa
stay with	hlala na---	hlaalaa naa---
steak	isiteki	eeseete´kee
steal (v)	-eba / yeba / ntshontsha	e´baa / ye´baa / ntsho´ntshaa
steam	isitimu	eeseeteemoo
step (v)	hamba	haambaa
step child	umntwana wokutholwa	oomtwaanaa wo´kooto´lwaa
stepladder	isitebhisi	eeseete´beesee
stew (n)	isitshulu	eeseetshooloo
stick (v)	namathela	naamaate´laa
stick	induku	eendookoo
stiff	lukhuni	lookoonee
sting (v)	tinyela / hlaba	teenye´laa / hlaabaa
stink	iphunga elibi	eepoongaa e´leebee
stir (v) - food	bonda	bo´ndaa
stir till thick	govusa kuze kushube	go´voosaa kooze´ kooshoobe´
stitch (v)	thunga	toongaa
stockings	amasokisi amade	amaaso´keesee aamaade´
stomach	isisu	eeseesoo
stone	itshe / ilitshe	eetshe´ / eeleetshe´
stop (v)	vimba	veembaa
store (n)	isitolo	eeseeto´lo´
store (v)	beka	be´kaa
storm (n)	isivunguvungu	eeseevoongoovoongoo
story	indaba	eendaabaa
stove	isitofu	eeseeto´foo
straight	qondile	qo´ndeele´
straighten (v)	qondisa	qo´ndeesaa
strange – odd	mangalisayo	maangaaleesaayo´
stranger	isihambi	eeseehaambee

strangle (v)	klikliza / klinya	kleekleezaa / kleenyaa
strawberry	istrobheri	eestro'be'ree
stray (v)	eduka	e'dookaa
street	isitaladi	eeseetaalaadee
strength	amandla	amaandlaa
stress (v)	qinisa	qeeneesaa
strict	qinile	qeeneele'
strict discipline	ukuphathwa	ookoopaatwaa
	ngokuqinile	ngo'kooqeeneele'
strictly	ngokuqinile	ngokooqeeneele'
strike (v) – hit	shaya	shaayaa
strike (n) - from work	isiteleka	eeseete'le'kaa
strike - go on strike	shaya umduvo	shaayaa oomdoovo'
strike (v)	teleka	te'le'kaa
string	intambo	eentaambo'
stubborn	nenkani	ne'nkaanee
student /	umfundi /	oomfoondee /
student	isitshudeni	eeseetshoode'nee
study (v)	funda	foondaa
stupid person	isiphukuphuku	eeseepookoopookoo
stupid - person	-yisithutha	-yeeseetootaa
stupid - he / she is	-nobuthutha	-no'bootootaa
stupidity	ubuthutha	oobootootaa
submarine	umkhumbi ohamba	oomkoombee o'haambaa
	ngaphansi kwamanzi	ngaapaansee kwaamaanzee
subtract (v)	susa	soosaa
succeed (v)	phumelela	poome'le'laa
success	impumelelo	eempoome'le'lo'
suck (v)	munca / munya	mooncaa / moonyaa
sudden /	masinya /	maaseenyaa /
sudden	sheshayo	she'shaayo'
sue (v)	mangala	maangaalaa
suffer (v)	hlupheka	hloope'kaa
sugar cane	umoba	oomo'baa
sugar	ushukela	ooshooke'laa
suicide	ukuzibulala	ookoozeeboolaala
suit (n)	isudi	eesoodee
suitcase /	isuthikesi /	eesooteeke'see
suitcase	ipotimende	eepo'teeme'nde'
sulk (v)	khunsa / qumba	koonsaa / qoombaa
summer	ihlobo	eehlo'bo'
summon	biza	beezaa
sun	ilanga	eelaangaa
sunbeam	umsebe welanga	oomse'be' we'laangaa
sunburnt	-shiswe yilanga	-sheeswe' yeelaangaa
Sunday	iSonto	eeSo'nto'
sunglasses	izibuko zelanga	eezeebooko' ze'laangaa
suntan (v)	thamela	taame'laa
suntan (n)	ukushiswa yilanga	ookoosheeswaa yeelaangaa
supper	isapha	eesaapaa

supply (v)	nika	neekaa
support (v)	sekela	se'ke'laa
suppose	cabanga	caabaangaa
sure	qinisekile	qeeneese'keele'
surgery	ukuhlinzwa	ookoohleenzwaa
surname	isibongo	eeseebo'ngo'
surprise (n)	isimangaliso	eeseemaangaaleeso'
surprise (v)	mangalisa	maangaaleesaa
surrender (v)	thela	te'laa
surround	zungeza	zoonge'zaa
suspect (v)	sola	so'laa
swallow (v)	gwinya	gweenyaa
swallow (n)	ukugwinya	ookoogweenyaa
swarm (n) - of bees	ibololwane	eebo'lo'lwaane'
swarm (v) bees	phithiza	peeteezaa
swear (v)	thuka / funga	tookaa / foongaa
sweat (v)	juluka	joolookaa
sweep	shanela	shaane'laa
sweet (a)	-mtoti	-mto'tee
sweet potato	ubhatata	oobaataataa
sweet	iswidi	eesweedee
swell (v)	vuvuka	voovookaa
swim (v)	bhukuda	bookoodaa
swimming pool /	ichibi lokuhlamba /	eecheebee lo'koohlaambaa
swimming pool	ichibi lokubhukuda	eecheebee lo'koobookoodaa
switch (v)	shintsha	sheentshaa
switch	iswishi	eesweeshee
sympathetic	-zwelayo	-zwe'laayo'
sympathetic person	umboneleli	oombo'ne'le'lee
sympathy	uzwelo / isihawu	oozwe'lo'/ eeseehaawoo
symptom	isibonakaliso /	eeseebo'naakaaleeso'/
	uphawu	oopaawoo
syphilis	ugcunsula	oogcoonsoolaa
syringe	isirinji	eeseereenjee
system	ihlelo / uhlelo	eehle'lo' / oohle'lo'

T

table	itafula	eetaafoolaa
table - set the table	deka itafula	de'kaa eetaafoolaa
table - clear the table	susa izitsha etafuleni	soosaa eezeetsha e'taafoole'nee
tablecloth	indwangu yetafula	eendwaangoo ye'taafoolaa
tablespoon	isipunu esikhulu	eeseepoonoo e'seekooloo
tablet	iphilisi	eepeeleesee
tackle (v)	qala	qaalaa
tadpole	ushobishobi	oosho'beesho'bee
tail	umsila	oomseelaa
tailor	umthungi	oomtoongee
take (v)	thatha	taataa
take care (v)	qaphela	qaape'laa
take out	khipha	keepaa
talent / gift	isiphiwo	eeseepeewo'
talk (v)	khuluma	kooloomaa
talkative person	isibhavubhavu	eeseebaavoobaavoo
tall	-de / mu+de	-de' / moode'
tame (a)	-fuyiwe / thambile	-fooyeewe' / taambeele'
tame (v)	thambisa	taambeesaa
tank	ithangi	eetaangee
tap	umpompi	oompo'mpee
tape	ithepu	eete'poo
tape measure	ithephu	eete'poo
tapeworm	ingcili	eengceelee
tar	itiyela	eeteeye'laa
tart - savoury	ikhekhe lephesteri	eeke'ke' le'pe'ste'ree
tart	ikhekhe	eeke'ke'
task	umsebenzi	oomse'be'nzee
taste (v)	-zwa / i+zwa	-zwaa / eezwaa
tasteless	-duma	-doomaa
tattoo (v)	chaza	caazaa
tattoo	umchazo	oomcaazo'
tax	intela	eente'laa
tax (v)	thelisa	te'leesaa
taxi	ithekisi	eete'keesee
tea	itiye	eeteeye'
teach (v)	fundisa	foondeesaa
teacher	uthisha	ooteeshaa
team	ithimu	eeteemoo
teapot	ithiphothi	eeteepo'tee
tear (v) rip / tear open	dabula / qaqabula	daaboolaa / qaaqaaboolaa
tear – tear in cloth	ukudabuka	ookoodaabookaa
teardrop	unyembezi	oonye'mbe'zee
tears (cry)	izinyembezi	eezeenye'mbe'zee
tease (v) /	gcona / sukela /	gco'naa / sooke'laa /
tease (v)	chukuluza	cookooloozaa
teaspoon	ithisiphuni	eeteeseepoonee
teat (nipple)	ibele	eebe'le'

156.

teeth	amazinyo	aamaazeenyo´
telephone	ithelefoni / ucingo	eete´le´fo´nee / ooceengo´
television	ithelevishini	eete´le´veesheenee
tell (v)	tshela	tshe´laa
temper	ulaka	oolaakaa
temperature	izinga lokushisa	eezeengaa lo´koosheesaa
tenant	umqashi	oomqaashee
tender - soft	thambile	taambeele´
tent	itende / ithende	eete´nde´
tepid	fudumele	foodoome´le´
terrible	esabekayo	e´saabe´kaayo´
terrify (v)	ethusa	e´toosaa
terror	ukwesabisa	ookwe´saabeesaa
terrorist	iphekulazikhuni /	eepe´koolaazeekoonee /
	umthothongi	oomto´to´ngee
terrorize (v)	thothonga	to´to´ngaa
test (n) /	isivivinyo /	eeseeveeveenyo´ /
test (n) - exam	ukuhlolwa	ookoohlo´lwaa
test (v)	hlola	hlo´laa
thank	bonga	bo´ngaa
thanks (n)	ukubonga	ookoobo´ngaa
thanksgiving	ukubonga	ookoobo´ngaa
that - so that	ukuze	ookooze´
that	lokho / lokhuya	lo´ko´ / lo´kooyaa
thatch (v)	fulela	foole´laa
thatch (n)	utshani wokufulela	ootshaanee wo´koofoole´laa
theatre - operating	ithiyetha	eeteeye´taa
their	. . .bo / labo / abo	. . .bo´ / laabo´ / aabo´
theirs	okwabo / awabo	o´kwaabo´ / aawaabo´
them	bona	bo´naa
then (time)	ngesikhathi	nge´seekaatee
there	lapho	laapo´
they	bona	bo´naa
thick & smooth	shelelezi	she´le´le´zee
thick (as in gravy)	shubile	shoobeele´
thick - layer	nohlonze	no´hlo´nze´
thicken (v)	enza kubeluhlonzi /	e´nzaa koobe´loohlo´nzee /
	shubisa	shoobeesaa
thief	isela	eese´laa
thin (figure)	zacile	zaaceele´
thin (watery)	ube manzi	oobe´ maanzee
thing	into	eento´
think (v)	cabanga	caabaangaa
thirst	ukoma	ooko´maa
thirsty	omile	o´meele´
this	lokhu	lo´koo
thorn	iva	eevaa
those	lezo / labo / abo	le´zo´ / laabo´ / aabo´
though	nokho	no´ko´
thread – wool / cotton	uhala / ukotini	oohaalaa / ooko´teenee

threat	usongo	ooso'ngo'
threat (v)	songa	so'ngaa
threaten (v)	songela	so'nge'laa
throat	umphimbo	oompeembo'
throb (v)	qaqamba / futha	qaaqaambaa / footaa
throne	isihlalo sobukhosi	eeseehlaalo' so'booko'see
throttle (v)	khama	kaamaa
throw	phonsa	po'nsaa
thumb	isithupha	eeseetoopaa
thunder (v)	duma	doomaa
thunder	ukuduma	ookoodoomaa
Thursday	uLwesine	ooLwe'seene'
tick (on a dog)	umkhaza	oomkaazaa
ticket	ithikithi	eeteekeetee
tidily	-ngobunono	-ngo'boono'no'
tidy (n)	-lungisiwe / -nobunono	-loongeeseewe' / no'boono'no'
tidy (v)	lungisa / hlanza	loongeesaa / hlaanzaa
tidy person	inono	eeno'no'
tie (n)	uthayi	ootaayee
tie (v)	bopha	bo'paa
tight	qinile	qeeneele'
tighten (v)	qinisa	qeeneesaa
time	isikhathi	eeseekaatee
tin	ithini	eeteenee
tin opener	isivulithini	eeseevooleeteenee
tinned food	ukudla kwasethinini	ookoodla kwaase'teeneenee
tire (v)	khathala	kaataalaa
tired	khathele	kaate'le'
tissue - paper	ithishu	eeteeshoo
title	ibizo	eebeezo'
to come out - oven / house	kuphuma	koopoomaa
to - direction / go to	ku.. / uku.. / e.. / kwa ..	koo.. / ookoo.. / e'.. / kwaa ..
toad	isele	eese'le'
toast (n)	ithosi	eeto'see
toaster	ithosta	eeto'staa
tobacco	ugwayi	oogwaayee
today	namuhla / namhlanje	naamoohlaa / naamhlaanje'
toddler	ingane encane	eengaane' e'ncaane'
toe	uzwani	oozwaanee
together	hlangene / ndawonye	hlaange'ne' / ndaawo'nye'
toilet paper	iphepha lasethoyilethe	eepe'paa laase'to'yeele'te'
toilet	ithoyilethe	eeto'yeele'te'
toll free number	inamba yamahala	eenaambaa yaamaahaala
tomato	utamatisi	ootaamaateesee
tombstone	itshe lesikhumbuzo	eetshe' le'seekoomboozo'
tomorrow	kusasa	koosaasaa
tongue	ulimi	ooleemee
too much	ningi / kakhulu	neengee / kaakooloo
too - also	futhi	footee
tooth	izinyo	eezeenyo'

toothache	ubuhlungu bezinyo	ooboohloongoo be´zeenyo´
toothpaste	umuthi wamazinyo	oomootee waamaazeenyo´
topic (n)	indaba / ingxoxo	eendaabaa / eenxo´xo´
torch	ithoshi	eeto´shee
tornado	isiphepho	eeseepe´po´
total (n)	isamba	eesaambaa
touch (v)	thinta	teentaa
tough	lukhuni	lookoonee
tour (v)	hamba	haambaa
tourist	isihambi	eeseehaambee
tow (v)	donsa	do´nsaa
towel	ithawula	eetaawoolaa
town	idolobha	eedo´lo´baa
toy	ithoyizi	eeto´yeezee
track (v)	landela umkhondo	laande´laa oomko´ndo´
tracksuit	itrekisudi	eetre´keesoodee
tractor	ugandaganda	oogaandaagaandaa
trade (v)	hweba	hwe´baa
trade union	inyunyana yezisebenzi	eenyoonyaanaa ye´zeese´be´nzee
traffic	itrafiki	eetraafeekee
traffic lights / robot	irobhoti	eero´bo´tee
train (v)	fundisa / qeqesha	foondeesaa / qe´qe´shaa
train – choof choof (n)	isitimela	eeseeteeme´laa
trainer (n)	umqeqeshi	oomqe´qe´shee
translate (v)	humusha	hoomooshaa
trap - snare (n)	isithiyo	eeseeteeyo´
trap (v)	thiya	teeyaa
trap (v) - set a trap	cupha	coopaa
trap (n) - police trap	umcuphi	oomcoopee
travel (v)	hamba	haambaa
tray	ithreyi	eetre´yee
tread (v)	nyathela	nyaate´laa
tread	ukunyathela	ookoonyaate´laa
treason	ukwambuka	ookwaambookaa
treasure	igugu	eegoogoo
treasure (v)	londoloza	lo´ndo´lo´zaa
treat – badly (v)	phatha kabi	paataa kaabee
treat – give a treat (v)	jabulisa	jaabooleesaa
treat – kindly (v)	phatha kahle	paataa kaahle´
treat – medically (v)	elapha	e´laapaa
treatment – medically	ukwelapha	ookwe´laapaa
treatment	impatho	eempaato´
tree	umuthi / isihlahla	oomootee / eeseehlaahlaa
tremendous - huge	khulu kakhulu	kooloo kaakooloo
tremor – earthquake	ukudikizela komhlaba	ookoodeekeeze´laa ko´mhlaabaa
trepidation	umxwayo	oomxwaayo´
trespass (v) / break in	eqa umthetho / fohla	e´qaa oomte´to´ / fo´hlaa
tribal	esizwe	e´seezwe´
tribal name	isibongo	eeseebo´ngo´
tribesman	owesizwana	o´we´seezwaanaa

tribute (n)	ukuthela	ookoote'laa
tribute (v) – pay to	bonga	bo'ngaa
tribute (v) - pay	thela	te'laa
trick (n)	impamba / icebo	eempaambaa / eece'bo'
trick (v)	phamba / yenga	paambaa / ye'ngaa
trick (v) - play---on	khohlisa	kho'hleesaa
trim (v)	nquma	nqoomaa
trip (v) - stumble	khubeka / guzuka	koobe'kaa / goozookaa
trip (v) - fall	khubeka / khuba	koobe'kaa / koobaa
trip - journey	uhambo	oohaambo'
tripe (n) - insides	amathumba	aamaatoombaa
triumph (n)	ukwahlula	ookwaahloolaa
triumph (v)	ahlula / nqoba	aahloolaa / nqo'baa
triumphant	nqobile	nqo'beele'
trolley	ingolovane	eengo'lo'vaane'
troop (n)	isigaba	eeseegaabaa
troop (v)	futhuzela / viva	footooze'laa / veevaa
troop the colours (v)	bonga ifulegi lebutho	bo'ngaa eefoole'gee le'booto'
troop - animals	umhlambi	oomhlaambee
troop - soldiers	ibutho	eebooto'
trot (v)	qhuba / dlela	qoobaa / dle'laa
trouble (v)	khathaza	kaataazaa
trouble	inkathazo / hlupha	eenkaataazo' / hloopaa
trousers	ibhulukwe	eeboolookwe'
truck	iloli / ithrogo / itilogo	eelo'lee / eetro'go' / eeto'lo'go'
true	qinisile	qeeneeseele'
trustworthy	thembekile	te'mbe'keele'
truth	iqiniso	eeqeeneeso'
try (v)	zama	zaamaa
Tuesday	uLwesibili	ooLwe'seebeelee
turkey	ikalikuni / igalukuni	eekaaleekoonee / eegaalookoonee
turn (n)	ithuba	eetoobaa
turn (v)	jika	jeekaa
turnip	utheniphu	oote'neepoo
type (a) - kind	uhlobo	oohlo'bo'
typhoon	ithayifunu	eetaayeefoonoo
tyre	ithaya	eetaayaa

U

udder	umbele	oombe´le´
ugly	-bi / mubi	-bee / moobee
umbrella	isambulela	eesaamboole´laa
un -	nga -	ngaa -
unaware	nganaki	ngaanaakee
uncertain / to be ..	ngaqondi / ngabaza	ngaaqo´ndee / ngaabaazaa
uncivilised	luhlaza	loohlaazaa
uncle	umalume	oomaaloome´
unclean	ngcolile	ngco´leele´
uncomfortable	nganethezekile	ngaane´te´ze´keele´
unconscious	qulekile	qoole´keele´
uncooked	luhlaza	loohlaazaa
undamaged	ngalimalanga	ngaaleemaalaangaa
under	phansi	paansee
under water	phansi kwamanzi	paansee kwaamaanzee
understand	qonda / zwa	qo´ndaa / zwaa
undo	qaqa	qaaqaa
undress	khumula	koomoolaa
uneasy	novalo	no´vaalo´
uneducated	ngafundile	ngaafoondeele´
unemployed /	ngenamsebenzi /	nge´naamse´be´nzee /
unemployed	ngasebenzi	ngaase´be´nzee
uneven - odd	-ngalingene	-ngaaleenge´ne´
uneven - not straight	akuqondile	aakooqo´ndeele´
unexpected /	zumayo /	zoomaayo´ /
unexpected	ngalindelekile	ngaaleende´le´keele´
unfit	ngalungile	ngaaloongeele´
unfortunately – bad luck	ngebhadi / ngeshwa	nge´baadee / nge´shwaa
unfortunately	ngelishwa	nge´leeshwaa
unfurnished	ngenayo ifenisha	nge´naayo´ eefe´neeshaa
ungrateful	ngabongi	ngaabo´ngee
unhappy – sad, tired	khathazekile	kaataaze´keele´
unhappy / worried	hluphekile	hloope´keele´
unhealthy	ngaphilile	ngaapeeleele´
uniform	inyufomu	eenyoofo´moo
union	inyunyana	eenyoonyaanaa
university	iyunivesithi	eeyooneeve´seetee
unkind	ngenamusa	nge´naamoosaa
unload	ethula	e´toolaa
unlucky	nebhadi	ne´baadee
unmarried /	ngaganile /	ngaagaaneele´ /
unmarried	ngashadile	ngaashaadeele´
unsafe	nengozi	ne´ngo´zee
untidy - dirty	ngcolile	ngco´leele´
untidy	mahlikihliki	maahleekeehleekee
untidy person	inuku	eenookoo
until	kuze ku ---	kooze´ koo ---
unusual / rare	-ngavamile	-ngaavaameele´

161.

unwilling	ngathandi	ngaataandee
up	phezulu	pe'zooloo
upset - hurt	thunukala / thunukele	toonookaalaa / toonooke'le'
upset (a)	phatheka kabi	paate'kaa kaabee
upset (v)	phatha kabi	paataa kaabee
upset (v) fall / spill	wisa / chitha	weesaa / ceetaa
upset (v)	thunukalisa	toonookaaleesaa
urge (v) / urge on	gqugquzela / qhuba	gqoogqooze'laa / qoobaa
urge (v)	ukuphokophela	ookoopo'ko'pe'laa
urge (n)	impisekelo /	eempeese'ke'lo'/
	impokophelo	eempo'ko'pe'lo'
urgent	phuthumayo	pootoomaayo'
urinate (v)	chama	caamaa
urine (n)	umchamo	oomcaamo'
us	thina	teenaa
use (n)	umsebenzi	oomse'be'nzee
use (v)	sebenzisa	se'be'nzeesaa
useful	nomsebenzi	no'mse'be'nzee
useless	-ngasizi /	-ngaaseezee /
	-ngenamsebenzi	-nge'naamse'be'nzee

V

vacancy	isikhala somsebenzi	eeseekaalaa so´mse´be´nzee
vacant	ngenalutho	nge´naalooto´
vacate (v)	thutha / phuma	tootaa / poomaa
vagina	imomozi	eemo´mo´zee
valuable	nenani eliphakeme	ne´naanee e´leepaake´me´
vary (v)	kushiyana	koosheeyaanaa
vase	ivazi	eevaazee
vegetable (greens)	amaveji / uhlaza	aamaave´jee / oohlaazaa
vein	umthambo	oomtaambo´
veld / open field	inkangala	eenkaangaalaa
veld	indle	eendle´
very	kakhulu	kaakooloo
vest	ivesti	eeve´stee
victim	umkhohlisi	oomko´hleesee
victimize (v)	hlupha / khohlisa	hloopaa / ko´hleesaa
video recorder	ividiyo	eeveedeeyo´
village	idolobhana	eedo´lo´baanaa
vinegar	uvinika	ooveeneekaa
vineyard	isivini	eeseeveenee
violence - rage	isidlakadla / udlame	eeseedlaakaadlaa / oodlaame´
violence – riot	udlame	oodlaame´
violin	ivayolini	eevaayo´leenee
virgin	intombi emsulwa	eento´mbee e´msoolwaa
visa	imvume yokungena ezweni	eemvoome´ yo´koonge´naa e´zwe´nee
visible (v)	bonakala	bo´naakaalaa
vision – ghost	umbono	oombo´no´
vision – sight	ukubona	ookoobo´naa
visit (n) /	ukuvakashela /	ookoovaakaashe´laa /
visit	ukuvakasha	ookoovaakaashaa
visit (v)	vakashela	vaakaashe´laa
visitor	isivakashi	eeseevaakaashee
vocabulary	amagama olimi	aamaagaamaa o´leemee
vocalist	umhlabeleli	oomhlaabe´le´lee
voice	izwi / ukukhuluma	eezwee / ookookooloomaa
volcano	intabamlilo	eentaabaamleelo´
volcanic eruption (v)	ukuqhuma kwentaba yomlilo	ookooqoomaa kwe´ntaabaa yo´mleelo´
volunteer (v)	volontiya	vo´lo´nteeyaa
volunteer	umuntu ozenzelayo	oomoontoo o´ze´nze´laayo´
vomit (v)	hlanza	hlaanzaa
vote (v)	vota	vo´taa
vouch (v)	qinisa / fakazela	qeeneesaa / faakaaze´laa
voucher	incwadi yokufakaza	eencwaadee yo´koofaakaazaa
vow	isithembiso	eeseete´mbeeso´
vow (v)	thembisa / funga	te´mbeesaa / foongaa
voyage	uhambo	oohaambo´

W

wage	iholo	eeho'lo'
wagon	inqola	eenqo'laa
wail (v)	khala	kaalaa
waist	ukhalo	ookaalo'
wait (v)	linda	leendaa
waiter	uweta	oowe'taa
wake (v)	phaphama / vuka	paapaamaa / vookaa
walk	ukuhamba	ookoohaambaa
walk (v)	hamba	haambaa
walk (v) - go for---	elula imilenze	e'loolaa eemeele'nze'
wall	udonga	oodo'ngaa
wallet	iwalethe	eewaale'te'
wander (v)	zula	zoolaa
want (v) – need	funa	foonaa
ward (hospital)	igumbi / iwodi	eegoombee / eewo'dee
ward - labour	igumbi lokubelethela	eegoombee lo'koobe'le'te'laa
warm	fudumele	foodoome'le'
warm (v) - warm up	fudumeza	foodoome'zaa
warn (v)	qaphisa / xwayisa	qaapeesaa / xwaayeesaa
warning /	isiqapheliso /	eeseeqaape'leeso' /
warning	isexwayiso	eese'xwaayeeso'
wash (v)	geza	ge'zaa
washing (n)	izingubo zokugezwa	eezeengooboo zo'kooge'zwaa
wasp	umnyovu	oomnyo'voo
waste (v) – squander	chitha	ceetaa
waste (v) – money	-ntamuza imali /	-ntaamoozaa eemaalee /
	chitha imali	ceetaa eemaalee
waste (v) – time	chitha isikhathi	ceetaa eeseekaatee
waste away (v)	bunda	boondaa
waste (n) - rubbish	izibi	eezeebee
waste (v) - to throw away	lahla	laahlaa
waster	umchithi	oomceetee
watch (n)	iwashi	eewaashee
watch (v)	bheka / buka / bukela	be'kaa / bookaa / booke'laa
water	amanzi	aamaanzee
water (v)	manzisa / chelela	maanzeesaa / che'le'laa
water rat	ilidwele	eeleedwe'le'
watermellon	ikhabe	eekaabe'
waterfall	imphophoma	eempo'po'maa
water consumption	amanzi asebenzile	aamaanzee aase'be'nzeele'
water pump – hand held	isigwedlo	eeseegwe'dlo'
wave (sea)	igagasi	eegaagaasee
wave – bye (v)	valelisa ngesandle	vaale'leesaa nge'saandlaa
way	indlela	eendle'laa
we	thina	teenaa
weak (fragile)	ngenamandla	nge'naamaandlaa
wealth	umnotho / ingcebo	oomno'to' / eengce'bo'
wear (v) - clothes	gqoka	gqo'kaa

weariness	ukukhathala	ookookaataalaa
weary	khathele	kaate´le´
weather	izulu / isimo sezulu	eezooloo / eeseemo´ se´zooloo
wed (v)	shada	shaadaa
wedding	umshado	oomshaado´
Wednesday	uLwesithathu	ooLwe´seetaatoo
weed	ukhula	ookoolaa
weed (v)	hlakula	hlaakoolaa
week	iviki / isonto	eeveekee / eeso´nto´
weekend	impelasonto	eempe´laaso´nto´
weekly	ngeviki / ngesonto	nge´veekee / nge´so´nto´
weep (v)	khala	kaalaa
weigh (v)	kala	kaalaa
weight	isisindo	eeseeseendo´
welcome (v)	emukela	e´mooke´laa
welfare	inhlalakahle	eenhlaalaakaahle´
well (satisfactory)	kahle	kaahle´
well (health)	phila	peelaa
well (n) (hole / water well)	umgodi onomthombo	oomgo´dee o´no´mto´mbo´
wet	manzi	maanzee
wet (v)	manzisa	maanzeesaa
what	yini	yeenee
wheel	isondo	eeso´ndo´
wheelbarrow	ibhala	eebaalaa
wheeze (v)	bhohoza	bo´ho´zaa
when	nini	neenee
where	-phi / kuphi / ngaphi	-pee / koopee / ngaapee
whether	noma	no´maa
which	-phi / yiphi	-pee / yeepee
while	ngenkathi	nge´nkaatee
whip (n)	isiswebhu	eeseeswe´boo
whip (v)	thwisha / shaya	tweeshaa / shaayaa
whisper	ukuhleba	ookoohle´baa
whisper (v)	hleba	hle´baa
whistle (n)	impempe / ikhwela	eempe´mpe´ / eekwe´laa
whistle (n) game	indweba / impempe	eendwe´baa / eempe´mpe´
whistle (v) blow up	shaya indweba	shaayaa eendwe´baa
whistle (v) -tune	shaya ikhwela	shaayaa eekwe´laa
white - colour	umhlophe	oomhlo´pe´
white meat -(chicken)	umkhwepha	oomkwe´paa
who	ubani	oobaanee
whole	onke	o´nke´
whose	kabani	kaabaanee
why /	ngani / elani /	ngaanee / e´laanee /
why	kungani	koongaanee
wife	unkosikazi	oonko´seekaazee
will (n) (testament / wish)	intando / isifiso	eentaando´/ eeseefeeso´
will (v)	-zo	-zo´
win (v)	wina / phumelela	weenaa / poome´le´laa
wind	umoya	oomo´yaa

window	ifasitela	eefaaseete'laa
windmill	ipitsi / ingwedlo	eepeetsee / eegwe'dlo'
wine	iwayini	eewaayeenee
winter	ubusika	oobooseekaa
wipe (v)	sula	soolaa
wire (n)	ucingo	ooceengo'
wise	hlakaniphile	hlaakaaneepeele'
wish	isifiso	eeseefeeso'
wish (v)	fisa	feesaa
with	nga-	ngaa-
withdraw (v)	khipha	keepaa
within	ngaphakathi	ngaapaakaatee
without	ngaphandle	ngaapaandle'
witness (n)	ufakazi	oofaakaazee
witness (v)	fakaza	faakaazaa
woman /	unkosikazi /	oonko'seekaazee /
woman	umuntu wesifazane	oomoontoo we'seefaazaane'
woman achiever	owesifazane ovelele	o'weseefaazaane' o've'le'le'
wonder (v) - amaze	mangala	maangaalaa
wonderful	mangalisayo	maangaaleesaayo'
wood	ukhuni	ookoonee
wooden spoon	ukhezo lokhuni	ooke'zo' lo'koonee
wool	uvolo	oovo'lo'
word	igama	eegaamaa
work (n)	umsebenzi	oomse'be'nzee
work (v)	sebenza	se'be'nzaa
worker /	isisebenzi /	eeseese'be'nzee /
worker	umsebenzi	oomse'be'nzee
world	umhlaba	oomhlaabaa
world cup	inkomishi womdlalo	eenko'meeshee wo'mdlaalo'
	womhlaba wonke	wo'mhlaabaa wo'nke'
worm (maggot)	impethu	eempe'too
worm (intestinal) /	isikelemu / isilo	eeseeke'le'moo / eeseelo'
worm (tapeworm)	ingcili	eengceelee
worm (earth)	umsundu	oomsoondoo
worry	khathazeka	kaataaze'kaa
worry (v)	khathaza	kaataazaa
wound - sore	inxeba	eenxe'baa
wound (v) - hurt	limaza	leemaazaa
wrap (v)	songa	so'ngaa
wreck - ship	umbhabhalala	oombaabaalaalaa
wriggle (v)	shobashoba	sho'basho'baa
wring (v)	khama	kaamaa
wrinkle (n)	umfingcizo	oomfeengceezo'
wrinkle (v)	fingciza	feengceezaa
write (v)	bhala	baalaa
wrong	ngalungile	ngaaloongeele'

X

xhosa	iXhosa	eeXho´saa
xray	i x-reyi	ee - e´xre´yee
xylophone	izilofoni	eezeelo´fo´nee

Y

yacht	umkhumbi	oomkoombee
yard (garden)	iyadi	eeyaadee
yawn (v)	zamula	zaamoolaa
year	unyaka	oonyaakaa
yearly	-omnyaka / ngonyaka	-o´mnyaakaa / ngo´nyaakaa
yearn (v)	langazela	laangaaze´laa
yeast	imvubelo / iyisti	eemvoobe´lo´ / eeyeestee
yell	isikhalo	eeseekaalo´
yell (v)	khala / klabalasa	kaalaa / klaabaalaasaa
yellow	phuzi	poozee
yelp (v)	klewuza	kle´woozaa
yes	yebo	ye´bo´
yesterday	izolo	eezo´lo´
yet – but / and yet	kanti / kepha	kaantee / ke´paa
yoke – cattle	ijoka	eejo´kaa
yolk (egg)	isikhupha seqanda	eeseekoopaa se´qaandaa
you - people	nina	neenaa
you	wena	we´naa
young	ncane	ncaanee
youngster	ingane	eengaane´
your (you)	-kho / kwakho	-ko´ / kwaako´
your (pl.)	-inu / kwenu	-eenoo / kwe´noo
yours	okwakho	o´kwaako´
yours (pl.)	okwenu	o´kwe´noo
yourself - by	ngokwakho	ngo´kwaako´
youth	ubusha / intsha	oobooshaa / eentshaa

Z

zebra	idube	eedoobe´
zero	iqanda / unothi	eeqaandaa / oono´tee
zig zag – sewing / walking	igwingcigwingci	eegweengceegweengcee
zig zag (v)	gwingciza	gweengceezaa
Zion	iZiyoni	eeZeeyo´nee
zip	uziphu	oozeepoo
zone	ibhande	eebaande´
zoo	izu	eezoo
zulu (person)	umZulu	oomZooloo
zulu (language)	isiZulu	eeseeZooloo

NATIONAL ANTHEM

NKOSI SIKELEL' iAFRIKA
MALUPHAKANYISW' UPHONDO LWAYO,
YIZWA IMITHANDAZO YETHU,
NKOSI SIKELELA, THINA LUSAPHO LWAYO.

MORENA BOLOKA SETJHABA SA HESO,
O FEDISE DINTWA LA MATSHWENYEHO,
O SE BOLOKE, O SE BOLOKE SETJHABA SA HESO,
SETJHABA SA SOUTH AFRIKA, SOUTH AFRIKA.

UIT DIE BLOU VAN ONSE HEMEL,
UIT DIE DIEPTE VAN ONS SEE,
OOR ONS EWIGE GEBERGTES,
WAAR DIE KRANSEANTWOORD GEE,

SOUNDS THE CALL TO
COME TOGETHER,
AND UNITED WE SHALL STAND,
LET US LIVE AND STRIVE
FOR FREEDOM,
IN SOUTH AFRICA
OUR LAND.